Sensational

Sparrow

Chrysalis: Maria Sibylla Merian and the Secrets of Metamorphosis

Tinkering with Eden: A Natural History of Exotic Species in America

AN ALLURING FRAUD

EXPOSED BY NELLIE BLY.

FOUR PAGES OF
Original Humor and Colored Cartoons.

'MONG GIRLS WHO TOIL

The Classification of Minneapapolis Women Who Are Bread-Winners.

Girls Who Work at the Manufacture of Overalls, Jumpers, Etc.,

In Illy Ventilated Rooms for Wages Little Less Than Starvation.

Eva Gay's Trip Through Upper Stories Where Girls

Marti is believed to have def United States.

SIGHTED THE SAME GUNB

This Time the Alliance Was Al to Proceed Unmolested.

The steamer Alliance arrive fternoon from Colon. Capt. Cro tated that he passed within five f the Cuban coast on last Mon 30 A. M.

The officer on the bridge right ame barkentine-rigged Spanish oat that fired on the Alliance revious voyage. This gunboa lose under the Cuban coast, hea he westward. She paid no at hatever to the Alliance, which s long on her usual course.

IGNORE BRIDGE BIDS

Delos E. Culver Making Contr Span the North River.

The four companies interested

ELESS AND POISONOUS.

y Drugs That Lurk in the So-Called "Aids to Beauty."

E LAURIE" EXPOSES THE DANGERS OF QUACK COSMETICS.

New Wor

SENSATIONAL

THE HIDDEN HISTORY
OF AMERICA'S
"GIRL STUNT REPORTERS"

KIM TODD

HARPER

An Imprint of HarperCollins Publishers

HarperCollins books may be purchased for educational, business, or sales promotional use. For information, please email the Special Markets Department at SPsales@harpercollins.com.

FIRST EDITION

Designed by Elina Cohen
Art from Shutterstock / impulse50

Library of Congress Cataloging-in-Publication Data has been applied for.

ISBN 978-0-06-284361-6

21 22 23 24 25   LSC   10 9 8 7 6 5 4 3 2 1

For the ink-stained Amazons

I write the truth because I love it and because there is no living creature whose anger I fear or whose praise I court.

—Nellie Bly, *The Evening World*, 1895

CONTENTS

Part III: Facing the Storm (1896–Present)

This is a work of nonfiction. The dialogue is taken from newspaper articles, letters, interviews, and reporters' memoirs. As required by their profession, some of these journalists could be quite self-mythologizing. Unless I have evidence to the contrary (such as a census record showing a woman couldn't have been born when she said), I take them at their word.

Also, I refer to some writers by their pseudonyms and some by their legal names (though marriages and casual attitudes toward consistent spelling render even these unstable). They created characters to conceal and reveal themselves, and sometimes the character overshadowed the woman behind her. Those known mainly from a single pseudonym—Nellie Bly, Nell Nelson, and Nora Marks—I refer to by their pen name. Those who used a pseudonym only sparingly or inconsistently, I refer to by their actual names. It makes sense to call Elizabeth Cochrane "Nellie Bly" when that was how the whole country knew her and how she signed many letters. It's less logical to refer to Elizabeth Banks as "Polly Pollock" when only a handful of articles at the start of her career carried that byline.

Sensational

THE CASE OF
THE GIRL REPORTER

Have I not been drinking moxie all this spring?

—Caroline Lockhart, *Boston Post*, 1895

In late November 1888, a young woman threaded her way through the grit-filled streets of Chicago's downtown, skirting horse-drawn cabs and wagons teetering under sacks of grain. When she finally arrived at the doctor's office, she sat hot-faced in the waiting room while her companion pulled the doctor aside and explained the nature of the problem. The physician, small and alert like a sparrow, turned to the girl and tried to calm her: "You must not be scared about it," the doctor urged. "It is perfectly safe. You suffer more from fright than you would the operation." The patient, still agitated, put off a full examination. She'd come back another day, she promised, to arrange the abortion.

A few days later, the young woman visited a different doctor. This one had a German accent and a diploma from a German university under crossed swords on his wall. She described her situation, saying she was from Memphis, and, like many girls, she'd taken the train to Chicago because of its reputation. Then she haltingly made her request. Did she have any other health problems, the doctor asked? Was she in pain? When she said no, to both, he wrote her a prescription for ergot, a fungus thought to induce premature labor. She should go to her hotel, he said, draw a warm bath, drink a hot toddy, and take two teaspoonfuls. Don't follow the dosage written on the prescription, the doctor warned, because it was wrong; otherwise, the pharmacist might get suspicious about the drug's true purpose. The physician looked her in the eye, handed her the slip of paper, said, "Remember how to take it tonight, do not be alarmed if it produce[s] pain," and sent her back out into the hectic city.

She went to another doctor after that. And another. In the course of three weeks, she visited more than two hundred physicians. Many agreed to perform an abortion, a surprising number as it was illegal. The police department surgeon, Dr. C. C. P. Silva, plump with a black goatee, highlighted the danger: "Inflammation might set in, and Lord knows what might follow." Then he swore her to secrecy and said he'd do it for $75. The head of the Chicago Medical Society rocked back on his heels, saying, "There are enough ways in this state for a man to get into the penitentiary without taking a crowbar and prying his way in," and refused to do it. But then he gave her directions to a man who would. Hundreds of girls have had abortions, a female physician assured her. And she added, "It will not do for you to feel so timid. . . . You must feel daring and brave."

The slight young woman with tidy dark hair recorded these facts, but also assumptions and attitudes—euphemisms, opinions on sex out of wedlock, the way doctors made her feel shame or comfort or alarm. One, fatherly, advised her to marry; one, leering with a tobacco-stained mouth, made her suspect that he felt more sympathy for her lover than he did for her. Some called abortion "murder" and "a sin." Another brushed away concerns about damnation, saying: "If I were a girl I would get rid of my trouble if I had to go to the devil rather than live in disgrace before my parents." Though she had assumed women seeking abortions must be poor, the doctors' fancy offices and high prices—ranging up to $250*—made it clear many patients must be

---

*   About $6,000 in 2020.

middle- or upper-class. All the walking and asking, occasionally pretending to weep, was tiring. Some days the encounters left the woman
filled with despair, even though she was not, actually, pregnant. But
usually a sense of righteous anger carried her through, as when a Dr.
Knox condescendingly brushed her aside. She fumed and imagined
her retort: "Don't prate of virtue to me; I am as good as the rest of
the world, only less lucky." Traveling from one end of the city to the
other, past boutique windows displaying lace-up boots and butcher
shops with pens of hissing geese, she captured what it might be like to
be a woman in a certain kind of difficulty, looking for a way out.

Though one physician suspected she was an "adventuress," none
knew she was actually an undercover reporter, bent on revealing the
extent of the city's abortion practice. When her exposé, a monthlong
project for the *Chicago Times*, hit the stands, the city editor quit in
disgust, letters of praise and outrage flooded the news desk, lawsuits
for libel piled high. Discussions of abortion, in a daily paper? Readers
found it repellent—and irresistible. They also found the message hard
to decipher. On the one hand, the writer referred to only as the "Girl
Reporter" condemned abortion in the strongest terms; on the other,
she published detailed instructions for how and where to get one, including which medicines to take and at what dosage. A heated discus-
sion blazed through the editorial pages about women's bodies and the
power imbalance between the sexes.

The Girl Reporter's series had such a wide reach because she dared
to talk about women and sex and the way it felt to be a woman talking
about sex—embarrassed, threatened, angry. Her *Chicago Times* series
took all these speeding trains—experiments in journalism, a demand
for women's rights, a medical field struggling to dilute the influence
of midwives—and put them on a collision course. In her articles, the
Girl Reporter also discussed the challenges of this particular assignment and of her role as a woman reporter. For example, after a long
day of playing pregnant and recording justifications and refusals, she
reflected on her weeks spent tromping from one doctor to another:
"Today I have been wondering whether, if I had to do it over again,

I would have taken a position on a newspaper staff. It used to be the dream of my childhood that I would some day become a writer—a great writer—and astonish the world with my work. And this dream had not entirely vanished yet, thank goodness."

Then she added, "But did I ever suppose that I would have to commence on a newspaper by filling an assignment like this?

"Well, no."

Entering journalism, a predominantly male field, meant competing with men on their own terms, she knew, and she was ready. But, ironically, for this story, one of her first, the reporter's sex was not a disadvantage; it was a necessity.

"A man couldn't have done it," she concluded.

The *Chicago Times*'s Girl Reporter might seem exceptional in her readiness to risk scandal to tell a story no one else would, but she was not alone. The same script was playing out in cities from coast to coast. She was just one of the nation's "girl stunt reporters," pioneering a new genre of investigative journalism, going undercover to reveal societal ills. Throughout the 1880s and 1890s, women from Colorado to Missouri to Massachusetts dressed in shabby clothes and sneaked into textile mills to report on factory conditions, slipped behind the scenes at corrupt adoption agencies, fainted in the street to test treatment at public hospitals.

At the time, American journalism, a field on the cusp of professionalization, was plotting its future. A revolution in printing technology made putting out a paper cheaper than ever before, and an influx of immigrants offered a tantalizing new audience. Newspaper rooms, from San Francisco's *Examiner* to New York's *World*, battled viciously for market share with weapons of scandal and innovation. In the process, they shaped the growing metropolis, reflecting it back to itself. On the one hand, cities were engines of opportunity; on the other, magnets for sin. They drew people seeking better lives and sometimes swallowed them.

Publishers were looking for a new kind of story to fill those numerous pages, to tempt those new readers, to stoke their anxieties but also feed their hopes. And when Nellie Bly's 1887 "Inside the Madhouse" series for the *World* hit the streets of New York, readers couldn't get enough. She had faked insanity to get committed to the asylum at Blackwell's Island so she could document the starvation and abuse of patients. Even more compelling than the situation she revealed was the way she told the story—a firsthand account from a charismatic narrator, filled with dramatic twists and laced with warmth and humor. The exposé sold thousands of copies of the *World*, resulted in the municipality committing $50,000 for better asylum management, and created a publishing sensation.

Slipping on a disguise and courting danger suddenly became a way for writers to get a foot in the door. By crafting long-form narratives that stretched over weeks and read like novels, using engaging female narrators to explore issues of deep concern to women, and promising real-world results, stunt reporters changed laws, launched labor movements, and redefined what it meant to be a journalist. These footloose exploits were so sought after by readers and publishers that reporters willing to attempt them commanded high pay. And, while in 1880 it was almost impossible for a woman writer to escape the household hints of the ladies' page (the kind of writing one female journalist termed "prostitution of the brains"), by 1900, papers were publishing more bylines by women than men.

Stunt reporters put a new female character in the headlines—not a victim of assault or murder—but a protagonist. Bravery was their brand. It was like they stepped out of the adventure tales that flew off the bookstore shelves, except that they were real.

But it was a disorienting sense of reality, as the freedom displayed in these stories was at odds with the limited rights of American women in the late nineteenth century. More and more were moving to the big cities, finding jobs, living on their own, but the Victorian ideals of a certain kind of womanhood still clung like a corset. Women couldn't vote. No laws protected them from sexual harassment or marital rape.

Wives, in particular, struggled to be seen as full citizens: under "coverture," a common law legal doctrine imported from Britain, their legal selfhood was subsumed under their husband's. In many states, married women couldn't own property, sign contracts, or earn a salary. When Myra Bradwell, denied the ability to practice law at the Illinois bar, took her case to the Supreme Court in 1873, Justice Joseph Bradley highlighted "coverture" in his response: "The natural and proper timidity and delicacy which belongs to the female sex evidently unfits it for many of the occupations of civil life." Bradwell lost her case.

And it wasn't just a legal issue. In a post-Darwin era fascinated with biology, women's inferiority was codified by science. Psychologists, physiologists, and sociologists all weighed in. Phrenology—the determination of character by skull shape—revealed women to be naturally childlike, as did analysis of their stature and rounded features. Their nerves—alleged to be smaller and more delicate—made them sensitive and impressionable. Doctors increasingly diagnosed hysteria, a uniquely female ailment that could result in a patient being confined to her bedroom or sent to an asylum.

Then there was the question of womanhood on the page. Writing by women has historically been devalued, though much read, and the nineteenth century was no exception. Budding novelist Nathaniel Hawthorne was so concerned that in an 1830 biographical sketch of the 1600s religious leader Anne Hutchinson for the *Salem Gazette*, he took a long detour to detail his fears about women writers in his own age. Why was their work so popular? What was the cost for creators of actual literature? He worried that "the ink-stained Amazons will expel their rivals by actual pressure, and petticoats wave triumphantly over the field" and mulled the "impropriety in the display of woman's naked mind to the gaze of the world." Nineteenth-century and early twentieth-century female writers fended off this kind of disparagement in a variety of ways, from adopting male pseudonyms, like George Eliot and the Brontës, to penning essays and stories where the sex of the narrator is obscured, like Mary Austin in her *Land of Little Rain*.

The stunt reporters challenged these views of what a woman should be. They couldn't cast a ballot, but they could interview presidential candidates. They couldn't sit on juries, but the *World* could impanel twelve female reporters and editors to offer their perspective on court cases. Anatomy textbooks might detail their weakness and frailty, but they could leap into the cold ocean and face down burly factory bosses. Under the guise of journalism, they adopted roles forbidden to them, demonstrating their fitness to serve on a search-and-rescue team or drive a train. Unlike female writers who masked their sex, the girl stunt reporters told the truth experienced by their bodies. They wrote about sexual harassment. They wrote about seeking abortions. They wrote about crushes and concerns about their hair. These reporters were deemed silly, sentimental, or sensational—all criticisms of "feminine" writing—but the power of their voices made Hawthorne's fears come true. They changed the journalistic landscape.

Rather than being an oddity of history, stunt reporters altered the trajectory of both traditional reporting and memoir. Along with other writers like Ida B. Wells and Victoria Earle Matthews, they developed techniques of "muckraking," a style of investigative journalism first condemned then embraced as a noble tradition. They employed the intimate tone and scene-based structure that would later characterize the "New Journalism" of the 1960s and '70s and the "creative nonfiction" that followed. Their disguises allowed them to go deep into the lives of their subjects, providing early examples of "immersion journalism." But while Bly is well known, most of the women who followed in her wake have been forgotten, their legacy obscured. The identity of the *Chicago Times*'s "Girl Reporter," for example, remains a mystery.

After a little more than a decade of headlines and book deals and newspaper profits, these writers faced a backlash that stripped them of their credibility and, ultimately, credit for their innovations. Their assignments shifted from public hazards to circus elephants and nights spent in a haunted house. Awareness of the body, both by the writers and in half-page illustrations, was criticized as indecent. Stunt reporting, which played a critical role in the 1890s circulation war between

Joseph Pulitzer and William Randolph Hearst, became synonymous with "yellow journalism." It was disdained as a particularly female variety of trash. As newspaper editor W. C. Brann wrote at the time, "A careful examination of the 'great dailies' will demonstrate that at least half of the intellectual slime that is befouling the land is fished out of the gutter by females." Turn-of-the-century advice books for aspiring women journalists warned them to steer clear of stunts. And these criticisms stuck, effectively ejecting these reporters from the journalistic tradition they helped forge. If the form is known at all, it is referenced with a sneer. Even today, one scholar describes the stunt reporter genre as "semipornographic titillation" that "cast a spell of infamy over the image of the woman journalist which only years of sober professional accomplishment finally exorcized."

Stunt reporters and their treatment raise the question of what it means to write in a female body, from an overtly female perspective, in their time and in our own. It is the same question that haunts many women who write honestly about their lives: how to tell the truth and still be taken seriously. In her 1931 lecture to the Women's Service League, Virginia Woolf described a writer as an angler, letting her line drift as she dreams over the water, hoping to hook something astonishing. But then the woman is violently jerked from her creative reverie, all writing halted, because "she had thought of something, something about the body, about the passions which it was unfitting for her as a woman to say." Woolf told her audience that, over the years, she'd solved many writerly problems, but "telling the truth about my own experiences as a body, I do not think I solved. I doubt any woman has solved it yet."

The issues faced by the stunt reporters and excavated by Woolf still play out today. Writing by women about women continues to be shunted into separate literary categories, those that are both high selling and low prestige, like romance novels, "chick lit," and memoir. Like stunt reporters, the authors of online personal essays are expected to write about their bodies and are punished for doing so with scorching criticism (and sometimes threats) in the comments section.

It's a no-win situation. In contrast, roles branded more "male" are held in high esteem, like war correspondent and investigative reporter. A decade ago, when the organization VIDA, Women in Literary Arts, started counting numbers of women and men published by the most prestigious literary publications, they found a 25/75 split in some places. What is considered respectable versus sensational or "literary" versus "popular" often remains centered on discomfort around female physiology, leaving writers who take women's lives as their subject to navigate the narrow, rocky passage between tame and scandalous.

By writing these reporters back into history, I aim to highlight the double standard that labels women as "stunt reporters" while men are "investigative journalists," even as they do the same work. I also hope to illuminate its consequences. If we let these groundbreaking women journalists be erased, allow "muckraking" to be the provenance of Lincoln Steffens and Upton Sinclair, leave unquestioned Tom Wolfe's assertions about the invention of New Journalism, and permit male writers to lay claim to launching "creative nonfiction," then we add fuel to the notion that women's articles, essays, and novels—and by extension, women's lives—are small, timid, unambitious. This dismissal cuts to the heart of women's credibility as witnesses of their own experience and of the world.

Many women authors and journalists I have interviewed ended our conversations confiding how inspirational they found Nellie Bly. Some have gone undercover themselves; others just aim to write fearlessly. Bly showed the way when, even a hundred years later, paths to meaningful careers are hard to find. But as vital and exceptional as Bly was, it is equally vital to know she was not the only one. Ordinary women from Boston to Omaha stepped up, willing to breach the bounds of propriety to uncover a truth, despite a nation of obstacles arrayed against them.

This is the story of how they did it.

AN ALLURING FRAUD
EXPOSED BY NELLIE BLY.

FOUR PACES OF
Original Humor and Colored Cartoons.

'MONG GIRLS WHO TOIL

The Classification of Minneapapolis Women Who Are
Bread-Winners.

Girls Who Work at the Manufacture of Overalls,
Jumpers, Etc.,

In Illy Ventilated Rooms for
Wages Little Less Than
Starvation.

Eva Gay's Trip Through
Upper Stories Where Girls

Martl is believed to have del
United States.

SIGHTED THE SAME GUNB

This Time the Alliance Was Al
to Proceed Unmolested.

The steamer Alliance arrive
afternoon from Colon. Capt. Cro
tated that he passed within five
of the Cuban coast on last Mon
.30 A. M.

The officer on the bridge sight
same barkentine-rigged Spanish
boat that fired on the Alliance
previous voyage. This gunboa
close under the Cuban coast, hea
he westward. She paid no at
whatever to the Alliance, which s
along on her usual course.

IGNORE BRIDGE BIDS

Delos E. Culver Making Contr
Span the North River.
The four companies interested

UELESS AND POISONOUS.

ly Drugs That Lurk in the So-
Called "Aids to Beauty."

HE LAURIE" EXPOSES THE DAN-
GERS OF QUACK COSMETICS.

New Wor

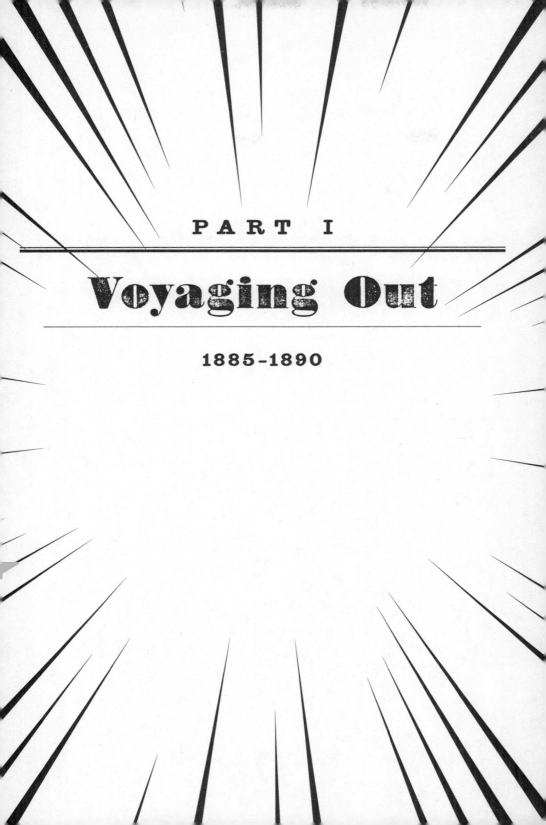

PART I

Voyaging Out

1885–1890

TRIALS OF A WORKING GIRL

Now and then a young woman with keen sense of the world's movements, who writes well, will look longingly to a great city paper with a desire to become one of its workers.

—*Good Housekeeping*, 1890

Somewhere in Allegheny City, Pennsylvania, in early 1885, a twenty-year-old woman chose her words carefully. Across the river, past the barges sliding by heaped with coal, the industrial engine of Pittsburgh churned out steel beams and glass bottles. Surrounded by hills that trapped the factory pollution, Pittsburgh was the "City of Smoke." Residents said it with pride; smoke equaled money. And the metropolis had money, but not much glamour, as the thick air smeared white gloves with ash. Not far beyond city limits, the tall buildings turned to hard-to-traverse hills and deep forest. Evergreen branches bent under heaps of snow, isolating the small towns, the kind where the young woman had grown up. But she was older now, and that day, on a large sheet of paper, she penned a letter to the editor of the *Pittsburg Dispatch*, hoping to write herself into a new life.[*]

---

[*] Throughout the nineteenth century, "Pittsburgh" was spelled both with and without the "h."

The *Dispatch* was a prosperous, forward-looking paper, known for opposing slavery during the Civil War and favoring increased rights for women. But one of the paper's columnists, Erasmus Wilson, who used the pseudonym the "Quiet Observer" and usually covered topics like the etiquette of umbrella usage, had recently taken the "women's sphere" as his theme. It was a topic hashed over in articles and lectures of the 1880s as suffragists urged that women should take part in public life—inventing, reforming, voting—while conservatives argued that they belonged in the home. But the suffragists had encountered a series of setbacks. Passed in the wake of the Civil War, the Fourteenth and Fifteenth Amendments had given citizens the right to vote regardless of race, but the Fourteenth Amendment had specified that the right belonged to "male citizens," the first time sex appeared in the Constitution as a voting criteria. Efforts to pass an amendment to allow for female voters had languished in Congress every year since the proposal was introduced in 1878.

Wilson joined those who felt biology and the Bible framed the female for domestic life. His columns expressed increasing annoyance with those who sought to expand their reach. "If women would just let up on this sphere business and set themselves to do that which they are best fitted for, and which their hands and hearts find to be done, they would achieve more for themselves and be greater blessings to the world," he wrote. A woman's focus should be making "her home a little paradise, herself playing the part of angel."

In January 1885, the Quiet Observer pushed his point even further. A man calling himself "Anxious Father" wrote in, asking what to do with his five daughters. In their teens and mid-twenties, they painted, collected money for the poor, played piano, but didn't seem fit for much else. He'd love to marry them off but didn't have many takers: "Now what am I to do with them?"

Wilson was remarkably unhelpful, suggesting that the father ask the *Dispatch*'s female columnist Bessie Bramble instead and noting, darkly, that in China they kill extra girl babies or sell them as slaves. When the father wrote Wilson back, unsatisfied with Bramble's advice (she idealistically suggested that in this modern age, there were no limits to what women could achieve, while Anxious Father saw limits everywhere), Wilson doubled down, stressing that the sooner a woman found a husband and got on with the business of housekeeping, the better. A woman who ventures outside her sphere and competes with men is "abnormal," "a monstrosity." If Wilson was playing the gadfly, it worked. Women wrote in, incensed, saying, "Your 'Quiet Observer' is a fool—to put it mildly. I used to like him real well, but since he got onto this woman question he is just as crazy as the rest of the men," and "We don't wish to wear the breeches, we simply want our rights, and that is to dispose of ourselves according to our own sweet wills."

For the young writer in Allegheny City, this idea of domestic bliss directly contradicted her personal experience. She'd heard her mother called "whore" and "bitch" by her alcoholic stepfather and watched as he choked her. Marriage made her mother wish she was dead. At fourteen, the girl fled the house, along with her younger sister, mother, and brother, when the stepfather leaped up from a dinner table argument, brandishing a gun. Over the course of several days, the stepfather barricaded himself inside and destroyed their home, smashing furniture and flowerpots, upending the table, kicking holes in wall plaster. Hard to play an angel in this domestic paradise.

She wanted something more, but what? Teaching was an option for smart young women, and so she'd started at Indiana State Normal School with high hopes. Her father left some money when he died, but the executor mismanaged it, and funds ran out after one term. She found herself back home. Factory worker, servant, shop clerk—fields open to women—had applicants lined up to apply. In the *Dispatch*'s Help Wanted section, things looked equally bleak. The city was recovering from a nationwide recession marked by a stock market crash, meager prices on corn and wheat, and a bank panic that shuttered the Penn Bank in Pittsburgh and left the streets crowded with the unemployed. So listings were thin. But still, that January, in the "Male Help" column readers could find:

**"Wanted—manager for art publications
for the best house in the trade."**

**"Wanted—Experienced press boy—that can make
himself generally useful in a printing office."**

**"Wanted—Agents in every county in
Western Pennsylvania, Western Virginia and Eastern Ohio,
to sell the celebrated Electric Light Lamp."**

But reading farther down to the "Female Help" listings, job seekers would find only:

"Wanted—Two good dishwashers at Horner's Chophouse."

"Wanted—a good girl for general housework."

**"Wanted—a chambermaid, from 25 to 40 years of age;
one that can make good soup."**

The letter writer saw herself in Anxious Father's daughters. How frustrating to be brushed off as useless when she had so much to offer. It wasn't fair.

The young woman, called "Pinkey" by friends and relatives, wrote the newspaper to say so. Her writing style was unpolished, to say the least, punctuation haphazard as hail, but she made a passionate argument, rooted in a real situation—her life. She wrote about applying for jobs, being treated badly and rejected over and over. She was too small. They didn't have any openings. The pay for women was less than half what a man might make, nothing one could live on. She signed it "Lonely Orphan Girl" and sent it off.

Flipping through the *Dispatch* several days later, she didn't find her letter, but this instead:

"If the writer of the communication signed 'Lonely Orphan Girl' will send her name and address to this office, merely as a guarantee of good faith, she will confer a favor and receive the information she desires."

The next day, a girl who struck those she passed as shy and rather frightened showed up at the offices of the *Pittsburg Dispatch*, out of breath from climbing the four flights of stairs, and asked to speak to the editor. Her meek voice and timidity were in contrast to her clothes—a floor-length silk cape and a fur turban—which projected, if not grandness, at least the idea of grandness.

Under her plush hat, the girl had hair cut with bangs, a round face, and a snub nose that would later be described as evidence of "a strain of sound North Ireland in her stock." Elizabeth Cochrane (originally "Cochran," but she added a final "e" to sound more distinguished), struck people, then and later, as not so much as beautiful but straightforward. There was nothing vague or unfocused about her curious glance. She asked for what she wanted. The editor, who had been impressed by the personality in her prose, despite the rough edges, hired her to write two articles. A working-class young woman would add a missing perspective.

Her first column, a direct response to Wilson's dialogue with Anxious Father, was called "The Girl Puzzle." Not all women marry, and not all have the skills, money, beauty, or connections to succeed as writers, doctors, or actresses, she wrote. The white-haired columnist's fantasy home life obscured the reality for many. She also pushed back against the abstract optimism of Bramble, who had painted endless possibilities for women, while in her view, there were hardly any. What women needed, she said, were better jobs. Why not have female messengers or office assistants, and allow them to work their way up as a young man might? Why couldn't girls be Pullman conductors or traveling salesmen? After all, she wrote, "Girls are just as smart, a great deal quicker to learn."

Her second article, "Mad Marriages," argued for a law that would

bar anyone who had taken public charity, or owed taxes, from marrying. At her mother's divorce proceeding, neighbor after neighbor
testified that they'd known for years the man she married had a foul
temper and propensity to drink. They should have been required to
speak up before the ceremony, the writer suggested. And divorce
should be outlawed, so that people wouldn't just leap into a wedding,
ignoring warning signs. All these steps would keep the unhappy
spouse from saying "I did not know," and allow the community (and
perhaps frustrated daughters) to say, "I told you so." For this piece, she
dropped "Orphan Girl," and picked up the pseudonym "Nellie Bly," a
nod to a song by Pittsburgh native Stephen Foster.

Elizabeth Cochrane, "Nellie Bly"

Through the late winter and early spring, Bly wrote a series on
"Our Workshop Girls." Week after week, she interviewed women
making money in fields beyond cleaning and cooking. Unlike her

pieces that would come later, exposing harsh factory conditions, Bly's implied argument was that women could do a lot more than generally thought, and do it well. She profiled women contributing to Pittsburgh's most iconic, manly industries, immersed in dirt and flame: the iron works, the wire works, the glassworks. These surprising stories, and her energetic recounting of them, spread beyond western Pennsylvania. The *Dispatch*'s New York correspondent copied the idea, noting that Bly's series "attracted considerable attention here."

It quickly became clear that behind the timorous girl who turned up and painted herself as a representative of the ordinary and unexceptional lurked someone else entirely, someone deeply determined. Not long after the *Dispatch* hired her, Bly found herself pushed into the society journalism traditionally offered to women. Reports on spring fashions and flower shows were painfully boring, and she took off to Mexico for six months as a correspondent, writing about hotels and cuisine, but also poverty and prison conditions. After Mexico, she gave Pittsburgh-based reporting another try, but her mind drifted elsewhere. Finally, in spring 1887, Bly wrote a goodbye letter to Wilson (who became a close friend, despite his infuriating on-paper attitudes), left the smoke and comfort of western Pennsylvania behind, and went to seek her fortune in New York City, home of legendary newspapers like the *Tribune*, founded by Horace Greeley; Charles Dana's *Sun*; and, most significantly, Joseph Pulitzer's *World*.

G angly with poor eyesight, Joseph Pulitzer had come to the United States from Hungary in 1864 to fight for the Union in the Civil War as a seventeen-year old. He then spent hard years scrambling for a job—tending mules, waiting tables—until making his way in the newspaper business, first as a reporter for the German-language newspaper in St. Louis, and ultimately as publisher of the *St. Louis Post-Dispatch*. It was here that he honed his ideas about the kind of paper he wanted. Positioning the *Post-Dispatch* as a friend of the common man against rich corporations, he published the tax returns of the wealthy to show they weren't paying their share and campaigned against railroad monopolies. He experimented with a different kind of storytelling, conducting investigations of gambling dens and fortune-tellers, sending a reporter to find a killer who had eluded the police (with no luck), and pushing his writers toward crisp, compact prose. As an editor and publisher, he was always in the office, always offering an opinion. His unruly dark beard was cropped close to his jaw when he was a younger man but, when he was older, flowed down his chest like that of a Victorian genius.

Joseph Pulitzer

In 1883, drawn to publishing's epicenter, he moved to Manhattan and bought the struggling *New York World*. A year earlier, his younger brother Albert had launched the 1-cent paper the *Morning Journal* in the same city. The *Journal* aimed for a "sparkling, breezy, good-natured tone" specifically to appeal to women and their advertising dollars. Failing to get a loan from his brother, Albert did a fundraising tour in Europe, came home with $25,000, and rented space and printing presses from the *New-York Tribune*. With its low price and coverage of dances and love affairs, the *Morning Journal* became known as the "chambermaid's delight."

But the moment Joseph Pulitzer arrived in New York, where he would upend the newspaper business, his hardnosed single-mindedness was on display. He hired away Albert's managing editor and two of his best writers. He then launched a radical and ambitious experiment with journalism in the public interest. Thin-skinned and demanding, willing to set employees against one another to compete for positions, he could be a tough man to work for. But he could also articulate a vision and carry it out. With the *World* (he dropped "New York" from the name), Pulitzer aimed to produce a paper that was "not only large but truly democratic—dedicated to the cause of the people rather than that of purse potentates—devoted more to the news of the New than the Old World—that will expose all fraud and sham, fight all public evils and abuses—that will serve and battle for people with earnest sincerity."

The *World* was forged as the United States was struggling with questions about citizenship—who belonged, whose hopes for the young country would prevail. Black men had only recently been provided citizenship and the ability to vote, but southern states were busy undermining these rights, using laws, propaganda, and violence. Many were fleeing to the North. And between 1870 and 1900, 12 million immigrants entered the country, the majority through New York: Irish fearing a second potato famine, Italians escaping serfdom, Russian Jews taking refuge from pogroms. The changing composition of the country inspired a backlash from those whose vision of America was a white, Anglo-Saxon, Protestant one. The 1882 Chinese Exclusion Act prohibited Chinese laborers from entering the United States for a decade after its signing (making the exception for merchants, intellectuals, tourists), and barred those already in the country from citizenship. American Indian tribes, whose members weren't considered citizens, were massacred and systematically stripped of their land by broken treaties. In 1877, the US government made a grab for the gold in Black Hills, overriding the Fort Laramie Treaty. The Dawes Act of 1887 laid the groundwork for transfer of even more reservation acreage to whites by dividing land into individual parcels.

In this demographic turmoil, Pulitzer, an immigrant himself, saw the potential of a vast new readership. Understanding the potency of symbolism, he used the pages of the *World* to raise $100,000 for a pedestal for the Statue of Liberty, after state and local governments had refused to contribute, and the gift lay in pieces in wooden crates. When the statue finally went up in 1886, it was a monument to Pulitzer's creativity and drive, as well as to the paper's sympathy for the plight of newcomers specifically and the underdog in general. This positioning paid off, and circulation soared, jumping from thirty thousand in 1883, when Pulitzer took over, to almost two hundred thousand in 1887. His paper was so identified with the interests of the poor, readers would write in offering tips on corrupt businesses and, sometimes, just flat out asking for money.

And in the years since Bly had started at the *Dispatch*, the allure of New York journalism had only grown. "Newspaper Row," across from City Hall, right near the courts, was the pulse of the city. Reporters sprinted down the sidewalk, toward fires and train wrecks. As soon as printing presses finished each morning, wagons piled with papers rattled over the bridge to Brooklyn and uptown to Harlem; newsboys scooped up the crisp sheets and scattered like pigeons in front of a streetcar. The press offices were right next to each other: the squat *Sun* with European gables in the roof; the *New York Times*, a cream-colored cube; the eleven-story *Tribune* with its flashy clock tower, like an English church, rising above the rest. The *World*'s reputation outshone its unimpressive home in the dingy Western Union Building. It was the ideal place to immerse oneself in cutting-edge journalism.

Its increasing circulation and audacious self-promotion drew letters from eager job applicants (or sometimes from their mothers),* flinging themselves at the light. But how to get in? All along the row, gate-keepers kept an eye out for hopeful young people bearing newspaper clippings and shooed them away.

One of those who made it past the front door was the young William Randolph Hearst. Freshly ejected from Harvard and just a year older than Bly, he was distinguished by eerily pale eyes, hair in a center part, and expensive taste in clothes that ran to glossy top hats. While his mother pleaded with the college president and paid tutors to prep him for tests in the hope he could graduate with his class, Hearst's mind was elsewhere. He was obsessed with the *Examiner*, the failing newspaper his father owned in San Francisco, and all the ways he might make it shine. He wanted it to be the *World* of the West, the kind of paper "which appeals to the people and which depends for its success upon enterprise, energy, and a certain startling originality and not upon the wisdom of its political opinions or the lofty style of its editorials." If his father would only let him run it, he'd redesign it, showcase gripping illustrations, and advertise it up and down the coast. In anticipation of this opportunity, Hearst spent the spring of 1886 at the *World*'s offices, learning how to put together a front page and how to pace a sensational story, eyeing the machinery, breathing in all that fresh ink.

Bly arrived in New York in spring 1887, also full of dreams of journalistic glory. In her letter to Wilson declaring she was off to the big city, she suggested with bravado—"Look out for me." But by early August, her money was running short, her plan to take Manhattan by storm going nowhere. The competition for the few reporter jobs was fierce. One desperate writer placed an ad: "Editor and popular author wants work; anything at any price." Though she hoped to turn her back on the *Dispatch*, Bly sent articles to her old paper, having few other takers. These offerings seemed increasingly like she was

---

* Elizabeth Cady Stanton sent in a plea on behalf of her son.

scraping the bottom of the barrel. Finally, a few days after writing a piece detailing a couple milking an obstinate cow in an alley, she had an idea that might get her inside the seemingly impenetrable newspaper offices. She would write an article on women in New York journalism and request interviews with editors of all the major papers. It was easy reporting; all she had to do was walk down the blocks of Newspaper Row (and climb many stairs and ride the rare elevator).

And it worked. After a summer of fruitless effort, she found herself in the inner sanctum, face to face with Charles Dana, the white-bearded editor of the *Sun* and former assistant secretary of war. Standing on his soft carpet, peering at the bookshelves that covered the walls, she asked in her western Pennsylvania drawl what he thought about women in journalism.

"I think if they have the ability," he said, encouragingly. But then he added that they rarely did: they lacked the right education, maintained only a loose relationship with the truth, and were constrained by the bounds of respectability: "While a woman might be ever so clever in obtaining news and putting it into words, we would not feel at liberty to call her out at 1 o'clock in the morning to report at a fire or crime."

The comment about lack of truthfulness stung, but she pressed on, circling closer to her real question, "How do women secure positions in New York?"

"I really cannot say," Dana replied, clearly never having given it much thought.

At the *World*, she confronted Colonel John Cockerill. Physically imposing, he had a round face, brown eyes, and a vigorous mustache. Among his peers, Cockerill had a reputation for voluminous cursing, drinking to excess, and mocking whoever had just left the table. Pulitzer moved him to the *World* from the *St. Louis Post-Dispatch*, partially for his editorial prowess, and partially because he'd killed a man. When a lawyer upset with the *Post-Dispatch*'s coverage of a political campaign stormed into the paper to complain, Cockerill shot him. He was exonerated, but the bad publicity depressed paper sales. The editor displayed a ruthlessness Pulitzer both despised and admired.

Cockerill looked up from his desk at the young interviewer and suggested she "get a bachelor and form a syndicate" of her own. Once again, here was the advice to leave journalism, marry ("form a syndicate" was a hokey metaphor, not a business plan), and busy herself with children. If she was frustrated, she didn't show it, quipping later that she declined to "relate a tale of blighted affections," and instead continued her mission, asking, "What do you think of women as journalists?"

Women didn't like the kind of things they were suitable for, Cockerill said. "There are society events which no man can report as well as a woman; yet they always claim to hate that style of work." Like Bly, other women reporters didn't hide their scorn for these assignments. J. C. Croly, who reported for the *World* under the pseudonym "Jennie June" had written to Pulitzer, asking for a better beat, complaining, "I cannot write the utter rubbish that seems to be expected from women—or columns about nothing." But with dozens of male applicants showing up each day, restless women weren't Cockerill's concern. The editor of the *Mail and Express* echoed these sentiments. Women were great for gossip, travel, dramatic criticism, but, he noted, "Their dress, constitution and habits of life keep them from the routine of a reporter's work."

Like Charles Dana, former Unitarian pastor George Hepworth of the *Herald* said he couldn't send a woman to police courts to cover crime and criminals, and even if he did, no one would talk to her. They were unsuitable for the sensations and scandals the public craved. Women needed to be respectable, and respectability was boring. Until "the public demands a different kind of news . . . women will be unable to serve as all-around reporters," he said. He added that with women in the office, men didn't feel free. They couldn't work in shirtsleeves, put their feet on their desks, or curse.

With Hepworth, Bly tried a different strategy, even more blunt and straightforward than she'd been with Dana.

"Dr. Hepworth, I want a position on the *Herald*."

"Yes?" he said. "What can you do?"

And, in what would become her career-defining trait—a splash of bravado, a hint of desperation—she answered, "Anything."

The *Herald* didn't hire her. And the article resulting from her interview tour, which Bly wrote up for the *Dispatch* to inform young women who long for "the empty glory and poor pay" of a reporter's life, wasn't encouraging to anyone with the same dreams. None of the male editors saw a place for women outside petticoat styles and party reports. Aspiring writers, mostly the qualified men whom editors preferred, were descending on the papers in thick flocks. No one offered her a job.

Nonetheless, these encounters provided food for thought. Though her interview subjects talked about education, experience, and writing ability, the front pages they published displayed a journalism that valued sheer nerve. The editors' view of what a woman could do was narrow, framed by convention. What if she could enlarge it? The editor of the *Telegram* had said, "Woman understands women, as men never can; so why should she not be able to write of their ways and habits?" He meant that they grasped intricacies of weddings and waltzes, but wasn't this true in other ways as well? Plenty of women crowded courts and jails; they just weren't reporters. Cockerill claimed, "No editor would like to send a woman out in bad weather or to questionable places for news." But what if the story was irresistible? Right in the middle of police stations and holding cells and other unseemly places? And what if it was something only a woman could do?

By September, Bly's purse had been stolen. Her rent was overdue. Pride wouldn't let her return to Pittsburgh and admit failure. She put on her lucky ring, a gold band around her thumb, and returned to Newspaper Row and the dirty, dilapidated building that housed the *World*. Somehow, she talked her way past the elevator operator up to the editorial department, saying she had an important story, and if the editor didn't want to hear it, she'd take it elsewhere.

Face-to-face with Colonel Cockerill again, she said he could send her out in bad weather. That she had no objection to "questionable places." That she wasn't going to quit and get married. She told him her ideas, including traveling in steerage class from Europe and writing about the immigrant experience. He gave her $25 to keep her from going to another paper while he thought it over.

Bly must have appeared sufficiently bold, or sufficiently reckless. When she returned, Cockerill asked whether she thought she could fake her way into New York's notorious insane asylum for women on Blackwell's Island, past the doctors, keeping up her role without discovery to report on conditions there. It was an opening, and Bly took it.

"I don't know what I can do until I try."

"Well, you can try," Cockerill said, "but if you can do it, it's more than anyone would believe."

OPPORTUNITY IN DISGUISE

Calmly, outwardly at least, I went out to my crazy business.

—Nellie Bly, *Ten Days in a Mad-House*

Blackwell's Island Insane Asylum for Women, a gleaming white building on an island in the East River, had been cloaked in rumors of beatings and neglect from the facility's opening in 1839. It was one of a constellation of institutions on the island—a penitentiary, a workhouse, an almshouse, a charity hospital—designed to shelter those the city wanted out of sight. The rapid current offshore thwarted escape. Sewers emptied into the river, drawing rats. When Charles Dickens visited the asylum, he noticed a suicidal patient locked alone in the dining room before he fled from the "naked ugliness and horror." The *New York Times* reported a girl forced to give birth while in a straitjacket.

A chill wind blew through New York City on September 23, 1887, as Bly headed toward a boarding house, the Temporary Home for Females, putting her plan in motion. The first step was to convince a group of strangers she should be committed. After practicing gazing wide-eyed into the mirror the night before, trying to capture what she imagined to be the vacant stare of the insane, she now adopted a different pose as she wandered down the street, and "assumed the look which maidens wear in pictures entitled 'Dreaming.'"

In the rest of the city, the New York Tennis Club's tournament went forward, despite the breeze. Dickens fans looked forward to a dramatic reading of *The Pickwick Papers* by the author's son in Brooklyn. In the harbor, *Alosia*, a ship from Naples with six hundred passengers onboard, had landed, only to be immediately quarantined for cholera. The sick were sent to Swinburne Island, those without symptoms to Hoffman Island: defending against the disease was a constant concern; an epidemic had broken out at Blackwell's Island not long before.

Illustration for Bly's article in the *World*, October 9, 1887

Once at the boardinghouse, a plain box with shuttered windows, Bly asked a surly blonde girl of about thirteen for lodging. She gave her name as "Nellie Brown," disguising herself, but keeping her initials. Inside, women with jobs and those seeking them ate an uninspired lunch of boiled beef and potatoes, served by the same brusque girl, then gathered in the back parlor on rickety furniture. As Bly sat, mulling her campaign, the assistant matron asked what was wrong.

"I can see it in your face. It tells the story of a great trouble."

"Yes, everything is so sad," replied Bly. No time like the present to start her ruse. She looked around at the other women knitting, tatting lace, listlessly scolding their children, and declared, "Why, they look horrible to me; just like crazy women. I am so afraid of them."

From there, she was off, saying she was afraid to go to bed, refusing to take off her gloves, claiming a headache and that she couldn't remember anything, and asking repeatedly, "Where are my trunks?"

Persuaded to go to her room, Bly worried if she fell asleep, she would awake refreshed, all her work undone, so she forced herself to stay up. She thought back over the events of her life, dwelling on old friends "recalled with a pleasurable thrill." Then she contemplated the future and whether she would "be able to pass over the river to the goal of my strange ambition." What would she find at the asylum, and did she have the strength to face what she saw? Were all the reports of mistreatment true? And once inside, would her editors be able to get her out?

Meanwhile, her insanity act gave another woman nightmares. Down the hall, someone woke screaming, saying Bly had been coming after her with a knife. In the morning, increasingly wary of this fraught guest who refused to leave, the assistant matron fetched the police.

O fficers escorted Bly to the police station house and from there to the Essex Market Police Court. Rival newspapers, trolling the courthouse for human interest stories, took note of the well-spoken young woman, wearing a black sailor hat with an illusion veil and gloves, alternately calling herself Nellie Brown and Nellie Morena, claiming to have been raised in Cuba and educated in a convent in New Orleans. She had only 33 cents and a notebook in her purse. Her dress might be wrinkled, but it was good enough quality, in both material and cut, to prompt curiosity. "Who Is This Insane Girl?" asked the *Sun*, describing her as "pretty, well dressed," and able to speak Spanish.

The presiding judge, the man who would decide her fate, was also taken by her outfit and her speech.

"Poor child," Justice Duffy said, "she is well dressed, and a lady. Her English is perfect, and I would stake everything on her being a good girl. I am positive she is somebody's darling."

The courtroom erupted into giggles. There were two types of woman and, despite playing insane, it was important for Bly, as a prisoner and a reporter, to remain on the right side of the line, the side of chastity and respectability. It was the constant lesson of novels, Sunday school sermons, parental lectures, and etiquette books: a fallen woman was ripe for abuse. Duffy's words implied that she had slipped to the wrong side of the line, that she was "kept." Bly stifled a guffaw in her handkerchief, making light of the comment, but maintaining her pure status was integral to her safety. And to her ability to experiment. As another undercover reporter would put it: "A good woman can do without blemish to herself many things that a doubtful or foolish one would blacken herself by trying to do."

"I mean she is some woman's darling," Duffy backtracked. "I am sure some one is searching for her. Poor girl, I will be good to her, for she looks like my sister, who is dead."

Here Bly's hewing to the line of "good girl" and Duffy's compassion for someone he recognized as his class—his symbolic adoption—almost undid all of her effort to get committed. When one of the policemen suggested, "Send her to the island," the matron of the woman's home, who had escorted her to court, answered, "Don't! She is a lady and it would kill her."

Judge Duffy waffled, asking the matron if she could keep Bly a few more days until the court could find her relatives, but the matron refused, and Duffy reluctantly referred Bly to Bellevue Hospital for more evaluation. From there, if doctors declared her insane, she would be sent to the asylum.

At Bellevue, her status started to fall in earnest. The hospital sat on a bleak street, populated by the destitute, diseased, and mentally ill, those waiting to see the doctors or waiting at the end of East Twenty-sixth Street for the ship to Blackwell's Island. Some, in despair after a Bellevue stay, went straight to the pier to jump off it. Bly was now a woman without relatives to protect her, exiled from mainstream society. A doctor saw her (feigned) distress and offered to accompany her to the office, where he turned in her paperwork. But when she was sent to the insane ward, and a burly man dragged her away, the doctor, despite her pleading, said he was needed at an amputation and left.

After evaluating Bly, Bellevue doctors remained puzzled. Maybe she had been drugged or suffered from depression or melancholia. At least one, though, determined she had "hysterical mania."

With this diagnosis, the doctors tapped into a centuries-long debate over women's health. Based on an ancient malady, cited by Hippocrates and Plato and centered on the notion of a "wandering womb" afflicting various parts of the body where it settled, hysteria in the second half of the nineteenth century had evolved into a unique strain. Symptoms included fits, nausea, vomiting, headaches, self-centeredness, sadness, laughter, depression, and yawning. Subcategories encompassed "neurasthenia," or nervous exhaustion; "greensickness," which today might be recognized as anemia or anorexia; "nymphomania," which struck, in particular, the small, dark, and buxom, as well as young widows and women married to cold men who lacked vigor. Hysteria's risk factors included taxing the intellect, "the sight of licentious paintings," "frequent visits to balls or the theatre," "the too assiduous cultivation of the fine arts," and living in cities. The most popular treatment had been dreamed up by Dr. Silas Weir Mitchell, who advocated bed rest without any distractions (like books), forced feeding, and electric shocks.

Easy to diagnose, yet impossible to define, the only sure thing about hysteria was that the primary risk factor was being female. Sometimes, that in itself was enough. "As a general rule, all women are hysterical and . . . every woman carries with her the seeds of hysteria. Hysteria, before being an illness, is a temperament, and what constitutes a temperament in a woman is rudimentary hysteria," claimed one physician. The nature of their bodies made sufferers unreliable.

Other doctors acknowledged, though rarely in so many words,

that the problem was sexual frustration, the struggles of a female body straitjacketed by Victorian ideals of femininity. Cures included pelvic massage, spraying upper thighs with water, and, when the technology developed, the application of vibrators to "dissolve the paroxysm."

But the patients receiving these treatments were the lucky ones, mainly wealthy, mainly white. Others ended up in the asylum. Like Nellie Brown.

O n the boat across the East River, in a dirty cabin, accompanied by attendants who spit tobacco juice on the floor, Bly took note of the other women consigned with her to Blackwell's Island. Tillie Mayard, a frail twenty-five-year-old with short hair who was recovering from an illness, stood out even at Bellevue. She seemed sane enough, just sick. Mayard thought friends were sending her to a convalescent home to recover from a "nervous debility" and was devastated to find out where she was going. Bly would keep an eye on her.

On shore, an ambulance took them along the river road, past sparse trees and a reeking building Bly determined was the kitchen. The L-shaped asylum itself, enormous and stark, was built of pale stone quarried on the island. Once again, Bly feared her performance skills might let her down. When she walked into Blackwell's grand hall, marked by a twisting staircase, her goal in sight, she wanted to shout in triumph. Seeing her expression, Mayard commented, "I can't see what has cheered you up so. . . . Ever since we left Bellevue you have looked happy."

"Well, we might as well make the best of it," Bly replied.

The first night, Bly eavesdropped as Mayard pled her case, asking doctors to test her for insanity, only to be ignored. Attendants slapped the newcomers, fed them bread with rancid butter, roughly bathed them in icy water in a cold room. In a more cheerful moment, Bly played "Rock-a-Bye Baby" on an out-of-tune piano, and Mayard sang along. Mayard plotted escape, telling Bly she would be obedient until she could make a plan, but the next morning confessed that, after a sleepless night, "My nerves were so unstrung before I came here, and I fear I shall not be able to stand the strain."

Settling into the asylum, Bly met many patients, like Mayard, who didn't strike her as insane at all. One immigrant woman with little English was locked up by her husband, according to the nurses, "because she had a fondness for other men than himself." Another, who described herself as "penniless" with "nowhere to go," had asked to be sent to the poorhouse but ended up at the asylum instead. A third, a young cook, had been committed after she lost her temper when someone dirtied the floor she'd just finished cleaning.

Immigrants, the poor, the adulterous, the angry, the sick. Like hysteria, the asylum seemed like a catch basin for women society didn't know what to do with.

Once inside Bly stopped acting "crazy" at all. It wasn't necessary. Despite Mayard's requests for evaluation, doctors paid scant attention to the patients. "How can a doctor judge a woman's sanity by merely bidding her good morning and refusing to hear her pleas for release?" Bly asked one doctor. She concluded, "Even the sick ones know it is useless to say anything, for the answer will be that it is their imagination."

In fact, the place seemed designed to turn sane women crazy. When nurses whisked patients out of sight, Bly gathered evidence of violence on their return: black eyes, choke marks on throats. And she hadn't even seen the worst, deciding that she wouldn't try to get into the Lodge and the Retreat, which housed the most violent prisoners. Her bravery had its limits. Noting that women were locked in their rooms with individual locks, a death sentence in a fire, she suggested to the assistant superintendent they install universal locks, like those in prisons, so all doors could be opened with one switch. He just looked at her with pity, wondering about her prison stay. After days of eating rotten beef, shivering by open windows, sitting all day confined to a straight-backed bench, staring at the wall, Bly concluded that there was no recourse for the sane. "The insane asylum on Blackwell's Island is a human rat-trap," she would write. "It is easy to get in, but once there it is impossible to get out."

Through all this, Bly struggled to do the work that drew her there, pleading for the return of the pencil and notebook that had been in her purse, only to be told, "You can't have it, so shut up." When she asked again, a doctor told her she hadn't brought a pencil and should strive to stop hallucinating. She stayed up late, trying to take in as much as she could, the whispers and shufflings of the asylum night. The nurses offered a narcotic to prompt sleep, and, when Bly refused it, they called the doctor who threatened to put it in her arm with a needle. Figuring once injected, the medicine would be in her blood for good, Bly drank it, but forced herself to throw up as soon as the staff left.

For Mayard, still not fully recovered, the unsalted and spoiled food, the cold baths, the inadequate clothing, took their toll. She grew steadily worse. One day, when they sat together on a bench, Mayard started shivering violently, then collapsed in what Bly referred to as a "fit." When the superintendent came in, Bly reported, "He caught her roughly between the eyebrows or thereabouts, and pinched until her face was crimson." Mayard was never the same.

After ten days, the lawyer from the *World* showed up, asking for the confounding Nellie Brown. Relatives were willing to take over her care, he told the asylum. Fetched from a walk with other inmates, pulled from the line and led through the grounds, Bly said an abrupt "goodbye" to those around her, and was free.

The departure of the sad girl from Cuba left the other papers in suspense. What was her story? How did all these strange parts add up? They would soon find out. The first installment of Bly's asylum exposé splashed across the *World*'s front page days later.

B ly worked fast. Rescued on October 4, she published the first of two Blackwell's articles on October 9, under the headline "Behind Asylum Bars." Illustrations of Bly, practicing insane faces in a mirror, standing before the judge, being grilled by the doctor, decorated the columns. Over the course of the lengthy piece (the two parts together spanned almost thirty thousand words), she wrote about the freezing cold, the inedible food, the cruel treatment of the prisoners, and the way the facility was completely incapable of telling who was sane or not. It was desperate for reform. At the end of the first installment appeared the signature "Nellie Bly." In the second installment, "Inside the Madhouse," published October 16, Bly's name moved to the subhead: "Nellie Bly's Experience in the Blackwell's Insane Asylum." This was quite a coup for a new reporter.

The tale of the pretty girl with amnesia had been compelling, but the tale of the young woman who faked her way into the asylum was explosive. *Sun* reporters scrambled to catch up, interviewing doctors, nurses, and others who had encountered Nellie Brown. They were writing about Bly writing about her asylum experience. Bly was so popular with readers that within a few weeks, the *World* highlighted her name in their promotion of upcoming issues. Her story crept into other advertisements, too. Under the headline "Can Doctors Tell Insanity?" and the subhead "Experience of the World's Reporter, Nellie Bly, Would Indicate Not," an ad for "Dr. Green's Nervura Nerve Tonic" offered to "restore tone, vigor, and vitality to the brain, rebuild and restore lost nerve force and power, and renew the strength and energies of the whole system."

From its epicenter in New York, the asylum exposé rippled outward. The rise of syndication and news transmission by telegraph meant the story stirred readers on San Francisco streetcars and benches in Tennessee. The *Salt Lake Herald* declared the articles had set "New York wild with excitement," and added, "It's a tale far more interesting than a romance." The *Hazel Green Herald*, out of Kentucky, reprinted an article under the headline "Smarter Than All of Them," that crowed, "The police, the Court, the nurses and physicians at the famous Bellevue Hospital, were all successfully duped by a mere girl." The *Ohio Democrat* concluded, "Miss Bly has undoubtedly performed a great work for the cause of humanity." The *Iola Register* reprinted a column that took Bly's performance as evidence for the competence of women. The whole piece was a rebuttal to the editors who told Bly women were only good for twittering about ball gowns. After recounting the stunt that "made a sensation from Maine to Georgia," the writer concluded, "There is no reason whatever, there can be no argument whatever, against girls working on newspapers."

And if praise and fame weren't enough, her articles had real-world effects. Bly testified before a grand jury, an experience she found gratifying: "I answered the summons with pleasure, because I longed to help those of God's most unfortunate children whom I had left prisoners behind me. If I could not bring them that boon of all boons, liberty, I hoped at least to influence others to make life more bearable for them." She also went along on an inspection of asylum facilities. To Bly's disgust, inspectors found better food, barrels of salt in the kitchen, polite nurses, and few of the patients she'd deemed mistakenly imprisoned. The institution had clearly prepared for their arrival. And Tillie Mayard? "I shuddered when I looked at her," Bly wrote. She seemed to have become genuinely insane.

Even so, the grand jury recommended the asylum hire at least three female doctors, install prison-style locks that could open with one motion, and receive increased funds. The Board of Estimate and Apportionment gave the facility an additional $50,000.

Though it was the kind of creative reporting he loved, Pulitzer wasn't enjoying the splash. He was strangely silent for reasons that soon became clear. One morning, a month after Bly's first asylum piece, he went to the *World*'s offices to pore over the editorial page, to see that each phrase met his high standards for vividness and clarity. He'd been stressed for some time, weathering constant criticism of the *World*'s exposures. Insomnia plagued him. When he held up the sheets, as he told a friend later, "I was astonished to find that I could hardly see the writing, let alone read it." A doctor ordered him to stay in a dark room for six weeks, and he did, but afterward, the prognosis was no better. The diagnosis was a ruptured blood vessel, then a detached retina. More rest was ordered. He was going blind.

Bly's wasn't the first undercover story, but it was inventive in all kinds of ways. In 1859, just before the Civil War, Mortimer Thomson of the abolitionist *New-York Tribune* posed as a buyer at an auction of more than four hundred enslaved men and women in Savannah, Georgia. Other abolitionist reporters went "blackbirding," signing on as crew on slave ships to write about what they saw.

In a famous stunt for London's new *Pall Mall Gazette* in 1866, writer James Greenwood slipped on an ill-fitting coat that closed with the help of a piece of twine and spent the night in the "casual" (or temporary resident) ward of Lambeth Workhouse. He described grim conditions, taking a bath in dirty water the color of "weak mutton broth," sleeping on a straw mattress stained with blood. But it was less an exposé of the institution than of the people who ended up there. They were ugly, dirty, lazy, and used shocking language, according to Greenwood. And his conclusion that "I have avoided the detail of horrors infinitely more revolting than anything that appears in these papers," implied the men were selling sex rather than just sharing bedding.

The *Pall Mall Gazette* continued undercover exposés with W. T. Stead's four-part 1885 series, "The Maiden Tribute of Modern Babylon." For this report on children being tricked into prostitution, drugged and kidnapped or sold outright by their parents, Stead used traditional techniques—interviewing a police officer, the owner of a brothel, and a former prostitute. But he also pretended to be a customer, requesting very young virgins, verified to have never had sex by a doctor, which the brothel owners repeatedly supplied. The age of consent at the time was thirteen, allowing many of these abuses, and his series helped get it raised to sixteen.

In the *Pall Mall Gazette* stories, as significant as they were, the women described were still powerless. At the time of Bly's stunt, women who made the news were generally murder victims or those fallen from virtue. Front-page stories from weeks just before and after Bly's asylum articles included "He Dug Her Grave, Shooting, Stabbing and Burying an Old Woman"; "Mrs. Robinson's Fatal Leap: A Louisville Woman's Suicide"; "She Ran Away from Home, Story of Niagara Girl Found Wandering in Boston Streets"; and "A Bride Choked with Gas." And the reporters who wrote about the enigmatic waif in the courtroom tried to fit her into one of those boxes. Was she a pathetic innocent? Or had she been seduced and abandoned?

If Bly's entry into journalism showed anything, it was that representation of women in newspapers altered women's lives. She got her start protesting Quiet Observer's thoughts about her sex's natural abilities. Two years later, Bly wrote about a new kind of woman, one who took action, did good, was brave. And this heroine was battling institutions. Judges, police officers, medical experts—all had been wrong. The Bellevue doctors were convinced that Bly was hysterical, but her whole experience undermined their authority to make this diagnosis. After she passed a second round of tests, she wrote, "I began to have a smaller regard for the ability of doctors than I ever had before, and a greater one for myself. I felt sure now that no doctor could tell whether people were insane or not, so long as the case was not violent."

Part of the asylum story's appeal was this kind of audacity, but another lure was its style.

W. T. Stead embellished his sentences with ornate clauses and classical references. At the start of the "Maiden Tribute," he wrote, "In ancient times, if we may believe the myths of Hellas, Athens, after a disastrous campaign, was compelled by her conqueror to send once every nine years a tribute to Crete of seven youths and seven maidens. The doomed fourteen, who were selected by lot amid the lamentations of the citizens, returned no more." Then he quoted Ovid in Latin.

Here is Bly, in the first paragraph of her Blackwell's exposé: "Could I pass a week in the insane ward at Blackwell's Island? I said I could and I would. And I did.'"

Bly shook free of the ruffles and hoop skirts of Victorian prose and made her sentences accessible to the less educated and to recent immigrants who might struggle with English—the specific readers Pulitzer coveted. While she advocated for serious reform, her writing was always a pleasure to read. She was funny. Up all night at the Temporary Home for Women, she spent hours watching the mice that landed on her quilt and crawled over her pillow and the cockroaches that struck her as unusually large and fast. "I believe I made some valuable studies in natural history," she wrote. Bly included ample dialogue. She was also unabashedly vain, and the humor is partially at her own expense. After her hair dried in knots following an asylum bath, a nurse combed it out, braided it, and tied it with a red rag. "My curly bangs refused to stay back," Bly wrote, "so that at least was left of my former glory." Though Bly's prose had its flaws, something in it invited the reader to come along for the ride.

For Bly, the stunt drove the story. The delight in fooling the powerful, the slipping disguise, the fact of her being a rather poor actress—it all added to the drama. In fact, that was most of the drama, as she often breezed by genuine hazards. When she was at Bellevue, a doctor came into her room as she got ready to sleep. He sat on the edge of the bed, put his arm around her, asked about Cuba, and said, "Don't you remember me? I remember you." In the article in the *World*, Bly mentioned that this doctor was particularly handsome and commented, "It was a terrible thing to play insane before this young man, and only a girl can sympathize with me in my position." But in the version she published as a book, a few months later, she acknowledged that his caress could be read the wrong way. "Some people have since censured this action," she wrote, "but I feel sure, even if it was a little indiscreet, that the young doctor only meant kindness to me." A sexual encounter, even against her will, would have bumped her out of the "good woman" class. Chastity meant credibility. Throughout her story, Bly downplayed real risks—disease, assault, drugging—and highlighted less significant ones—that her hair was a mess, that she might burst out laughing and blow her cover.

This strong first-person point of view immersed readers in the narrator's experience. Bly's tone was confiding—a whisper to a trusted friend rather than the assertions of a disembodied observer—and the body she inhabited was specifically young and female. The reader was right next to her, shivering, thrown into the icy bath, smelling spoiled meat, responding to a handsome doctor, hiding behind a veil. This vivid narrator, full of life, moral but not preachy, was clearly enjoying herself. And if this little scrap of a person—this "mere girl" as the *Hazel Green Herald* put it—could take on the whole system of institutions with wit and compassion and negligible acting ability, what couldn't be done? A stunt reporter had real power.

Suddenly, everybody wanted to hire one.

Or be one.

DETECTIVE FOR THE PEOPLE

Detective: B. n. One whose occupation it is to discover matters artfully concealed.

—Oxford English Dictionary

All across the country, throughout late 1887 and 1888, girls took notice. They opened the paper as they ate their eggs, read headlines as they stood in line at the corner store to buy butter, glanced at a father's desk as they tidied it, or grabbed an abandoned page on a street-car seat.

One of these was Eva McDonald, a voracious reader in Minnesota with a rebellious streak, who would discover the potential of stunt reporting as an activist tool. Small with a dark fringe of bangs, McDonald had a round, pale face and thick, ink-swipe brows. A bout of diphtheria when she was nine left her heart weak, but she was anything but frail. If there was a beehive to be poked with a stick, McDonald wasn't going to stand around eating store-bought honey. On some women, the frills and ribbons of the time flowed naturally, but photographs show McDonald stuffed uncomfortably into puffed sleeves and lace collars. With her cropped hair, even at twenty-one she looked like a twelve-year-old boy, more likely to be whitewashing a fence for Tom Sawyer than writing newspaper articles.

McDonald lacked polish, and she felt it. When her mother, who claimed aristocratic roots and had high-class aspirations for her daughter, sent McDonald to a nun for piano lessons, student and teacher quickly agreed she was hopeless. Declaring her "a terrible tomboy," the nun offered to teach her elocution instead. And her pupil agreed, sensing that speaking well might come in handy to accomplish what she wanted to do, though she wasn't yet sure what that was. She told herself that if her family had only stayed in Maine rather than moving to Minnesota, she would have gone to college like her friends, maybe even become a lawyer, stunning the courtroom with her arguments. But now, her education disrupted, that avenue was closed to her. When she tried to get a job as a teacher, the school board rejected her as too scrawny and told her to "go do something else for two or three years until you grow up." She had a talent for recitation, particularly comic poems, but there wasn't much money in that. Typesetting paid well but was tiring.

She knew what she didn't want to do, though, which was take care of any more siblings. One of eight with five younger brothers, two younger sisters, and a mother who doted on the latest baby but left the others to McDonald's care, she was overwhelmed and resentful. Minnesota was full of things to do. Sledding, ice-skating, swimming in the lakes and rivers—it all happened just outside the window, and she wanted to be out in it. Or haunting the library in pursuit of religious histories to fuel arguments with her Catholic-school teachers. Or making forays into union organizing as a member of the Ladies' Protective Association, Local Assembly 5261, Knights of Labor. McDonald also belonged to the Typographical Union. But, as the oldest, she was usually stuck inside, trying to read while rocking a cradle-bound baby to sleep.

So when an editor for the *St. Paul Globe* showed up at her house, saying he'd seen her in a local theater production—maybe as Mother Foresight in *Danger Signal* or Mrs. Arabella Blowhard in *The Persecuted Dutchman*—and asked if she'd like an assignment where she could put her talents to good use, she said yes, thankful that her mother wasn't home. He wanted her to investigate conditions for working women by sneaking into factories. It was hardly proper, and her mother would have disapproved. Her carpenter father, indifferent, said she could do what she liked. Here was a chance to get out of the house, escape the sticky fingers and tidying, earn money, and turn her political convictions into action.

Eva McDonald

So March 1888 found McDonald picking her way through treacherous downtown Minneapolis, pursuing her first newspaper story. The late-winter blizzards had stopped, leaving icy ruts and ankle-deep pools of slush. Textile warehouses and flour mills powered by St. Anthony Falls lined the railroad tracks along the Mississippi. Boardinghouses, some cheap and run-down, others more spruce, housed the women who came to town from the cornfields and prairies that rippled over much of the state. They were drawn by the promise of regular wages and the excitement of city life. Like them, McDonald was increasingly interested in standing at the center of things.

At the Shotwell, Clerihew & Lothman clothing factory, one of her first stops, McDonald took the freight elevator up. A little over a year before, Karl Marx's daughter, Eleanor Marx, had visited town to lecture on socialism. Facing a packed crowd, she used female Minneapolis factory workers as an example of those abused under the current system. Some earned $1.50 to $2 a week for ten-hour days, she said. The audience and the newspapers scoffed at her claims—wages couldn't possibly be that low—but McDonald herself knew stories about mistreatment at factories throughout the city, and Shotwell, Clerihew & Lothman in particular. In January, an exposed sewing machine mechanism installed in the floor of Shotwell caught a woman's skirt and dragged her to the ground, causing permanent injury.

Wage details could be hard to come by—some companies posted guards at the factory doors or enlisted supervisors to eavesdrop on those who might be complaining to reporters or union representatives. The women themselves were reluctant to talk, afraid of being fired or embarrassed by their meager pay. Going undercover was a way in, and McDonald adopted the pseudonym "Eva Gay."

At Shotwell, more than two hundred women hunched over sewing machines at long tables, making overalls, jeans, and wool pants—sturdy clothing for miners and farmers. Neat paint on the walls couldn't hide the sewage smell or sweltering temperature of the overheated room. A woman with a German accent explained that the water rarely ran in the toilets, and they couldn't open the windows because of the cold. When McDonald, feeling woozy, asked if it made the girls sick, the woman said every day some of them requested a pass from the foreman to step outside for fresh air. McDonald asked why they couldn't go out without permission and got a suspicious glance in return.

"Don't know. What do you want to know for anyhow?"

McDonald moved on.

As she conducted more sly interviews, McDonald found wages even lower than she expected. A girl sweating over a pile of calico shirts earned 3.5 cents per shirt—the ones the boss didn't rip up as subpar—about $1.75 a week at a time when a week's lodging alone might cost $3. Women were paid as though their income was a bonus, supplementing that of husband or father, but many provided their family's only money and had younger siblings to support. And wages were only going down. Cuts had come in January, and the company threatened more. A girl sewing overalls who used to receive 12 cents per pair now earned only 7.

But more than the smell and the wages and the long hours, the women at Shotwell objected to their boss. The superintendent, H. B. Woodward, begrudged them pleasure and seemed to relish their humiliation. If he met an employee in the street wearing a nice dress, he'd sneer that she imagined herself a lady. Clearly, she earned too much, he'd say, and suggest cutting her wages even more. Violent, he threatened to kick one employee down the stairs. When men in other departments leered at the women, Woodward ignored it. He hired one candidate to work as a supervisor, then never gave her the promotion. The woman would say later, hinting at what couldn't be stated outright, that she wasn't sorry "when she learned some of the qualifications necessary outside of skill."

"If your foreman insults you, why don't you complain to the proprietors?" McDonald asked.

"What's the use?" another replied. "If we don't want to put up with the way we're treated, we are told we can leave. They can find plenty glad to get a chance to work at any wages."

The mid- to late 1880s were a charged time for American labor. In 1885, the Knights of Labor, the first national industrial union in the United States, had established its power by striking and forcing railway companies to rescind a wage cut. The organization threatened another strike in the fall when railroads planned to lay off union activists, and the company backed down again. These high-profile successes led to Knights of Labor's membership increasing from 104,000 in July 1885 to 703,000 the next year. Unlike the competing organization, the American Federation of Labor, the Knights admitted women. They, and other unions, were gaining momentum. But in spring 1886 in Chicago, a nationwide protest in favor of the eight-hour workday spilled out of control. On May 3, police shot strikers at the McCormick Reaper Works. The next day, at a rally in Haymarket Square, someone threw a bomb, and, in the rioting afterward, eleven people were killed, including seven police officers. Known anarchists, several of whom had been elsewhere at the time, were rounded up, tried with little evidence, and hanged.

In some minds, unions became associated with criminality, dynamite, and explosions, even if they hadn't been directly responsible for the Haymarket violence. In light of the bad publicity following the anarchists' trial, Knights of Labor membership declined. Union issues, like the eight-hour day and the promotion of strikes, became increasingly polarized. And the question of women in factories performing physically demanding work became a particular focus. In the fall of 1886, a year and a half before McDonald became Eva Gay, Helen Stuart Campbell's series for the *New-York Tribune*, "Prisoners of Poverty," had detailed the lives of garment industry workers, paid by the piece for such low amounts that they struggled to feed themselves and support their families. Campbell didn't wear a disguise, but she conducted interviews of the women trying to make ends meet by hemming shirts and sewing buttonholes. Campbell had the heart of an economist and pointed out that the cheap, fashionable clothing heaped on bargain counters came at the expense of the poor who made it, in airless conditions, for pennies. Campbell also highlighted women's particular plight: They had little leverage. Because they couldn't vote, politicians didn't even have to pretend to care about their troubles or opinions.

But the power of exposure was a tool available even to those without access to the ballot box, a particularly potent one when backed by a newspaper with a large circulation. In New York, Bly continued to use smooth talking and costumes to ferret out corruption. In March, she posed as the wife of a patent medicine manufacturer. A bill in the state legislature would force makers of these concoctions (many useless, some dangerous) to file a list of ingredients with the Board of Health. She met lobbyist Edward Phelps at his Albany hotel and offered him $2,000 to kill the bill. He said he'd do it for $1,125, then ticked off the names of six politicians whose votes could be bought. Needless to say, as the *Buffalo Times* (which called Bly a "petticoat detective") declared: "Statesmen Shaking at the Knees and Red with Rage Denouncing a Metropolitan Newspaper."

In their use of deception and disguise, stunt reporters echoed another phenomenon of the time: the rise of the private detective, particularly as embodied by the Pinkerton National Detective Agency, an organization with origins in 1850s Chicago. The Pinkertons, an extensive network of investigators, worked mostly as corporate spies. Railroads used Pinkertons to eavesdrop on disgruntled conversations and then break unions. Streetcar companies hired them to ride the lines and catch conductors who let passengers slide without paying a fare. Stunt reporters, like the Pinkertons, infiltrated organizations, looked for clues, ferreted out secrets, and interviewed witnesses. But the reporters presented themselves as sleuthing from the other side— investigators for the people—catching businesses as they acted unethically and thwarted laws. Along with the *Buffalo Times*, papers like the *Times-Picayune* pointed out similarities between the jobs, responding to Bly's exploits by objecting to "the spectacle of a brilliant young woman in the role of a private detective." And one of the appeals of stunt reporting to its readers was its similarity to detective novels. The first Sherlock Holmes story, "A Study in Scarlet," came out the same year Nellie Bly published her initial investigation for the *World*.

Though clearly inspired by Bly (the headline of her first story echoed language from a Bly article published several months earlier), McDonald took her own approach. Her writing style was spare, mostly records of conversations, but she doggedly pestered reluctant subjects to talk. Bly loved to chart her elaborate cover stories. McDonald made only the faintest pretense of seeking work. Her preferred technique was to slip onto the factory floor while the superintendent was distracted, ignoring NO HANDS WANTED and NO ADMISSION signs, then wander through, sidling up to anyone who looked willing to talk. Scrawniness had its uses.

McDonald's sensibility was different than Bly's, and the results were different, too. McDonald's piece sparked not a governmental investigation but a strike. This was another power available to those without the vote. Despite worker demands, Shotwell had refused to return wages to 1887 levels and then owners cut wages again—by an average of 17 percent. While the *St. Paul Globe* suggested ministers and charitable donors get involved, on April 18, less than a month after McDonald's first *Globe* article, Shotwell's female workers stood up from their sewing machines and walked out.

Later in the afternoon, they returned to the factory at First Avenue South and Second Street, to collect their pay. The door was locked. When it finally opened, only a few were let in at a time, leaving a mass of women on the sidewalk. As they waited, they felt damp drops down their collars, in their hair. But it wasn't spring rain. They looked up to find their male colleagues, several stories up, pelting them with wadded-up bits of paper, cemented with spit.

Over the next few weeks, strike organizers raised money for women out of work, sought support from other local unions, held meetings to plot strategy. They wanted higher wages, but they also wanted Superintendent Woodward fired. As one worker commented, "If we do go back it will be with the understanding that the dude clerks shall stop ogling us and trying to mash us when we go to and from work. We call ourselves respectable and want to be treated as if we were."

At one meeting, 175 women showed up drenched from the pouring rain. The organizing committee had met with the company and shared its report: Shotwell, Clerihew & Lothman would only hire one hundred women back, and Woodward threatened more rules for those who returned—no talking during working hours, 9.5-hour work days, the firing of women who couldn't sew fast enough to make $6 a week. In response, the women threatened a boycott. Union men, who supported the strike, were a big market for overalls and jeans.

They pitched their case to the public at another meeting. With a theatrical flourish, strikers decorated a drop curtain with overalls and shirts and pinned two numbers to each, a comparison of pay at Shotwell to a comparable factory in St. Paul. A blouse bore the labels SHOTWELL, CLERIHEW & LOTHMAN, 6 CENTS and ST. PAUL 9 CENTS. A lecturer from a local home for unwed mothers warned that girls who couldn't earn living wages "have only the option of ruination or destruction." (This was a common line of reasoning, one that McDonald embraced early on then left behind as old-fashioned. The argument went: without good working conditions, women would become prostitutes, as if the only reason to treat them fairly was to preserve their virtue.) A minister said he refused to preach about angels when laborers, like these women, lacked basic necessities. Attendees voted to request that the firm put the matter of pay to arbitration.

These wide-ranging strategies built support, which the women desperately needed. The firm didn't sit idly by. It pushed back from several angles. The Jobbers Association wrote up a report saying the girls were actually well paid—one girl making $6.96 for cheap shirts, another $9 a week for jeans. In addition, the investigators reported that "charges of ungentlemanly conduct on the part of the superintendent were completely groundless." Several workers wrote to the paper, complaining that the strike leaders hadn't distributed donated funds fairly. A man named Christian Tingwold claimed to have heard the strike leaders insult the coworkers who had returned to Shotwell, saying they had "no character, no principle." These strategies drove a wedge between women ostensibly on the same side. The strike ground on, and more and more workers slipped back to their sewing machines.

The *Minneapolis Tribune*, the *Globe*'s competition, found the Jobbers' report particularly convincing, lauding it as "made by a body of men who could not be trifled with, and in language too plain to be misunderstood." The workers at the factory were happy, the *Tribune* suggested, until "along comes a St. Paul newspaper interloper, [who] begins a series of tirades against the horrid condition of working women of Minneapolis." McDonald's articles, the paper argued, "practically became the direct cause of the strike." The *Tribune* called the reporter a "walking delegate," implying she was a union representative bent on agitation.

The strike leaders denied all of it. The president of the Jobbers Association, they pointed out, was Clerihew of Shotwell, Clerihew & Lothman. Tingwold, like the Jobbers report, was an industry plant, they suspected.

But the *Tribune* was onto something. The charge of "walking delegate" was apt; McDonald knew the strike leaders well; they sat on union committees together, including the reception committee for the Painters and Decorators Protective Association Ball. As early as January 1888, McDonald had given a speech urging factory women to organize. Whatever the *St. Paul Globe's* purpose in hiring McDonald, she had her own agenda. She used the character of "Eva Gay" to educate readers about tactics and labor terms. Gay was much more naive about strikes than union-member McDonald must have been, asking innocently at one point, "What is a boycott?"

Just as all this unfolded—as the company refused to budge, as more women returned to making shirts, as the list of firms agreeing to boycott grew longer—McDonald traveled north to Duluth to give her first major union speech on the shore of Lake Superior. At

Eva Gay promotion in the *Saint Paul Globe*, March 31, 1888

the same time she'd been writing, she'd been learning to lecture. The talk on "Labor Organization" started off inauspiciously. Poor weather kept many away, and only four of the attendees were women, the very group she hoped to inspire. But she spoke anyway, transforming the observations she'd made as a reporter into a rallying cry. Women often worked not just ten-hour days but twelve- to fourteen-hour days and for much lower pay than men. The best they could hope for, if they spent all this time laboring and "never indulging in laughter," was $4.25 a week and a $25 annual bonus. Their efforts to improve their lives were undermined because they "do not ask for what they want or, if they do, they ask in the wrong way," McDonald said. If they co-operated and organized, like the men, like the Shotwell strikers, they might get what they wanted.

Political lecturing blended all of McDonald's skills—elocution taught by the nun, acting instincts honed on the community stage, a fierce commitment to the working class and women's rights, and a certain lawyerly fire. "The greatest little 'Labor Agitator' in the west," a friend later wrote about her on-stage magnetism. "Maybe the best speaker I have heard."

Though she held up the Shotwell strikers as an inspirational exam-ple, back in Minneapolis, the strike was collapsing. This was because Shotwell, Clerihew & Lothman was collapsing. Financial troubles had surfaced early in the year, and the firm responded by understat-ing its debt. By June, Theodore Shotwell was borrowing from one bank to pay another, writing checks in the hopes he could convince friends in the East to lend him money to cover them. By mid-June the company stopped paying its bills, and the *Globe* headline declared: "The Firm of Shotwell, Clerihew & Lothman Embarrassed." New York sources decribed debts much larger than previously thought. A bank account supposed to guarantee loans was empty. Shotwell, so distinguished with his gold-headed cane, so upstanding, head of the company the *Tribune* declared "one of the most responsible in the city," appeared suddenly in a less flattering light. In early July, Shot-well, Clerihew & Lothman were arrested.

By October, notices appeared in the paper advertising deep discounts on flannel, buttons, wool suits—all the "large Bankrupt Wholesale Dry Goods stock of Shotwell, Clerihew & Lothman." And the factory workers who hadn't been able to find other jobs drifted back to the winds and big bluestem, sky blue aster, and buffalo grass of the prairie, and the farms carved out of it.

Throughout the rest of the year, McDonald continued her exposés (as well as running, and losing, a race to be the first woman on the school board). She had a job, elocution lessons, and the ability to make people pay attention to what she had to say. The *Globe* took pride in her reporting, calling the series "a crusade for women." Increasingly, she left behind her younger siblings and explored her freedom. Shocked by her daughter's latest splash and by her moving into a boardinghouse and wandering all corners of the city, her mother would say, "Well, we've come to a fine pass when I got to look at the morning paper to see where my daughter was yesterday."

McDonald interviewed laundry workers who stood on damp floors, slogging through the winter in wet shoes. She visited another facility where the owner repeatedly "forgot" to pay his workers. She ate dinner with chambermaids at a hotel that featured ants in the sugar bowl and flies in the mustard. She charted further wage inequity, reporting that while female telegraph operators were paid $50 a month, males received $85. At a knitting factory, the girls warned that her notebook would reveal her identity as everyone was checked as they left to be sure they weren't stealing. But once again, McDonald somehow slid by, and, as she noted, "joyfully made my escape."

HUNGER FOR TROUBLE

There is hardly an editor in New York who is not bothered with young women who want to disguise themselves and go into unusual places with the idea of making newspaper stories out of their experiences.

—*Buffalo Morning News*, 1888

The year Nellie Bly went into the asylum was a low point for the *Chicago Times*. A Democratic Party organ for decades, its criticisms of Lincoln and the Union cause in the Civil War were so aggressive that General Ambrose Burnside sent soldiers to stop the presses. The *Times* hewed relentlessly to the wrong side of history, referring to Lincoln's Gettysburg Address as "silly, flat, and dishwatery utterances." The publisher, Wilbur Storey, whose journalistic goal was to "print the news and raise hell," pioneered an incendiary style. His paper was infamous for spewing inflammatory rhetoric and unearthing things best left buried. A former reporter summed up its early years this way: "Scandals in private life, revolting details from the evidence taken in police court trials, imaginary liaisons of a filthy character, reeked, seethed like a hell's broth in the *Times'* cauldrons and made a stench in the nostrils of decent people."

At his death in 1884, suffering from dementia, Storey left a will that would be fought over for years, becoming the kind of news he loved to cover. His paper, enterprising and original, whatever else you might say about it, descended into a sorry rag with a front page overrun with ads—True Bay Rum, gentlemen's underwear, Dr. Shephard's London Toilet Water. The rest was wire stories written elsewhere, railway timetables, snoozy editorials.

Into this chaos rode a white knight with a saintly backstory who bought a majority interest in the *Chicago Times* for a million dollars. At twenty-nine, James J. West presented himself as a self-made man. A poor boy with aspirations to be a minister, he started work at the Western Publishing Company at a salary of $500 in the hopes of raising money for his education. Three years later, he was a full partner and oversaw the publication of a book that sold more than a million copies. He had the erect posture, strong jaw, and straight nose of Greek statuary, an impression only slightly marred by a plaid bowtie. Still part pastor at heart, West claimed never to drink anything stronger than lemonade.

Despite the desperate situation of the newspaper, the ugly front page, the general aura of neglect, West determined that it would soon be "one of the ablest and handsomest journals in the world" and cast about for ways to make that happen: new type; thrilling fiction by the British adventure writer H. Rider Haggard; a *Times*-sponsored plan to find bison in Texas, domesticate them, and save them from extinction. A writer would file exclusive reports by carrier pigeon.

West hired away the *Chicago Tribune*'s star reporter, Charles Chapin, who'd tracked opium smugglers across the Canadian border. Chapin had written an exposé of a gang of virtue vigilantes who dragged adulterous couples out of their houses and whipped them. In his latest feat, he'd been on the scene, conducting an interview, when a wife shot and killed her cheating husband. Chapin disarmed the woman, went for the doctor, and wrote up the murder in gripping prose. That was the kind of initiative West was looking for. A week after the story ran, he offered Chapin the position of city editor, a promotion he couldn't refuse.

Nothing worked to boost the *Times*, though, until Chapin hired a schoolteacher-turned-reporter named Helen Cusack, pseudonym

"Nell Nelson." ("Nell" recalled Bly and was also a nickname for "Helen.") For some reporters, a stunt was their first assignment, a cannonball into the profession. But Nelson was an experienced journalist. In addition to preparing lessons, she wrote for the *Inter Ocean*, the *Herald*, and the *New York Evening Telegram*. In 1885, she served as vice president of the newly formed Illinois Woman's Press Association. She and her two younger sisters, Marcella and Virginia, all teachers and close in age, lived together during much of the 1880s. She was known for looking after her family, possessing a regal bearing, and wielding "a particularly caustic pen."

Nell Nelson in the *Journalist*, January 26, 1889

Stunt work represented a new opportunity. In July 1888, Nell Nelson donned a shabby frock, arranged her brown veil, swept her hair back in a twist called a "Psyche knot," and went looking for a job. It was a rainy, humid summer, with reeking trash piling up. Headed down State Street, she applied at two feather factories and three corset makers without any luck before going upstairs to the Western Lace Manufacturing Company. Here, in a lobby displaying samples of hand-crocheted products—doilies, collars, pillow covers—she took a seat and waited to submit an application. The lobby was watched over by a young man with a mustache. Nelson described him as the "pretty blonde secretary." His good looks, though, were spoiled by a constant scowl.

A girl brought in a dozen crocheted mats and asked for her pay. The accountant is out, the secretary told her. She'd need to wait. Nelson chatted with the girl, named Martha, and asked to see her contract. Perhaps as befits a teacher, Nelson focused on the math. The contract specified, in order to start manufacturing lace, an employee needed to pay $3–$2 for "lessons" and $1 as a "deposit" to be returned once $15 had been earned. After six months of crocheting at roughly 60 cents a week, and paying 10 cents each way in streetcar fare every time she needed to deliver the goods, Martha finally made her $15. Now, as the minutes ticked by, she wondered whether she would ever get paid at all.

While Martha waited, Nelson inquired about a position. The secretary handed her a flyer with all the details, and she proceeded to grill him.

"What's the $3 for?"

"Can't you read?" The secretary answered. "The $2 is to pay for the samples and instruction and the $1 as a security for our material. I don't know who you are and if I gave you the thread I might never see you again."

But she knew how to crochet and didn't want the sample, Nelson persisted. Could she start work without the deposit? No. She asked to see a list of customers and pointed out there weren't many. The Chicago market didn't seem overwhelmed with a desire for handmade crocheted goods.

The blond secretary grew increasingly flustered and finally refused to talk with her anymore.

"Why? Is it a secret organization, a sort of Masonic—?"

But eventually she let him be. She turned her attention to the employees, peppering them with questions. None made more than 20 cents a day. When she wrote up the episode, under the headline "City Slave Girls," Nelson commented: "I learned that many women paid $3 and gave up the work when they saw it was not possible to make the $15 necessary for the rebate." She called the business "a concern legally incorporated to grind the life out of the women and girls unfortunate enough to patronize it." With her focus on the economics, she uncovered an early model of a multilevel marketing scheme, like Herbalife or essential oils, where the real profit is made not from consumers but from those who think they are employees.

In factories and sweatshops, over the course of weeks, she stitched coats and shoe linings; interviewed her fellow workers in sweltering, unventilated spaces; and continued reckoning. At the Excelsior Underwear Company, she was handed a stack of shirts to sew—80 cents a dozen—and then was charged 50 cents to rent the sewing machine and 35 cents for thread. Nearby, a forewoman scolded an employee for leaving oil stains on chemises. She'd have to pay to launder them. At one facility, Nelson was told she'd need to work six weeks for free to gain experience.

The summer of 1888, Nelson was in her late twenties. Perhaps age and experience gave her confidence. Inspired by Eva McDonald's stories for the *Globe*, Nelson had a distinct style, wisecracking and intrigued by human nature, much more sophisticated than McDonald's. Like the best stunt reporters, her personality was an integral part of the story. (Unlike others, Nelson didn't leave any writing besides her newspaper articles, so it's hard to gauge the distance between how she presented herself in public and what she confided in a private letter or journal entry.) She never let a good digression slip by. At the Never-Rip Jersey factory, when a young woman at her table mentioned her hopes that her telegraph operator boyfriend would propose, Nelson offered tips on ways to catch him. They hatched a plan to be deployed, over chocolate cake, at a picnic in a park that evening. Nelson was confident in the recipe for commitment, though admitted she'd never tried it.

Like Bly, Nelson wrote from a close, first-person perspective, pulling readers into her bodily experience.* She included intimate details: the corsets hanging on nails, removed so the women could move more freely; the cold pancakes employees packed for lunch; a girl so tired she fell asleep in the filthy bathroom. When Nelson tried her hand at making dusters, she ended up covered in feathers: "They stuck in my woolen waist, got between my teeth and into my mouth and eyes till I could see nothing but flukes and stems." Like McDonald, Nelson wrote overtly about sexual harassment. One day, she forgot her streetcar fare and borrowed it from a well-dressed stranger. When she hopped off near a vest maker she wanted to investigate, he followed, asking where she was going, if she worked in the neighborhood, and eventually pressing so close, as she described it, "the sleeve of my 'never-rip' jersey was pressed against the waist-line of his light grey suit." She tried to shake him off, saying if he would give her a card, she'd be sure to reimburse the fare. When he finally offered one and asked for her contact information in return, she wrote, "Reporter, The Times," on the reverse and handed it back.

"Didn't think it was so late, have an engagement at 9:45," he said, and walked off, briskly.

The revelation that one has been underestimated is one of the pleasures of undercover reporting, particularly for young women, so often underestimated: "You thought I was part of your story, but really you are part of mine." It's a moment, like the ones where Nelson confronted employers in ways an employee might not be able to, that gave female readers a vicarious thrill.

The harassment Nelson uncovered was pervasive. At one company, where both sexes worked together, the men constantly jostled against the women, and Nelson observed the resulting exhaustion and anger. A "miserable bullet-headed sapling" tipped over a box where she was

---

* As Jean Marie Lutes, author of *Front-Page Girls, Women Journalists in American Culture and Fiction*, told me in an interview: "One of the paradoxes of the way that women journalists like Bly worked was that they took the thing that was used to disempower them—their physical vulnerability and the way they were objectified—and turned that into an asset."

sitting. At a cigar factory, she walked in to find a big boy chasing the female employees around the room, aiming to tickle them. At a coat factory, frustrated by lack of instructions on how to sew and the unwillingness of the forewoman to tell her how much she'd be earning, she got in a fight with one of the owners. He raised a fist to hit her before she ducked out. A seamstress told her she'd rather work at home than in a factory because of all the abuse.

"I don't think I can tell you how many ways there are to insult a girl. I have had a foreman just give me a look as I passed in to my machine or handed in my sewing that made me wish I was dead," she told the reporter.

In her travels, Nelson also encountered those far too young for factory work. In a rough part of the city, on a pitted road lined with garbage, she found thirteen-year-olds sewing frantically at a long table. In another sweatshop, a girl of about twelve brought seamstresses water. "But worse than broken shoes, ragged clothes, filthy closets, poor light, high temperature, and vitiated atmosphere was the cruel treatment by the people in authority," she wrote. Her series, "City Slave Girls," went deep into August. Businesses grew increasingly wary. One, armed with her description, refused to hire her and quickly dispatched a representative to the paper to contradict anything she might say about her brief time on the premises. When the *Times* sent a male reporter to take her place, even he was met with raised eyebrows.

"Aren't you from the *Times*?" a woman at a book bindery asked him.

"Do I look like a woman?"

"You might be Nell Nelson disguised in pants for all I know," she answered.

Demand for the *Chicago Times* soon strained the capacity of the printing presses. West must have been thrilled. What did it matter that the Never-Rip Company sued the paper for libel, asking $50,000?* Letters to the editor praised "the true knight errant of today . . . a

---

* A suit the company ultimately abandoned.

lady reporter for THE TIMES." The editorial pages hosted a robust debate about the situation of factory women, offering a variety of solutions. They should unionize, or rely on higher tariffs. Many told young women to hire themselves out as servants in the country, suggesting they were only drawn to Chicago by a desire for frivolous entertainment. "If they prefer working at starvation wages in the city . . . let them stay and work. They won't get my commiseration," one man wrote in.

This prompted a reply from a woman who'd been a servant on country farms. The wages were terrible, she reported. Sexual harassment was no less rife in rural areas. She had to leave one situation because the master "made himself obnoxious to me," she reported, and another where one of the sons became "insolent."

One letter writer delicately pointed out how many proprietors with Jewish last names Nelson frequented. He warned the paper against leading "an anti-Semitic crusade under the pretense of assisting poor working girls," and offered to take reporters to many establishments run by Christians. The dominance of Jewish last names lessened a bit.

If editors hadn't already been intrigued by undercover possibilities, Nelson's stunt proved their potential. The *Globe* congratulated itself that Eva McDonald's articles had been influential—"The highest compliment paid them was in the duplication of their character and scope by such newspapers as the *Chicago Times*"—but Nelson's made a much bigger splash. The *Times*'s rival, the *Chicago Tribune*, hired Eleanor Stackhouse, another teacher turned reporter, who took the name "Nora Marks," to do stunt after stunt throughout the fall of 1888, including testing out employment agencies and working in a meat-packing plant.

Reporter Eliza Putnam Heaton took up the challenge that Cockerill deemed too dangerous for Bly—she traveled from Liverpool to the United States in steerage, documenting the experience of immigrants coming from Europe, an account that appeared in papers, including the *Brooklyn Times*, in October. In the cramped, claustrophobia-inducing lower deck on the *Aurania*, she met a miner's wife on her way to join her husband in Pennsylvania, a youth in a cowboy hat with his heart set on Texas, a bevy of Irish girls aiming to work as servants in Boston and New York. Despite arriving exhausted, hollowed out from seasickness, and desperate for fresh fruit, she found the experience a positive one: "I think I shall always be a better American citizen for my emigration. This is still the land of promise." The piece was subtitled "A Sham Emigrant's Voyage to New York."

That fall, the *Buffalo Morning News* ran a story about the flood of girls seeking newspaper work in Bly's wake. (For all the stunt-generated debate about whether women should be factory seam-stresses or servants, many women themselves seemed to think they should be reporters.) The *Morning News* highlighted Nelson as one of these aspirants. A little more than a month after the series ended, she published a book of her collected columns and made her way to the larger playing field of New York. The *Morning News* was dismis-sive of Nelson's ambitions, perhaps not yet realizing the popularity of the new genre: "Occasionally her stories get into print, but like most of her sex who try to enter the newspaper ranks, she finds that the demand is limited."

But if Nelson struggled at first, it wasn't for long. The *World* had its feelers out, detecting any vivid writing anywhere, and the paper sensed her potential and hired her. Nelson started by re-creating her Chicago investigations in New York.

Pulitzer famously fired his newsroom with competition, often set-ting illustrator against illustrator and hiring two editors for the same job. Throughout the fall of 1888, Nelson and Bly jockeyed for space in the *World*'s Sunday pages, sometimes one taking the prime feature spot, sometimes the other. Bly was a star, but that didn't excuse her from churning out daily racing prose. As a colleague noted, "She suf-fered the penalty paid by all sensation-writers of being compelled to hazard more and more theatric feats." He added, "Nothing was too strenuous nor too perilous for her if it promised results."

Drawing attention away from Nelson's exposés, in an article that gently mocked a society-woman profile—"Hangman Joe at

Home"—Bly offered a portrait of the executioner for the state of New York. The electric chair had just become the preferred mode of capital punishment, so part of his job was obsolete. He was not interested in an interview and responded gruffly when Bly showed up, but she took it as a challenge: "Nothing is very good that is easily gained."

In a room filled with furniture he made himself (he was a carpenter, he stressed, though his signature construction was gallows), the hangman blamed the newspapers for romanticizing crime and making heroes of criminals, as Bly looked through his scrapbook of hangings. Did he have much contact with those scheduled to die, she asked. (He avoided them.) Always pursuing the "women's sphere" angle, Bly asked whether women could observe hangings. (No.) When the executioner complained about newspapers further, she shrugged it off.

"It is the age of exaggeration, you know," she said as she shook his hand and left.

No matter how thin the topic, Bly could excavate something worthwhile. She made a formidable competitor for newspaper space because she refused to be boring. "Should women propose?" she asked notable thinkers of the day a few weeks later. Listing professions now open to women, she wrote: "Is it just that an able (woman) lawyer shall be allowed to plead for everything except the hand of the man she loves?" And: "Shall (women) writers only woo imaginary people in their studies—propose only in stories?" In places, Bly seemed to rebel against the frothy assignment. Interviewing Chauncey M. Depew, a railroad magnate, she strayed from her purpose to ask his opinion on the recent presidential election. Republican Benjamin Harrison had unseated incumbent Democrat Grover Cleveland a week earlier. Then she caught herself and recorded his view that women should, indeed, propose. While Bly generally presented the back-and-forth as fluffy fun, she also noted that these chivalric customs encourage deceit, teaching women that "it is proper and good form to express everything but that which they honestly feel."

It's hard not to speculate about Bly's love life. Her persona was so sparkly and flirtatious, never failing to record a comment about her beauty, never shy about complimenting a good-looking man. In her early twenties, she must have seen her peers marrying. It would have been on her mind. In her asylum stories, she had gone out of her way to praise Frank Ingram, the assistant superintendent at Blackwell's, who chatted with her at length and moved her to a quieter ward. Papers at the time noted his kind expression and attractive mustache and wondered at the developing closeness between the reporter and assistant superintendent. Was this series a trial run for making a proposal of her own, like asking newspapers where she wanted to work how their editors felt about hiring women?

Meanwhile, Nelson moved ahead with her factory investigations, anger and naked outrage displacing some of the Chicago humor. In "Horrors of a Slop Shop," she described Freedman Brothers as a place where "modesty is mocked at, virtue debased, decency outraged, self-esteem murdered, and all that makes womanhood lovely and lovable crushed to death." Women worked alongside men, the men at the sewing machines, the women finishing collar and cuffs and other details. The men pinched the women and ran their hands over their bodies. When one complained on behalf of another, she was told to stop wasting time. Cockroaches crawled across the paper wrapping a

Nell Nelson promotion in the
Evening World, October 20, 1888

girl's lunch. A boy, to her skeptical look, insisted he had documents proving he was fourteen.

In "They Work in an Inferno," sewing beaver and chinchilla fur coats, Nelson met a seventeen-year-old named Anna who invited her to visit the tenement where the young woman lived with six brothers and sisters. Overcrowded, substandard housing was increasingly a hazard in New York where people crammed into poorly lit, unventilated spaces. Nelson didn't stay long. Anna's mother didn't speak English or seem to want the reporter there, so Nelson dropped off a beefsteak and left. But what she saw formed the moral center of that day's reporting. She ended with an overt call for action:

> When a family of eight can thrive in one room, when five cents a day will board the father and half a pound of prunes with butcher's scraps provide a soup for the maintenance of wife and children; when $3 is accepted as a fair compensation for seven days of labor of eleven hours each; when a foul-smelling, overheated, ill-ventilated, ratty fire-trap is regarded as an ideal workshop—then it seems that the time has come for action of some kind.

And people were listening. Back in Chicago, Nelson's work had lingering effects. Industry in the area was roaring—its central location meant the riches of the West, in the form of logs, grain, and cattle passed through—but the city itself struggled to provide basic services. In August, when Nelson was still pacing Chicago alleys in search of sweatshops, the Women's Federal Labor Union held a meeting to discuss Nelson's articles. Were her *Chicago Times* reports true? If so, members should campaign for living wages, factory inspection laws, a reduction in child labor, and sanitary workplaces. One member whose sister had tried and failed to pay her bills on $2 a week, proposed a committee, in conjunction with other like-minded organizations in the city, to investigate. By October, they and twenty-six other Chicago associations, from the swanky Chicago Women's Club to the African American literary society the Prudence Crandall Club, formed the Illinois Women's Alliance. Numbers gave them power. And the rise of unions made citizens like these Chicago women more bold in requesting changes to city and state laws. In December, the IWA launched a campaign to appoint school inspectors to ensure children between eight and fourteen attended class at least twelve weeks per year.

Meanwhile, as Nelson forged her path in New York, Bly exposed a quack "magnetic healer," and the Illinois Women's Alliance agitated to fine factories employing underage workers,* the *Chicago Times* cast about for its next sensation.

---

* Their efforts would eventually result in the passage of the (short-lived) 1893 Illinois Factory Law that limited women to an eight-hour workday and restricted child labor.

RECKONING WITH THE EVIL OF THE AGE

My judges preach against "free love" openly, practice it secretly.

—Victoria Woodhull, *New York Times*, 1871

In the fall of 1888, as Nell Nelson headed for New York, newspaper readers were caught up in a story from overseas. This one also featured women's bodies, but not strong ones, capable of striding through the city, of performing hard and dexterous labor, of engaging in deception, but those displayed on a slab at a morgue. A killer, soon dubbed "Jack the Ripper," was ranging through the Whitechapel District in London. From early morning of September 1, when a cart driver stumbled across Polly Nichols on his way to work, columns flooded with descriptions of throats cut to the spine, sliced noses, a missing uterus, severed breasts. Here the women were dismembered by the papers and displayed for the public gaze as a warning to those who ventured into the city without money, without male protection. The urban landscape, rather than a locus for opportunity, became a field for predation. For many reporters, mostly male, the unsolved murders inspired a journalism obsessed with the identity of the killer who evaded capture and sent taunting letters to newspapers. Writers credited Jack the Ripper with an almost diabolical intelligence.

The *Chicago Times* reprinted Jack the Ripper articles but didn't have an assigned reporter in London to give the paper an edge. Inspired by the circulation surge from "City Slave Girls," though, editor James J. West doubled down on stunt reporting. One day, he approached Charles Chapin, his city editor, and revealed his newest brainstorm. Horrified, later calling it the "yellowest" idea he'd ever heard in a newspaper office, Chapin refused to have anything to do with it.

Chapin thought West had forgotten about it, even when the publisher requested a "bright man and a woman reporter" for a special assignment. But in early December, Chapin recalled, he went into the composing room and saw the headline: "Chicago Abortioners." He quit before the edition hit the streets. (That exact wording doesn't appear in the series, but Chapin's memory might have faded: he wrote his account thirty-two years later, in Sing Sing, where he was serving time for murdering his wife.)

In the initial articles, under the all-caps headline "INFANTICIDE," a male reporter asked cabmen where he could find relief for a relative who had been "led into error." Midwives were notorious for knowing how to end pregnancies, and he sought out German and Scandinavian practitioners in the poorer section of the city and made his case. Some proposed medicines and places for her to stay during recovery. Others said they could help with adoption. But most demanded to see the young woman in question.

Enter the Girl Reporter. It would be hard, the *Times* admitted, to find

INFANTICIDE.

The Girl Reporter of "The Times" Takes in a Batch of Physicians.

Several of Them Prove to Be More than Willing to Commit Abortion.

Some Ready and Anxious to Proceed with the Horrible Crime Without Any Delay.

Prominent Physicians Who Have Not the Stamina to Stand Up for What They Know to Be Right.

Among Them Drs. Knoll, Carr, Davis, Atwood, Tooker, and Sharpe.

The Black List Rapidly Growing Larger—A Corrected Classification Up to Date.

What "The Times" Started Out to Do and What It Hopes to Accomplish Through This Inquiry.

Headline for the abortion series in the *Chicago Times*, December 23, 1888 just the right person for the delicate job, someone willing to "parade her shame" in front of multiple doctors and the male reporter who escorted her, "a young woman of intelligence, nerve, and newspaper training." But somehow they did. Writing under the byline "Girl Reporter," the female journalist and her male colleague refined their story over the next few days, switching from midwives to prominent doctors, claiming she was six weeks pregnant rather than two or three months, stressing to physicians that money was no object.

The Girl Reporter spent long days going from office to office. She visited Dr. Sarah Hackett Stevenson, the first female member of the American Medical Association, who treated her kindly but advised her to have the child and get married, even if it would be "but a step toward divorce." She interrupted Dr. John Chaffee at his lunch, and he urged her to have the operation right away, telling her, "Thousands are doing it all the time. The only thing to do when one gets into trouble is to get out again." (A few days later, Chaffee was arrested for giving a woman an abortion that killed her.) Dr. Edwin Hale, a controversial figure since publishing his pamphlet "On the Homeopathic Treatment of Abortion," gave the reporter a bottle of big, black (and harmless, the doctor assured her) pills to take before admitting herself to the hospital. That way, when he was called to her bedside and performed the operation surreptitiously, they could blame the medication for causing a miscarriage.

The Girl Reporter's voice was as unique as the topic of her research. She was determined: "I felt that there was some big ruffians to be brought down yet, and I was anxious to have a composed mind and a strong heart." She was weary: "Tonight as I write this I am sick of the whole business. I did not suppose there was so much rascality among the 'reputable' people." Her prose teemed with self-conscious literary

Illustration of medicine offered to the Girl Reporter in the *Chicago Times*, December 18, 1888 flourishes—puns and alliteration, references to Shakespeare and the *Aeneid*. This, alternating with casual exclamations, like "ugh" and "really swell," the gushing enthusiasm for favorite novels and her Sunday-school moralizing, all seemed like the first attempts of a big reader and beginning writer. She wrestled with the constant need for disguise, feeling more compassion for the distraught woman she pretended to be than she expected: "I manage somehow or other to lose my own individuality all together. I really don't recognize myself half the time." There was the sense of a real person trying to figure things out.

It wasn't chance that, of the almost thirty daily newspapers in Chicago during the 1880s, the *Chicago Times* was the one to give her this assignment. Notoriously trashy, the *Times* generated as much scandal among its staff as it reported in its pages. Many male *Times* reporters haunted the Whitechapel Club, an organization named after Jack the Ripper's hunting grounds, admiring photographs of beheadings on the walls, drinking out of cups made from skulls, and nurturing their literary aspirations.

This willingness to flout societal rules and journalistic standards made for some wretched reporting; it also opened a door to topics that no one else dared cover. Sometimes, an allegiance to propriety and respectability becomes a tool for censorship. For the *Chicago Times*, the unprecedented nature of the debates about reproductive rights was accidental, an artifact of shamelessness and the desire to sell papers by whatever means necessary. Only a paper with nothing to lose could write about abortion so frankly.

For most of the country's history, abortion before quickening (the moment at about twenty weeks when a woman could detect fetal movement) had been accepted. But at the time the Girl Reporter wrote, laws were growing more restrictive and knowledge of abortion techniques more actively suppressed. This crackdown was partially the result of the fact that throughout the nineteenth century, birth rates were declining and abortion was on the rise. Increased population density in cities allowed remedies to spread by word of mouth.

The printing boom resulted in mass-produced anatomically informative pamphlets, magazines, and journals, giving women information they needed to control their fertility. Some estimates put the figure as high as one in five pregnancies in some areas ending in abortion, starting in the mid-nineteenth century, while early in the 1800s, the rate was closer to one in twenty-five. Resolve built to shut down the practice: in 1800, no states had antiabortion laws, while in 1900, all but one did.

And over the course of the century, it would become clear that regulating women's reproductive options—whether by laws, shame, or misinformation—was intimately related to regulating their speech. Censorship of abortion discussion specifically and women's health information in general created the need for journalists like the Girl Reporter, who wrote about female bodies frankly, and the hunger to hear what they had to say.

The first wave of antiabortion legislation appeared in the late 1820s and 1830s. In 1828 in New York, providing medicine or an operation that produced abortion before quickening became a misdemeanor and after quickening became a felony—unless the procedure would save the life of the mother or had been signed off on by two physicians. At the time, those with rigorous training who published in the top-tier journals considered themselves the real medical experts. They were attempting to distinguish their practices from both quacks with pieces of paper from diploma mills and from midwives. Midwives often had the most experience with childbirth, and women often preferred them, stealing what doctors felt was their rightful business. But midwives often had no formal training at all. (And formal training would not have been available to them, as most medical schools did not admit women.) Antiabortion legislation was one way to make sure business flowed into the "legitimate" doctors' offices.

In addition to agitating for antiabortion laws to guarantee their market share, early nineteenth-century physicians trafficked in misinformation to undermine the authority of midwives. Maintaining patient ignorance was part of their strategy. They suggested that drugs used to cause abortions didn't work. They disparaged savin and pennyroyal—known to every midwife as abortifacients—as "useless" or "dangerous," writing that no medicines could safely provide that kind of relief. Enslaved women used cotton root to control fertility, doctors observed, and they searched for medicines that would stop a cotton-root-caused abortion and force the pregnancy to go through. (Women who read medical journals also took note and requested cotton root from their pharmacists.)

Newspapers supported the physicians' campaign with tales of evil abortionists and innocents taken in. The *Daily Commercial Advertiser* in Buffalo in 1837 featured the story of a Chicago woman, pregnant by her brother-in-law, who went to a Michigan hotel for an abortion, only to then be poisoned by her sister. "They have both been excommunicated from the church," the paper noted. The same year the *Long-Island Star* covered a doctor who performed an abortion on his lover, killing her. In 1843, the *Courier* reprinted an article from the *New York Sun* describing "the infernal plot" of a pastor who slept with a young woman in his church and then gave her drugs to cause an abortion. And as reporters and editorial pages involved themselves in these campaigns, abortion—its fascination, its hidden nature, its ubiquity—became intertwined with the development of journalism.

The same papers where these stories appeared were often funded by ads for abortion-causing medicines. Their financial security depended on the procedure they pretended to despise. For example, among offers of quills, coal, and beauty potions, readers of the *New-York Tribune* in 1841 could be tempted by "Genuine French Female Monthly Pills" promising "astonishing success in cases of irregular and obstructed" menstruation or the "Female's Friend," designed for "relieving and removing all those complaints peculiar to females." The *New York Herald* featured ads for "Dr. Van Hambert's Female Renovating Pills, from Germany" which noted, slyly, "They must not be taken during pregnancy, as they will produce abortion."

Even stories that appeared about something else entirely often had abortion at their root; the issue was everywhere. In 1841, Mary

Rogers, a young New York woman who worked behind the counter selling tobacco in a store in Lower Manhattan, so pretty she'd been dubbed "the beautiful cigar girl," disappeared one Sunday afternoon. She was found dead, several days later, floating in the Hudson. In one of the last sightings of Rogers alive, an innkeeper said she'd been drinking lemonade with several young men. The coroner determined she'd been raped and strangled. Who could have done it? A lover from the boardinghouse her mother kept? A marauding gang? The *Herald*, known (and condemned by competitor journals) for frank descriptions of bodies and sex, embraced and ran with the story. Not long after the corpse was recovered and the *Herald* printed a detailed coroner's report, a petticoat, shawl, and handkerchief with "Mary" on it were found in the woods.

With graphic descriptions of the corpse, the *Herald* and other papers grasped the potential of mysteries implied by the body of a dead, young, beautiful girl, the same potential exploited by the Jack the Ripper reporters decades later. As anyone who has walked through a forest littered with mouse bones or along the seashore peppered with shells and crab carapaces knows, to be dead is to have lost the ability to hide. The body is exposed to the wandering eyes and wondering thoughts of whoever may encounter it. It will reveal its clues, its secrets, if only we look hard enough. While killers might have peered at this body obscenely, readers tell themselves they look on it in righteous pursuit of justice. In this, the papers hit on a formula that would be a staple of murder mysteries and police procedurals far into the future.

Over time, many people wondered whether Rogers died not of murder but of an attempted abortion, a suspicion buoyed by the deathbed confession of the innkeeper, who changed her testimony to say that Mary had turned up with a doctor who planned to help her with a "premature delivery." The innkeeper's son helped dispose of the body.

At the same time, the troubles of another, very different woman dominated the newspapers—one who was decidedly alive and in charge of her destiny, too in charge for some. Madame Restell, an alias for businesswoman Ann Lohman, was on trial for providing an illegal abortion. Her advertisements in papers in Philadelphia, Boston, and

New York for pills that offered a remedy for "obstinate and long-standing cases of derangement in those functions of nature" called to "females in delicate health." One of her clients, dying of consumption, revealed to her husband that she'd become pregnant and sought out Madame Restell. Her husband told the police, and they arrested Restell and threw her in jail. As New York watched the Mary Rogers mystery unfold, Restell's case wound its way through the New York courts.

Restell, her faux French flair and constant press coverage, was famous enough that she inspired a new vocabulary. Abortion and its promotion was "Restellism." Competing papers deemed the *New York Herald*, which included many ads for abortifacients and dogged coverage of the trial, "Madame Restell's organ." When Mary Rogers was dragged from the river, she was (rightly) feared to be a victim of the "Restell school."

Restell appealed her case to the New York Supreme Court in 1842. And her letter to the newspapers on that occasion showed all the reasons the male physicians would want to put her out of business. One witness testified that a man had attended the operation. Restell scoffed: "In no case do I engage a 'man' or physician, for the simple and all abundant reason that, whatever I undertake, I feel myself competent, as well by study, experience and practice, to carry through properly." In fact, many pregnant women prefer to be treated by a woman, she wrote. And propriety demanded a lady, "provided always she is skillful, should attend in preference to a gentleman."

Not long after the Restell trial, both New York and Massachusetts passed stronger antiabortion legislation. New York's law banned advising, administering, or prescribing abortions. Seeking abortion also became a crime, making a criminal of the patient for the first time. As the antiabortion campaign of the doctors accelerated, it continued to be fueled by newspaper coverage. In 1871, the *New York Times* ran a series of articles called "The Evil of the Age" about a reporter and a female friend pretending to seek an abortion and their reception at various doctors and midwives. Unlike the *Chicago Times* pieces, only the man, Augustus St. Clair, wrote his interpretation of events; the woman was just a prop. St. Clair described guns brandished in his face and aborted fetuses left to disintegrate in vats of lime.

In St. Clair's account, he targeted newspapers advertising abortion as much as the practitioners themselves: "The mails go burdened with the circulars of such people, and come laden with money enclosures for pills, 'drops,' and other vile humbugs. The best home firesides in the land have been invaded by these advertisements, either in the newspapers or in letters." In a jab at the *New York Herald*, the couple used addresses listed in the paper's medical advertisements as a map of places to go, following their lead throughout the city. Their reporting took them to see Dr. Mauriceau, a relative of Madame Restell, at one of her offices. They visited Madame Restell at another. She started to talk with them but was interrupted by her daughter, who pulled her out of the room to confer. When Restell came back, she was dismissive. Apparently, the reporter's disguise needed work. He then stopped in to see a man with a thick German accent who went by both "Dr. Rosenzweig" and "Dr. Asher." Pale faces of patients peered through the blinds, St. Clair reported.

Soon, things became much worse. One of these patients, allegedly spotted by St. Clair in Rosenzweig's office, turned up dead a few days later, her body in a trunk bound for Chicago, leading to a week's worth of headlines about the "trunk murder" and the arrest of Dr. Rosenzweig.

These kinds of grisly rumors (the reporting is highly questionable) aided the passage of even stricter antiabortion statutes and ramped up enforcement. At the time, an 1869 New York law banned "articles of indecent and immoral use," as well as advertisements for them. This included not just playing cards with naked women on the back, racy daguerreotypes, and dildos, but contraceptives and abortifacients. It was a hard law to uphold, though, because while the good men of the YMCA's Committee for the Suppression of Obscene Literature took it very seriously, the police didn't. In April 1872, though, the YMCA found its own detective. Anthony Comstock, a Brooklyn man dismayed by the printing houses peddling smut in his neighborhood, was the ideal enforcer—energetic and fired with holy motivation. He began ordering scandalous books and arresting those who sold them, amassing a mountain of photos, pamphlets, catalogues. Each year, he printed details of his haul in a booklet: 181,600 obscene photos and pictures, 6,000 dirty watch charms, five tons of bound books. He also included numbers of arrests of manufacturers and dealers; even their deaths were tabulated—in the credit column.

**New York Society for the Suppression
of Vice annual report, 1880**

The federal Comstock Act passed two years later, in 1873. Comstock had campaigned for it by going to the Capitol and showing senators his collection of obscene books. And here the prohibition against certain procedures veered into a serious, nationwide campaign of censorship. The act forbid publishing advertisements, books, pictures, pamphlets, or other printed matter deemed "obscene," as well as sending any such materials through the mail. And again, the definition of obscenity included mentions of abortion and birth control. So not just the practice of controlling women's fertility was outlawed; writing about it was as well. The federal law specified a minimum prison sentence of one year, while the New York law allowed for only a fine.

Some states went further, attempting to outlaw even talking about abortion and birth control.

But despite jail time that resulted in her spending a year on Blackwell's Island, despite tightening laws, despite harassment by the newspapers, Madame Restell kept taking out advertisements, advising patients, giving them what they wanted. Her lavish house (bane of her Fifth Avenue neighbors), her flashy sleigh pulled by four horses, and her net worth were all constant subjects of criticism—to no avail.

Eventually, though, Comstock caught up with her. In January 1878, he showed up at Restell's famous mansion to launch an under-cover sting of his own. When the sixty-six-year-old woman answered the door, Comstock claimed to be a poor man seeking medicine for his wife. This time, her sense for disguised enemies deserted her. She gave him pills, and he returned again waving a warrant, flanked by police officers. They found medical tools and waiting patients. The judge denied bail and she was taken to the Tombs. Eventually bail was allowed but Restell, perhaps fearing a return to Blackwell's Island, slit her own throat in the bath and bled to death before trial.

Comstock was unrepentant. The Society for the Suppression of Vice (whose logo proudly featured a gentleman burning books) gloated: "It is a cause for profound thanksgiving that this city is rid of the disgrace of this woman and her murderous business, which for so many years has been flaunted with bold defiance on one of the most prominent avenues of the city."

And still, after decades of suppression of the practice and discus-sion about it, by the time the Girl Reporter made her rounds in 1888, abortion was everywhere. There was the sad, coded story from the *St. Paul Globe* in 1889 about a girl found dead in her sweltering board-inghouse room. Originally from Minneapolis, she'd gone to Montana eight months before, only to have returned to rent a room for herself and her husband, who never showed. Several days before she'd taken ill, she'd visited a Twin Cities doctor because of "uterine trouble." He suspected she may have died of "an internal hemorrhage." Maybe she took some drug or the cause was her smoking cigarettes, the paper speculated. But it doesn't seem much of a mystery. There were the ads that persisted, despite decades of campaigns against them. The same month as the Girl Reporter's exposé, December 1888, the *Boston Globe* touted the ability of "Wilcox's Compound Tansy Pills" to "afford speedy and certain relief." Birthrates for white women* were slipping from an average of 7 children per woman in 1800 to 3.5 in 1900. And there was the rebellion triggered by all these restrictions and revealed by the Girl Reporter's series for the *Chicago Times*. Doctors, midwives, and women rich and poor traded secrets, recipes, and information in coded language and a private economy.

The Girl Reporter and the other stunt journalists offered an inverted version of the Mary Rogers narrative and the novels it inspired—female detectives were now the ones unraveling mysteries of the male world. And in writing about abortion in particular, revealing how commonplace it was, the Girl Reporter showed the lie at the heart of the idea that women could be divided into good and bad, fallen and chaste. Those with the means used abortions to conceal premarital sex or affairs. In writing about the operation and its uses, the Girl Reporter broke a powerful taboo.†

And as is often the case with writing that breaks a taboo, everyone read it. The assistant state's attorney for Illinois insisted he hadn't, but mentioned that the streetcar he took to work was filled with people poring over the *Chicago Times*. Dr. Oscar Coleman De Wolf, commissioner of health, claimed that the exposé reached from "St. Lawrence to the Golden Gate." Like many others, he expressed concern that readers got the wrong message, and that the Girl Reporter painted a damaging portrait of Chicago: "I don't exaggerate the influence and wide spread circulation of *The Times* when I say that every woman who

---

* Statistics for other populations are less available.

† Abortion is famously the thing that can't be talked about—see Hemingway's "Hills Like White Elephants," a 1927 short story often used to teach the concept of subtext.

is in that kind of trouble, from Maine to California, knows just how easy it is to get relief in this city."

For some, the Girl Reporter had pushed stunt reporting way too far. The *Buffalo Daily Times* speculated she must be "lost to shame and womanly feeling," and added, "the method adopted by the *Chicago Times* to acquire the information desired is so revolting and horrible as to inspire disgust instead of praise." Female writers began to wonder if assigning editors had their best interests at heart. But for De Wolf, as well as others, the issue was not the Girl Reporter's deceptions or the impropriety of her pretending to be "fallen," but the raw information she provided. "A Friend of the Times" was blunt in his distress: "Some of the young girls will learn more out of *The Times* in a few weeks than they could get out of a medical work in a year." A father wrote in to say he had originally shielded his eighteen-year-old daughter from the articles but decided he needed to "take the bull by the horns" and let her read them.

Letters to the editor poured in deep into January, bubbling with praise and outrage and frank evaluations of relations between the sexes. Another letter, under the title "Bring the Husbands to Book," raised the issue of rape. Still another, from a female doctor, said patients had asked her for abortions three hundred times in her first year of practice. A doctor who didn't sign his name confessed that the Girl Reporter's entreaties might have swayed him. He had turned a woman away, only to be called to her family's house days later, after she had killed herself. "It is our duty to preserve life whenever possible. Did I do it?" he asked.

Dr. Sarah Hackett Stevenson, who had refused the Girl Reporter an abortion, wrote in a letter to the editor that the burden of parenthood should be shared: "The social order that permits a father to disown his child without the loss of public esteem is the very social order that permits a mother to destroy her child. Destruction is the mother's only method of disowning." One way to make men face consequences, another female physician suggested, would be to outlaw sex out of wedlock.

The December 17, 1888, meeting of the Chicago Medical Society overflowed Parlor 44 of the massive castle of the Grand Pacific Hotel. Attendees waited, perhaps jostling, perhaps impatient, perhaps shoved into the hall, through debate on new members, through a paper on "A Novel Treatment of Gonorrhea" and a display of specimens of pathological lesions resulting from typhoid fever.

Finally, they carved into the meat of the meeting: the claims unfolding in the *Chicago Times* over the past week. The paper implicated many society members, including the president, Dr. Etheridge. According to the published story, he had told the Girl Reporter, when she asked for an abortion, "I don't handle such cases. . . . You know it is lawbreaking," and sent her to see a man at the corner of Wabash and Harmon Court. The very day of the meeting, the *Times* started publishing names and addresses of doctors under the headings "Physicians who would commit abortion" and "Physicians who would recommend others who would commit abortion."

No one knew who would be named in the next issue. Tempers flared. The doctors must have been running through all their recent patient encounters in their heads. Some suspected a doctor was behind the whole thing, colluding with the *Times* to put competing physicians out of business. A Dr. Franks insisted the society needed to support its members, ignoring "what any woman might say who went sneaking around like a snake, trying to make a reputation." Her disguise and ambition made her inherently untrustworthy. A medical journal suggested, sneeringly, that she told her sad story with "many a pearly tear trembling on her pretty little eyelids." On the other hand, Dr. N. S. Davis said, if no one was held to account, the whole series became just a big advertisement for abortionists listed.

In the end, the Judiciary Committee was instructed to investigate three doctors only: E. H. Thurston, F. A. Stanley, and C. C. P. Silva. The case against the society president was dismissed with a unanimous vote in his support.

Earlier, Etheridge had met with a cooler reception at the newspaper office, where he'd gone to justify his actions, maybe to have the *Chicago Times* make a correction. When he explained that he only referred the Girl Reporter to the other doctor to catch him in the act, a reporter pressed him. Was Etheridge saying he set up a trap?

Not a trap, exactly, Etheridge fumbled. He knew her "brother" would find someone eventually, so he might as well send him to an office where he knew the address. If "anything happened I could locate it and we could get a hold on him." Etheridge seemed to imply that if the Girl Reporter died, police would know which doctor to arrest. The paper found this a thin excuse, and published, along with the letter, an editorial scornful of doctors whose only interest was in keeping their hands clean.

At the January meeting, the Judiciary Committee kicked Dr. E. H. Thurston out of the society but declared another doctor innocent. The society then decided to stop looking into the *Chicago Times* reports unless a doctor requested it. Despite the vocal stance many had taken against illegal abortion, their priority was shielding their own. At the meeting after that, they stopped investigating entirely. And at the meeting after *that*, they resolved to inform the State Board of Health of their concerns about personal cleanliness among midwives.

All in all, the *Chicago Times*'s abortion exposé was owner West's dream—a sensation. The paper, which eight months before had run ads for an abortifacient marketed as Chichester's English Pennyroyal Pills, packed its editorial page with demands that abortion be stamped out.

The situation was particularly dire, the paper argued, as American-born Caucasian women, wanting small families, vibrant social lives, and careers, took advantage of abortion more than others, a trend that threatened to give "control of our government and country to the foreigner." The paper proposed remedies. Women needed instruction on the delights of motherhood. Maybe there should be a lying-in

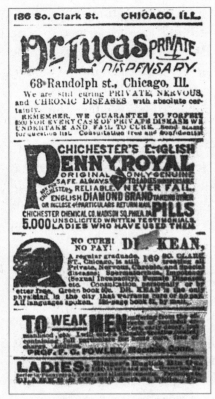

Ad for abortion-causing pills in
the *Chicago Times*, April 1, 1888

hospital. Or doctors should meet stricter certification requirements. Preachers shouldn't be squeamish about addressing abortion from the pulpit.

Though the *Times*'s editorials railed against the evils of "infanticide," the paper's reportage raised more questions than it answered. For example, there was the case of the father who wrote in and said he'd reluctantly decided to let his eighteen-year-old daughter read the articles. What was she supposed to think? Despite the paper's moralizing, it would be hard to avoid the impression that abortion was common, available to anyone who could steel herself to ask for it. She might even meet with kindness and understanding. As many readers dourly predicted, no one was arrested, though Dr. C. C. P. Silva was fired as police surgeon.

This building tension about a practice that was publicly condemned, privately embraced—a practice that it was illegal even to write about—split politically engaged women in the same way stunt journalists divided their reporter peers. The same question lurked at the heart of each divide. Was it manipulation at the hands of unscrupulous men, or a way for women to seize control of their lives? Suffragist Susan B. Anthony, in an 1875 speech, portrayed abortion as another example of women's victimization by men's drunkenness and lack of self-control, citing "the newspaper reports every day of every year of scandals and outrages, of wife murders and paramour shooting, of abortions and infanticides." It's important to note, too, that part of her sense of women's experience came from headlines. But, as the *Chicago Times* reporting showed, many women sought out abortions on their own, telling doctors they wanted to wait to have children, or to have only two. Even the Girl Reporter was conflicted, adamantly opposed to abortion, adamantly in favor of women's equality. When one doctor, sympathetic, justified offering the operation by saying, "A woman should have the same chances as a man has and society makes it much harder," the Girl Reporter added "amen," in parentheses. Then she went ahead and published his name for public scorn anyway.

Never missing a chance for self-promotion, the *Times* capitalized on curiosity about the Girl Reporter. An illustration on the editorial page showed five sketches of thin, dark-haired women with bangs in front and a bun in the back, wearing an apron over a collared shirt. The figures looked down, or up, with expressions pensive or half-smiling, line-drawn Mona Lisas. "For the Doctors," the caption taunted. "Guess which one of the above is the 'girl reporter'?"

Illustration featuring the Girl Reporter in the
Chicago Times, December 21, 1888

Students at one college sent her a bouquet; students at another sent her a gold pen, a "small token of esteem in appreciation of the services you are rendering in the medical profession and the world at large." The paper published her bashful letters of thanks and her fiery letters refuting doctors who claimed she'd misunderstood their intentions. On December 26 and 27, she wrapped up her findings, declaring, with a tone of relief, "My pilgrimage of disgrace is ended." And then, in late December 1888, while her story spread from its Illinois epicenter, the Girl Reporter disappeared from the *Chicago Times* pages and from the public record.

"Many of the brightest women frequently disguise their identity, not under one *nom de plume*, but under half a dozen," wrote a male editor for the trade publication the *Journalist* in an issue about female reporters in 1889. "This renders anything like a solid reputation almost impossible." Some who used pseudonyms parlayed their disguises into decades-long careers. Some, like the Girl Reporter, never emerged from undercover.

While Bly's exposé was an inspiration for many aspiring writers, the Girl Reporter's was more of a cautionary tale. That kind of assignment, those kinds of topics, were a line one might not want to cross. Yes, she received applause for her bravery, but the condemnation of the reporter as indecent was what lingered, at least in the minds of young journalists like Elizabeth Banks. Writing for the society pages of the *St. Paul Globe*, Banks was keenly aware of class. Such distinctions weren't supposed to exist in America, but every time an upper-class woman offered to have lunch with the reporter, as long as she didn't let anyone know, or she was made to wait for her ride home shivering outside in the cold after getting details of a party, the lines appeared, like invisible ink revealed by heat. It intrigued and repelled her.

But at least she was writing, finally.

Banks had been dreaming about it for years. Born in 1865 in

Trenton, New Jersey, Elizabeth Banks was the fifth child of Sarah Ann Brister and John Brister, a house painter. When Elizabeth was eleven, her mother died, and the girl was packed off to live with relatives in Wisconsin. She was raised on an "experimental farm" where her uncle pored over *The Scientific Farmer*, trying various techniques that never were successful enough to pay off the mortgage. Rural life had its charms. A boy who lived nearby pulled her on a sled through a snowy field. Oak trees filtered the sunlight, and a creek slicing through the meadow offered a cool place to dangle bare feet on a hot day. But most of her memories centered on dragging out of bed at four a.m. to boil potatoes for breakfast, the first chore of a day full of them—feeding chickens, shucking peas, picking currants, washing dishes, weeding onions—and the sting of being hit if she left silk on an ear of corn.

Respite came through animals, which she loved, telling her troubles to the cows and mourning every dead chick, and through reading. She savored Bible tales, short stories serialized in the weekly news-paper, and, especially, Elizabeth Barrett Browning's "Aurora Leigh." The epic poem told the story of an orphan sent to live with an aunt who tries to make a lady of her, dismissing the young Aurora's thirst to be an artist like Keats or Byron. Aurora Leigh's attraction to books is beyond passionate. They save her. Early in the saga, Aurora Leigh turns down the chance to marry her wealthy cousin and moves to London to launch her writing career. Elizabeth Banks had no trouble imaging herself as the heroine, struggling with an oppressive aunt, taking refuge in books. As she gathered and sold eggs and watched over neighbor's babies to scrape together money for college, certain lines echoed:

"A harmless life, she called a virtuous life.

A quiet life which was not life at all."

After attending Downer College in Fox Lake, Wisconsin, where she paid her way by ironing and washing dishes for the school, Banks wrote editors all over the country, but no one offered her a reporting job. She settled for typing for a grocer in St. Paul, Minnesota, a move that got her away from the farm and let her use some of her college skills. But in her spare time, she wrote up a piece about the life of a typewriter girl and sent it in to one of the papers. She basically interviewed herself, writing about a typist for a mercantile company who pays $5 of her $8 a week in rent, and sends out her laundry, leaving not much left of her take-home pay. But the article did the trick, and soon ink from her very own words smeared her fingers.

Exhilarated, she quit the grocer's. She headed straight to the office of the *Globe*, a glowing redbrick and terra-cotta building, the tallest in St. Paul. Her article had been published, and now that she knew her writing was good enough, she wanted to be a newspaper girl, she announced to the paper's owner.

The white-whiskered man told her the writing wasn't that good, then pondered her request.

"A newspaper girl, a newspaper girl."

He paused, then continued, more forcefully, "Don't think of it my poor child! Be anything, but don't be a newspaper girl."

But when Banks threatened to go to Chicago, the wickedest city in the Midwest, the one whose dangerous glamour tempted innocent girls from small towns to catch trains to their ruin, the editor relented. She could do office work in the mornings, and in the afternoons she could pitch stories to the editors.

A bubbly fashion article earned her a desk in the newsroom and the pseudonym "Polly Pollock." For months, Polly Pollock stayed late at society balls to record the cut of hostess's dress sleeves, wrote about disappointing Christmas gifts, and lamented the persistence of the bustle.

Elsewhere in the *Globe*, Eva McDonald, writing as Eva Gay, hired herself out as a lady's maid. She put on a servant's dress and penned a long-running series, funny and full of misadventure with its descriptions of coddled pugs and society women smoking opium cigarettes. What an excellent way to puncture the pretensions of the moneyed class. Elizabeth Banks took note.

The closest Banks came to a "stunt" was attempting to act like a "womanly woman" for an entire day, an expectation endlessly detailed in the Woman's Kingdom (the page where her articles appeared) and one she constantly failed at in her personal life. In this role, with instructions plucked from society parties and novels, she prayed, gossiped, sang a love song and played the piano as accompaniment, planned her winter hat while daydreaming at church, then offered praise for the sermon over dinner. That night she prayed some more: "Please make me a mean, rascally, wicked man, or even a masculine woman with a mission—anything, O, Lord, but a sweet, womanly woman!"

It wasn't the kind of writing Elizabeth Banks wanted to do. To learn what else might be possible, she continued to read. When she'd been at the *Globe* only a few months, on December 20, 1888, the paper ran the article "The Chicago Sensation," telling the story of the Girl Reporter who sought an abortion from prominent doctors. The stunt appeared to bear out all the editor's fears of what might await a young female journalist intent on proving herself in the big city. Banks was shocked. The indecent assignment seemed to show no care for the reporter's reputation. Who would do that? As a woman who aspired to write, she observed carefully how other female writers were treated—what earned censure, what garnered praise. And many found the abortion stunt appalling. Later, she would call the exposé an example of articles that "are so hideous and disgusting as to make one wonder how in the land of America, where chivalry of man towards woman is supposed to have reached its highest point, men can be found willing to take editorial positions which necessitate their assigning a woman to go out and degrade herself for the sake of making 'space.'" The response of the *Globe* itself was more temperate: "The exposure made by the *Times* of the existence of the crime of infanticide seems to have been done thoroughly and conscientiously, as it surely was an exhibition of fearless newspaper enterprise."

NEW TERRITORY

Go to work, and stop sentimentalizing about "woman's sphere." Any woman that is a woman carries her sphere with her wherever she goes—be it in a ballroom or newspaper office.

—Winifred Sweet, *San Francisco Examiner*, 1890

Stepping off the boat from Oakland in the spring of 1889, Winifred Sweet found herself at the head of Market Street, the broad cobblestone thoroughfare that sliced the heart of San Francisco, from the Ferry Building on the water, past storefronts and advertisements for beer, paper boxes, and artificial limbs. Streetcars lurched on rails embedded in packed dirt; horses pulled gilt-painted cabs. San Francisco was metropolitan, bustling, but it could feel a bit hollow, like a mining town thrown up in haste at the first glint of gold. Outside the urban core, treeless hills and sand dunes rippled to the ocean. A visitor from New York described a city of low buildings and oozing mud, characterized by the fact that no one had been there long. "The whole atmosphere of the place is charged with a vigorous, disrespectful sort of youth," the observer concluded.

The want ads of the *San Francisco Examiner* and other local papers sketched the dangers for someone like Winifred Sweet, a young woman with few friends, arriving in an unfamiliar place. Concern about sex out of wedlock and its revelation by pregnancy was constant. A slew of ads made the usual promises to cure "monthly irregularities." A Rev.

J. W. Ellsworth suggested that, "Women who have fallen and wish to reform can find a Christian home and friends" by writing him a letter. And finally, in the personals: "Minnie . . . come home; all is forgiven."

But Winifred was not one to be intimidated. Orphaned at fourteen, when her mother died not long after her father, she'd grown up in the Midwest under her older sister Ada's care. The two sisters looked alike, with the same unruly reddish-blonde hair, but their temperaments could not have been more distinct. Ada had the military bearing of her father, a Union solider, and portraits show sober clothing, serious expressions.

Ada Sweet

In contrast, Winifred preferred to bedeck her head with towering constructions of feathers and velvet. While Ada Sweet arranged for Winifred to attend the staid Mary A. Burnham girls' boarding school in Northampton, Massachusetts, Winifred had been swept up by the desire to be an actress and spent several years on the road. As a performer she struggled, playing roles like "ZoZo, the Magic Queen" rather than Ophelia, and it left her discouraged but not daunted. She'd already navigated New York City and been stranded in small towns with rickety theaters. She had taken the train across the country to find a missing brother, fending off marriage proposals along the way, locating him on a ranch in the southwest. Her sister Minnie had died a year and a half before, and now she'd come to California to visit her brother-in-law.

Ada, a noted Chicago reformer who supported her younger siblings by working as a United States pension agent, had urged Winifred to give up her attempts at an acting career and try reporting. Deeply invested in pulling Chicago from the muck and making it a healthy, compassionate city, Ada saw how the Women's Club responded to Nell Nelson's daring journalism. It fired them up, so that the society women were suddenly engaged in the lives of factory girls and poor children missing school. The bravura required by journalistic stunts might be a perfect fit for her younger sister, who, with her acting career languishing, needed another way to make a living. Winifred might be impetuous, but she was a good writer, as evidenced by her letters home, some of which Ada had arranged to be printed in the *Chicago Tribune* as a series on "Confessions of an Actress" by "Columbine."

On the page, Winifred poked fun at herself, admitting that while she considered herself a "heaven-born genius" as an actor, her friends generally thought she was a "stage-struck idiot." She mocked her own inexperience, reporting that she delivered her first-ever line, "My Lord, the carriage awaits," with such a tone of tragic intensity that she almost got fired. And when she finally landed a leading role and strode to center stage so the villains could abduct her, her fellow actors missed their cue. No one showed up for so long, she confided, "I began to think I should have to abduct myself." Though her dream of being a romantic heroine with the need to "weep and denounce" hadn't panned out, she knew she wanted a life that would let her roam. And in San Francisco, she found it. She immediately determined to stay and, since her first attempts had met with laughter and her sister's approval, try to make her way as a writer.

For someone considering a journalistic career, the *San Francisco Examiner* would have been hard to miss. In the spring of 1887, just as Bly headed to New York, William Randolph Hearst took his own risk. For at least two years, he'd been haunting the *Examiner* offices when he was home from college, sending his father, the wealthy Senator George Hearst, letters of advice on the paper's management. He'd been studying Pulitzer's *World* like a textbook, hiring college friends from the *Harvard Lampoon* to write columns, urging his father to spend more freely, chiding him: "The paper must be built up," and noting "cheap labor has been entirely ineffectual." After this lengthy campaign, and when it appeared he never would return to Harvard to finish his degree, the twenty-three-year-old had gotten what he wanted—a newspaper of his own. On March 4, a change appeared on the masthead. In a boastful note under "Ownership of the Examiner" was the comment: "The Examiner, with this issue, has become the exclusive property of William R. Hearst, the son of its former proprietor."

It's no surprise that the visitor who described San Francisco's atmosphere as "charged with a vigorous, disrespectful sort of youth" had spent an afternoon with *Examiner* reporters. Hearst himself had the intensity of a frontier priest or a prizefighter. Both characters held sway in his personality—a teetotaler known for a love of hunting and fishing, restless and ruthless in his desire to dominate the newspaper business. His techniques could be those of a broad-shouldered bully, while his soft voice was, according to a colleague, like "the fragrance of violets made audible." Bartenders all over the city knew the name of the *Examiner's* sharp-witted editor S. S. Chamberlain, as careful in his dress as Hearst, with Paris tastes and a gardenia in his lapel, but a hard drinker. In Chamberlain's small warren of an office, the reporters and editors, some from Hearst's Harvard days, some hired at high salaries with his father's backing, flung ideas like darts. They constructed elaborate and expensive schemes as if they were sand castles that could collapse without consequence. There always seemed to be more money.

The *Examiner* was evolving, testing out what might be possible with a printing press, creativity, and a mine full of gold. Editors masterminded exposés of police bribery and morphine clubs in Oakland. And in a strategy Hearst learned at the *World*, the *Examiner* ferreted out stories that, rather than focusing on power plays of senators, revealed scenes of life in factories, criminal courts, prisons. Like Pulitzer, he positioned himself as a champion of the poor and overlooked. Whether this reflected a deep-held political conviction on Hearst's part or not is hard to tell. More than one colleague commented he seemed willing to try anything, adopt any stance, to boost circulation. One reporter, with the kind of backhanded compliment that followed Hearst like hungry strays, said the publisher had "a very sure instinct about the seamy underside of human nature and what it would feed on with gusto."

Hearst's studying of Pulitzer paid off, though he had a distinctly more nativist bent. The *Examiner* advocated for continuation of the Chinese Exclusion Act, opened an employment agency for white applicants only, and referred to Chinese laborers as "the common enemy." This was a noted difference from Pulitzer, an immigrant himself, whose paper raised money for the pedestal of the Statue of Liberty and touted its message of welcome. The same month it published Bly's asylum exposé, the *World* hosted a debate between Wong Chin Foo, editor of the *Chinese American* newspaper, and Denis Kearney, an Irish immigrant and labor activist, over the Chinese Exclusion Law. (Kearney was trounced.)

For the next two years, Hearst and his staff explored how far a paper could go. Could it act as a police force? A rescue squad? A charity? The *Examiner* sponsored contests, threw parties. When reports came in that a fisherman was stranded on a rock near Point Bonita, his boat smashed and four companions dead, two *Examiner* reporters staged a rescue. One jumped into the heaving waves to bring the survivor a rope (though one of the boat's crewmen actually got it to him). The subhead read: "The Examiner Does the Work of the Life

Saving Service." Reporter Allen Kelly headed into the coastal mountains to capture a live grizzly bear to prove the giants weren't extinct in California. Kelly spent many fruitless months engineering and setting traps, building a series of enormous pens with pine trees as corner posts. Eventually, rumor that some rich San Francisco publisher would pay for a bear reached the high-country communities and a group of shepherds caught one. Kelly bought it, then faced the task of getting the massive, snarling, enraged animal four hundred miles to the *Examiner*. He did it, though. Hundreds came out to view the animal the first day it was on display in Woodward's Gardens, a San Francisco zoo and amusement park. The bear, named "Monarch" for the paper that called itself "Monarch of the Dailies" was chained, thin, and covered with bare patches where ropes had worn away the fur, but he became another Hearst triumph.

This was the environment of the *Examiner* office when Winifred Sweet showed up, all wild red hair and bluster. She was an experienced newspaperwoman, she assured the paper's city editor, and she "would cover not only myself but the paper with glory if only he'd give [her] a chance."

He gave her a chance, but her copy revealed the lie. One of her first assignments was to cover a flower show, and, nervous, she stayed up all night before it appeared only to find that the printed version contained completely new opening paragraphs. She'd neglected to include the location, the organization, the prizewinners—all of the actual news. Other stories came back with paragraphs crossed out in blue pencil and critical notes written in the margins, including "Don't moralize. Get at your story." But she kept at it, gaining confidence, a sense for the telling detail, the ability to infuse an article with personality, until, one day, the editor asked if she'd like a regular job as a reporter for $15 a week.

"Yes, sir," she said, and then, as she later described in a memoir, Winifred Sweet "walked out into the quiet of a sunny Sunday afternoon hardly knowing where I was or what I was doing."

Strangely, though peers described her as "wholesome and pink and white as an apple blossom" and "wholesome as a May morning," Winifred Sweet fit right in to the *Examiner*'s alcohol-fueled, extended bachelor party. She liked the reporters; she liked the publisher. Covering a children's celebration at Golden Gate Park, she watched a man in a light-gray suit and blue tie patiently entertain a boy who couldn't find his parents. Back at the office, the man in the suit—tie askew and damp spots on the knees of his pants from kneeling to a child's level—asked what happened with the lost boy. That was her introduction to Hearst, a man she described as "the best boss, the kindest friend, and the simplest-hearted, wisest, most understanding, most forgiving, most encouraging human being it has ever been my luck to know."

William Randolph Hearst

She caught Hearst's eye, too. Unlike East Coast editors who, as Bly discovered, could balk at the impropriety of hiring women, Hearst saw no obstacle. Whatever worked. The *Examiner* had tried using "girl stunt reporters" before, but the stunts were tame, and the narrators didn't capture the public imagination. But now this forceful young woman had shown up with her lavish hats and fearlessness. She was self-deprecating on the page and possessed of a good sense of humor off it. In this neophyte, Hearst saw his answer to Nellie Bly.

Winifred hadn't been working for the *Examiner* for long before Bly attempted one of the most audacious stunts to date. In November 1889, Bly volunteered to beat the time for circling the globe laid out in Jules Verne's novel *Around the World in Eighty Days*. She'd hatched the plan on a Sunday, brainstorming ideas for the *World*'s Monday editorial meeting, and fantasizing about a vacation. Somewhere far away, like the other side of the globe.

"If I could do it as quickly as Phileas Fogg did, I should go," she told herself. Maybe she could do it faster. That would be a story. When she proposed it—fact literally challenging fiction, a stunt to see whether what people could do might surpass what they could imagine—her editor put her off, saying the paper had already considered that idea and wanted to send a man, who wouldn't need an escort or much luggage. But a year later, she got the go-ahead, if she could be off in two days. And she was, in a long plaid jacket, a snug cap like a newsboy might wear, with no chaperone and only a small satchel for her spare dress and a light raincoat.

Just as Bly boarded a ship from Hoboken to England, *Cosmopolitan* magazine sent their own writer, Elizabeth Bisland, around the world in the other direction, speeding on a train from the East across the United States, in an attempt to beat Bly home.* You can almost feel the twist in Hearst's gut. Why didn't his paper have a girl racing around

---

* A conspiracy-minded reader might wonder whether the *World* also was behind Bisland's trip. The story gains tension and drama as a race against a real woman as well as the fictional character of Phileas Fogg. And Bisland is listed as part of the editorial department in the *World*'s 1889 office directory.

the world? The coupons where readers could guess the winning time? The prizes? The spectacle? It was everything he craved, yet someone else had dreamed it up.

Nellie Bly in her traveling clothes

The *Examiner* was stuck playing catch-up, like everyone else, but the editors made the best of it. The stormy, muddy day Bisland arrived in San Francisco, *Cosmopolitan* urged the steamship, the *Oceanic*, to leave immediately for Yokohama so she could be on her way, but the owners of the ship wouldn't budge. Bly was speeding across the Atlantic, bearing down on Europe. But the *Oceanic* would launch as scheduled, stranding Bisland on land for a few days with nothing to do but watch the minutes tick by. *Examiner* editors invited her to take a much more leisurely train ride than her recent four-day bullet across the continent, through the western reaches of the city out to lunch at the Cliff House, perched at the edge of the Pacific. With nowhere to go, Bisland admired the flaring sunset, the fat sea lions, the witty male journalists. With the rest of her San Francisco stay, Bisland slept in the Palace Hotel, shopped for light blouses to wear in the upcoming heat, bought silk for "fancy work" for when she got bored on the long ship passage, and talked with a young reporter—Winifred Sweet. Here Winifred, a stunt-reporter-in-training, came face-to-face with an active practitioner, almost as if she was taking notes on what to do, how to be.

If Sweet read other articles about the two racers, she would have gotten an education about the conflicting messages that swirled around stunt reporters. As Bly's fame grew, so did the pushback against her and what she represented. Her previous work was described, tepidly, as "distinctive"; profiles highlighted her "peculiar personality" and rather straightforward face saved by her animated smile: "She is a plain every-day girl, with a wonderful head and warm heart."

Even Bly, who always seemed to be enjoying herself, had learned to adopt a tone of apology for her fame and her stunts, using the need to support her mother and younger sister as an excuse. She told one paper that two paths faced her as a young writer: "One was the regular routine of fashion articles and the namby-pamby duties usually assigned to women in newspaper offices, and the other lay in doing something always startling, if not always original. I foresaw that the latter involved many things distasteful to me, but that I could earn more money, and I had two persons dependent upon me. I fully realized the vulnerability of my vocation—the exposure to charges of indelicacy of both action and motive, but horrible as it was to me I swallowed that, resolved to do my duty according to my conscience."

Much easier to praise the more conventional career and beauty of Bisland, who, according to the *Examiner*, "has never done anything

of the Bly order and a great deal of curiosity and surprise was shown
here when it was known that she had started on a trip of this kind."
Bisland had been a literary editor and book reviewer. One reporter
wrote, "Miss Bisland is universally regarded as one of the handsomest
women in New York. [Hers] is a distinctively southern beauty, the
soft eyes and long lashes which raise languidly to look at you, the full
mouth, the gentle outline of her figure, her dainty small hands and
feet all pointing to the South."

Bisland herself stressed her feelings of ambiguity at such a high-
profile role. Papers spent paragraphs detailing the reporters' appearance and outfits. She told Winifred, of the trip, "I didn't realize what
a public character it would make me when I started, but everything
has its drawbacks, they say. Does it always rain this hard in San Francisco?" And then, with the speed that characterized the whole trip,
she was off to Japan to catch Bly, who was racing toward London.

B ack in Illinois, Winifred's sister Ada had become an even more
passionate advocate for improving Chicago, campaigning for
cleaner streets and a ban on child labor, among other causes—and
would soon be referred to as "The Star-Eyed Goddess of Reform."
Spurred by Nell Nelson's articles, she planned a Women's Club lecture on "Influence of the Daily Press." She saw how newspapers and
activists could collaborate to spark change.

Nelson's old paper, the *Chicago Times*, wasn't going to be much help,
though. The paper was crumbling. Rather than reporting scandals,
it was the scandal. Rival papers trumpeted the downfall of James J.
West, the self-made millionaire who rescued the *Times*, sent Nelson
into the factories, and gave the Girl Reporter a list of suspect doctors.
In January 1889, a scant few weeks after the abortion exposé, the paper accused police officers of fencing stolen goods. The officers sued
West for libel and had him arrested, though he soon was out on bail.
Private detectives guarded the *Times* office. Editors and reporters
carried guns. Things spiraled out of control. On a trip to Washington

in the summer of 1889, West showed up at the hotel of his former city editor, Charles Chapin. According to Chapin, the panicked West carried a suitcase full of cash and begged Chapin to flee with him to Europe. Chapin convinced him to go back to Chicago, where he was arrested again, this time for issuing duplicate stock certificates, and writing checks backed by the paper for his own expenses. In late 1889, a judge sentenced West to five years in jail and a $5,000 fine, but this only launched a series of courtroom defeats and victories until he left the publishing business to try his luck in overseas gold mines.

While West scrambled to stay ahead of the law, Eleanor Stackhouse of the *Chicago Tribune* continued her investigations as "Nora Marks," sometimes in disguise, sometimes out. She had great potential as a partner in Ada Sweet's scheming, and the women knew each other because Ada occasionally served as the *Tribune*'s literary editor. Like other reporters doing stunts, Marks was in her mid-twenties, courageous, and curious about the hidden side of her city. One slushy January weekday in 1889, she stopped in at the Cook County jail. In the absence of any juvenile facility, young boys were kept there for weeks until they had a trial, or even after, if they weren't old enough or their crimes serious enough to be sent to reform school. Since the county jail housed only men, she couldn't trick her way in, so she walked up to the jailer with a letter of introduction.

WHERE HAS "NORA MARKS" BEEN

During the last two weeks? Not idle surely! She has had a new adventure—more unique than any ever before undertaken by a newspaper reporter. Begin to read her story in Sunday's TRIBUNE.

Nora Marks promotion in the
Chicago Tribune on October 12, 1888

"Well, what do you want?" The man with a large ring of keys stared her down.

"To see the boys in here and get your opinion of their being here."

"O, they're all right. This is the place for them. They've been bad."

Unimpressed with his level of concern, Marks requested a tour, and followed him through the barred door.

Here a teacher stood in front of twenty boys with messy hair and ragged clothes, trying to pretend they weren't curious about the reporter. It seemed clear the boys housed with adult criminals had more opportunity to pick up bad habits than to master grammar and arithmetic. Marks caught the teacher's eye.

"You don't approve of this?"

"It's a disgrace to the City of Chicago," the teacher said.

Marks noticed a ten-year-old with only a beginner's book.

"Haven't you got further along than that?" she asked.

"I can't read," he volunteered, but added that it didn't hold him back from his job selling newspapers. He learned the news of the day at the office. And if he forgot, he just yelled something about fire, a murder, or anarchists, and the papers sold.

The boys mocked the reporter's aspirations for them, hollering out their crimes as if they were career paths: That boy stole a lead pipe because he wanted to be a plumber, this one stole pants so he could be a tailor. But she launched into a story about her recent stunt in the stockyards, describing the techniques for making cans, wheel by wheel, belt by belt, and they fell silent, awed by the complex machinery.

Marks thought of herself as a vehicle for reform, the kind of "inconvenient individual who keeps abreast of the moral sentiment of his age and pushes his nose ahead of reform into existing institutions." Others viewed her this way, too. A month and a half later, the mayor declared the West Madison Station would be repurposed as a separate house of detention for boys. The Women's Club launched a campaign to raise money for the Norwood Park School, a privately funded industrial school that Marks visited and praised as a good place for boys to learn career skills.

Ada Sweet had her eye on Marks and on the need for an ambulance in Chicago. She asked the Women's Club to raise money for the cause, welcoming an amount as little as one cent. But she didn't stop there.

A month after Bly and Bisland set out, in December 1889, as Bly sampled curry in Ceylon and Bisland heaved on a storm-tossed ship headed to Hong Kong, the *Chicago Tribune* featured a new stunt. Nora Marks stepped off a streetcar and pretended to faint, falling into the chaotic intersection of Madison and Halsted, crowded with commuters, ringing with streetcar noise, blazing with electric lights. When bystanders attempted to rouse her, they got no response. Checking her purse, they found no clue to her identity, only change and a handkerchief. She was taken on a bone-shaking ride in a patrol wagon to Cook County Hospital. At the hospital, Marks collected herself enough to declare her name was "Annie Myers," and request her employer be sent for. Then, when the staff didn't do it immediately, she emphasized how worried her friends would be in her absence (and revealed how little she wanted to spend the night at the county hospital).

When the "employer" showed up to take her home, it turned out to be Ada Sweet. The activist played the scene with a gusto that her sister Winifred, the former actress, would have applauded.

"I can't see that there is anything the matter with her," the doctor told Ada. "She may have fainted—she acts a little peculiar."

"She is a little odd sometimes," Ada agreed.

Ada Sweet had teamed up with Nora Marks to pull off an exposé to raise awareness of the need for an ambulance. Nora would fake an illness that would result in her being transported to the hospital, and Sweet would get her out. And then, to drive home the point, Ada wrote a piece on the same page as Nora's story (which was entitled "All Jolted Alike"), explicitly advocating for better transportation: "The city should at once organize within the Police Department an ambulance corps, its members to be trained and drilled in the temporary care, handling, and transportation of sick and injured people. Squads detailed from this corps should be stationed at certain central police stations throughout the city, where they could be reached by the police alarm telephone service."

Proud of her work, Ada must have clipped the article and sent it to her sister. A suggestion? A script.

As it turned out, San Francisco also needed an ambulance. Hospital trips in the police wagon featured wrenching bumps. A carriage ride might take an hour. On Christmas Day 1889, a man hit his head on the cobblestones on Montgomery Street. By the time he got to the City Receiving Hospital, he had to go to the morgue instead. The next day, another man had a fit and died on the way to the hospital. A week into the New Year, timbers fell on a third man, who suffered internal injuries and broken bones. He didn't make it to a doctor. Neither did a fourth, who had shot himself.

But if they had survived, more trouble awaited them at this particular hospital, an emergency facility next to the jail. Rumors suggested things were particularly bad for women. Like those locked in an insane asylum, nameless patients were at the mercy of the system—often unconscious or too sick to advocate for themselves. A local doctor, "simply sick of hearing these things continually related of the Receiving Hospital," kept dropping in unannounced, but couldn't catch anyone misbehaving. Some contacted the newspapers, relating "queer doings" suffered by a friend. Other times, the victims approached the *Examiner* themselves. As usual, the precise nature of the problem was obscured. "Young girls wandered in with ugly stories," Winifred Sweet recalled.

And so, on a drizzly Friday afternoon, January 17, 1890, Winifred Sweet slipped on a worn dress, put a dime and several help-wanted ads in an old purse, asked a doctor friend to administer belladonna eye drops to widen her pupils so she seemed ill, and got on a streetcar. Disembarking at Kearny and Market, she put her acting training to good use, weaving and pretending to feel weak. A police officer ignored her. A passerby suggested she head home. Staggering down the sidewalk, she eyed a cluster of men around a cigar shop, and a pile of boxes that might cushion her landing and keep her out of the mud. But she hesitated. As she wrote later: "I kept walking away from it and then back again. I thought I'd have to give it up—that I hadn't the courage to do anything so dreadful. But I knew that it was my duty as a reporter to go through with it and that if I wasn't ready for such things I had better choose another business."

As she wavered, one of the cigar-shop men asked if she was ill.

"I am so sick—oh, my head," she said, then took a breath, clenched her teeth, and fell. He caught her before she hit the boxes.

The man carried her into a doorway, where a crowd gathered, trying to revive her. One offered to call a carriage. People generally took such good care of her, she worried she'd never make it to the hospital and the stunt would be ruined. But when the police showed up, they dragged her back outside and put her in a covered police wagon, the same one used to take prisoners to jail. The ride was uncomfortable, but she finally arrived at the Receiving Hospital. Here, though she followed Ada's playbook, things began to veer from the script.

At first, they checked for sobriety.

"I can't smell any whiskey," said the policeman.

"Say, did you take opium?" asked someone else.

Smelling her breath and determining she wasn't drunk, the medical student and nurse wondered whether she'd been poisoned. She should drink hot mustard water to throw up. Sweet resisted, but they held her nose and forced her head back against the chair until she swallowed some, leaving her teary-eyed and retching.

The assistant police surgeon, Dr. Harrison, a tall man with a scarred face and surly expression, came in.

"What's the matter with her; is she poisoned?" Dr. Harrison asked.

"We don't know, Doctor. We're just giving her an emetic on general principles," one of the caretakers said. "But we can't get her to take it."

"Give her a good thrashing and she'll take it," the doctor said. Then he gripped her head so hard she screamed, then grabbed her shoulder, scraping the skin off, and threw her down on a cot.

"Let her lie there, and if she makes any fuss, strap her down," he added, and left.

If there's any doubt about her sister's invisible hand pushing her out

into the street, there's the name Winifred gave when asked for identification by hospital staff: "Annie Myers," the same one used by Nora
Marks in Chicago. Winifred's article, with the byline "Annie Laurie"
(like Bly's pseudonym, taken from a song), ran under the headline "A
City's Disgrace." Unlike Marks's ambulance-focused story, though,
Winifred's article underscored the vulnerability of female public hospital patients at the hand of abusive male doctors.

In the aftermath, Dr. Harrison revealed himself as even worse
than Annie Laurie's account described. When another journalist confronted Dr. Harrison about Sweet's report, the doctor said, "She was
treated right, and she'll get the same treatment again if she comes
here."

"For what was she treated?"

"Hysteria," Harrison said. When pressed, he added that forcing
a patient to drink hot mustard and water was the proper treatment,
"that or a good, strong cathartic or an injection of spirits of turpen-
tine." In the face of the reporter's astonishment, he doubled down:
"Yes, anything to give her something else to think about. . . . The best
thing for a young woman like that is_____." Regarding the blank
space, the reporter commented, "The suggestion that Dr. Harrison
made is not printable. It was couched in language such as one would
expect from an inmate of a drunk cell."

A rival paper, which knew the rumors of hospital abuses, editorialized that "all the numerous complaints made recently against the
Receiving Hospital are to be visited on Harrison, who will be presented as a burnt offering to the indignant public." Maybe so. When
he showed up to the *Examiner* offices to question their motives in
running the story, the city editor punched him in the face. After pressure from the governor and questions from doctors with more conventional methods of treating hysteria, Dr. Harrison was suspended
and eventually dismissed. The police commissioners sent to Chicago
for a single, used ambulance, which arrived several months later.

The hospital article ran the same day as "The Race Grows Exciting," which hyped the approaching finish line of the round-the-world

caper. After keeping pace with Bly almost the whole way, Bisland had just missed her boat from France by three hours and would have to take a much slower one.

While the global contest was a boost for women's sense of independence, it also turned Bisland and Bly into curiosities rather than authors with something significant to say. The power of stunt reporters had originally been that with their first-person focus they increased the number of female voices telling stories and female characters featured on the front page. But while Bisland and Bly would write books later, for the duration of the round-the-world stunt, they were almost exclusively written about rather than writing themselves, except for their brief telegraph dispatches. This pushed stunt reporting into increasingly uncomfortable territory, and Bly chafed at it. In a January 22, 1890, *Examiner* article documenting Bly's arrival in San Francisco, she was figured as an inanimate object: "The most precious bit of freight that the *Oceanic* brought into this port yesterday morning came consigned to the *Examiner*. It was a package of Pretty Girl, with more brains than most girls who are not pretty and it was invoiced as One Globe-Trotter: Nellie Bly." The reporter asked Bly whether she had the chance to write anything. She said no, and a bit of frustration seeped through: "What was the end of the Cronin trial?* I want to interview you. I don't want to be interviewed." Then she hopped on the Southern Pacific, a special bound for Chicago.

The *Examiner* editorial page the same day outlined the stakes of the trip, saying that what might be most surprising to a European audience was "the fact that two young, unmarried women should start on a three months' journey unchaperoned. That is a peculiarly American feature of the affair. It is not so much that they should be going around the world, although that, of course, is remarkable, but that

---

* Chicago physician Dr. P. H. Cronin had fallen afoul of a group of Irish extremists, and his body ended up in the sewer. His murder in May 1889 and the resulting trial captivated the country. It is interesting to note that he was one of the many who wrote a letter in response to the Girl Reporter's exposé, pointing the paper to a case where a husband coerced his unwilling wife into having an abortion.

they should be going some thousands of miles in any direction alone. But to Americans that is not strange at all." And it offered a hint of things to come, adding, "If the *Examiner*'s Annie Laurie should be detailed to-morrow to go to Central Africa and interview Tippoo Tib, she would start off as soon as she could pack a valise and think nothing about it."

PART II

Swashbuckling

1890–1896

UNDER THE GOLD DOME

But Mr. Dashwood rejected any but thrilling tales, and as thrills could not be produced except by harrowing up the souls of the readers, history and romance, land and sea, science and art, police records and lunatic asylums, had to be ransacked for the purpose. Jo soon found that her innocent experience had given her but few glimpses of the tragic world which underlies society, so regarding it in a business light, she set about supplying her deficiencies with characteristic energy.

—Louisa May Alcott, *Little Women*, 1868–1869

On January 25, 1890, as thousands of people thronged the Jersey City Depot, Bly disembarked. When her boots hit the New Jersey platform, stopping the clock, cannons fired. Roses and lilies, thrown from the crowd, pelted her. The three official timekeepers checked their pocket watches, determining she had circumnavigated the globe in seventy-two days, six hours, and ten minutes. Jersey City mayor Orestes Cleveland stopped her on the way to her carriage, welcoming her, making a speech, though struggling to be heard over the din.

"The American Girl will no longer be misunderstood. She will be recognized as pushing, determined, independent, able to take care of herself alone and single-handed wherever she may go," he announced.

Bly, once so isolated in small-town Pennsylvania, had chatted with Jules Verne in Amiens, gambled in an Egyptian city near the Suez Canal, visited a camel market in Aden, bought a monkey in Singapore.

At some point, as Bly was speeding through the heartland, it became clear she was going to do it. The speeches had already begun as a special train carrying her mother and reporters from the *San Francisco Examiner*, the *Boston Globe*, and the New York *World* met her in Philadelphia to ride with her the last hundred miles. Behind on her sleep as she raced the clock all the way across the country, she still had enough energy to give an interview to a "little newspaper girl" from Nebraska, joke with the men of the Chicago Press Club, and pull off her cap and wave it at the crush of people at train stations from Fresno, California, to Dodge City, Kansas.

Then police carved a path through the crowd so she and her mother could board the ferry for Manhattan, where she threaded through the packed streets of Park Row to the *World* offices to bask in the congratulations of friends and colleagues.

Some sniped at her, at the unseemly self-promotion of it all. But if the admiring glances, and cheers, and heaps of flowers and congratulatory telegrams were any evidence, the trip was a triumph. Once again, she'd sized up a task that seemed impossible, taken a perilous leap, and landed on her feet with grace. Maybe this would make her career and her financial situation more secure. And she won. Elizabeth Bisland had missed a fast boat from Le Havre in France, then a German steamer from Bremen, and was bobbing somewhere in the Atlantic, on a slow ship from Liverpool, days from shore.

But that spring, supposed to be on a victory tour, giving lectures to a crush of fans, Bly didn't feel triumphant. After all the publicity she generated, the board games, the contest, the banner headlines from coast to coast, the *World* refused to pay her what she was worth. She'd fought with her editors before leaving for the West; it seemed the paper just wanted to squeeze all they could out of her and then toss her aside. Her love life was in turmoil. Rumors had her engaged to Frank Ingram, the assistant superintendent of Blackwell's asylum who'd been kind to her there. Simultaneous reports had her engaged

Nellie Bly game in the *World*, January 26, 1890

to James Metcalfe, an editor at *Life* magazine who'd shown up on the train at Philadelphia to escort her on the last leg of her round-the-world jaunt. She denied both commitments, and no marriage was forthcoming. Empty seats plagued her lectures. In late March, she missed her train from Chicago and had to pay $100 for a "special" out of her own pocket to make her scheduled talk at the Milwaukee Press Club.

So when a gushing young woman, all naive confidence, approached her in Milwaukee and confided that she was about to board a train herself to start a job at the *World*, then declared she wanted to write straight news, not perform stunts like Bly, perhaps the veteran reporter wasn't in the mood to exhibit her trademark cheer. Bly was only a year older than the woman who waylaid her, twenty-five to her twenty-four, but had much more life experience, much less raw en-thusiasm. Though the woman described Bly's and Nelson's exposés as "wonderful things," she was pulling moral rank. While it had been a genre for only three years, stunt reporting was already considered not quite respectable. As the young woman remembered it, her chat with Bly took on "a delicate layer of frost."

Not long before, the woman, named Elizabeth Jordan, aspired to be a nun. Something about the quiet intensity of the life of the Con-vent of Notre Dame in Milwaukee, where she'd gone to school, called to her. The walled garden with its fountain. The trees and the paths that wound through it. The ritual by which the novices took vows to enter the cloistered order that shunned the public unless called to ac-tion. It drew her in.

But not everyone was convinced. In the photography studio for her graduation picture, Jordan conveyed a certain sense of contra-diction. Yes, she had dressed in all white, looped a cross around her neck, and wore a sober expression. But her jaw was still rounded with traces of childhood. Her dress, far from severe, featured a skirt of stacked ruffles, trailed lace at the sleeves. Holding a jaunty umbrella, an explosion of curling white plumes on her hair, Jordan looked more prepared to stroll a fashionable boulevard than sink to her knees on a chapel's stone floor. Hearing her religious aspirations stated out loud could make her friends burst into laughter.

Her parents were similarly skeptical. While Banks's editor told her to be anything but a newspaper girl, Jordan's parents had another problem altogether. Her father, a Milwaukee real estate developer, and her musician mother who made Jordan practice her piano for two hours a day, had other hopes for their bright, bubbly daughter. Please let her be anything, they thought, but a nun.

One night, when she was seventeen and recently graduated from the convent school, her father sat at the desk in his study and made her a deal: if she would put aside thoughts of the convent for four years, he would bankroll her other dream—to be a writer—even as far as helping her to Chicago and New York, if that's what she wanted. The hustle of a newspaper office would test her religious resolve. And his plan seemed to be paying off. In Milwaukee, she edited the women's page for *Peck's Sun*, then wrote for Chicago papers, and finally took a "vacation" to New York that found her in the editorial offices of the *World*, asking the gruff, foul-mouthed Colonel Cockerill for a job. And he agreed. Six months later, she was on her way.

Like Chicago, in 1890, New York high society rested on top of a subterranean world of poverty. The wave of immigration throughout the previous decade meant that four-fifths of city residents were born elsewhere or children of those born elsewhere. And the city was straining to house them all. Whole families lived together in single rooms in tenement houses with little light or fresh air. Strangers paid 5 cents a night for space on a mattress or a corner to sleep in. Fire and disease were devastating in these closely packed quarters. In the summer, residents fled the stifling rooms and slept on the roofs. In the winter, homeless boys clustered around Newspaper Row, sometimes picking up work selling papers, sometimes just jockeying for space on the grates emitting heat from the underground printing presses. Narrow alleys offered space for gangs to gather, gangs that exploited the poor for economies of drugs and prostitution.

Stunt reporters discovered creative ways to cover hazardous housing, and others followed. Jacob Riis, a police reporter for the New York News Association, had been documenting life in the tenements. In Dickens-inflected, apocalyptic language he described his encounters: "A horde of dirty children play on the broken flags about the dripping hydrant, the only thing in the alley that thinks enough of its chance to make the most of it; it is the best it can do. These are the children of the tenements, the growing generation of the slums."

But his real innovation was photography. He often arrived in tenements unannounced and caught his subjects unawares. They frequently had surprised or bleary expressions, as if they'd just been jerked out of sleep. The technique wasn't kind, but the resulting images felt very candid, very real. Since January 1888, when he'd compiled a hundred photographs and presented a slide show called "The

Other Half: How It Lives and Dies in New York" to the New York Association of Amateur Photographers, he had been offering wealthy New Yorkers a view into the homes of their less fortunate neighbors. Not long before Jordan came to Manhattan, Riis published an article in *Scribner's*, soon to be a book, called "How the Other Half Lives."

When Jordan finally arrived in spring 1890, after dreaming of this moment for six months, she encountered the *World* in the middle of one of its biggest reinventions. No longer content with the dim, rented building where Bly talked her way onto the elevator, Pulitzer was constructing the most grandiose structure he and his architects could conjure. The man himself was rarely on-site, roaming the globe, increasingly blind, constantly sick, sometimes with his wife and four children, often without. But he still wanted the polish on each marble column to reflect his vision of what journalism could be. It wasn't there yet, though. Naked beams and a maze of scaffolding created a sense of disarray. And things felt ragged inside, too.

Bly was away lecturing and, as a result of her blowup with management, wouldn't be coming back. Her book *Around the World in 72 Days* would be out soon, and she had a contract to write serialized fiction for the *New York Family Story Paper*. Nell Nelson, who continued to produce a steady stream of articles, was distracted. Her younger sister had vanished. In March 1890, a headline in the *Chicago Tribune* read: "Miss Virginia Cusack Missing." On Sunday morning, Virginia said she was going to church but never came home. Her family was particularly alarmed, because Virginia didn't seem well, distraught over a disagreement with her principal that resulted in her reassignment to a new school. The next day, though, a telegram arrived from Niagara Falls, saying that, instead of showing up for her new class, Virginia had boarded a train to New York, where she was planning to stay with her journalist sister, Nell.

Nelson at the time had been advocating for a New York State bill that restricted working hours of women to ten a day and provided for eight female factory inspectors to check for functioning fire escapes and bathrooms with running water. Inspectors also could keep an eye out for sexual harassment and child labor. Stunt reporters' investigations showed the importance of women watching out for vulnerable populations. Their work inherently made the case for female doctors, prison matrons, factory inspectors. Nelson continued to cover other topics as well—a few days after her sister's arrival, she wrote up a lecture advocating against corsets—but family troubles often occupied her mind. (Whatever ailed her sister Virginia, it must have been serious; she died at the end of the year.) Perhaps that's why Jordan, who admired Nelson, described her as "cordial" but someone who "kept very much to herself and had no intimates."

A new arrival, Jordan found herself caught between two editors, the veteran Cockerill, who hired her, and the upstart Ballard Smith, who was edging Cockerill out as circulation slipped. Smith had little time for a Cockerill protégé like Jordan. Struggling to get into print, Jordan was given trivial assignments, which, often as not, went nowhere. Before long, Jordan was ejected from the main office and sent to write about Long Island summer resorts for the *World*'s Brooklyn edition. The demotion, after all her big plans to awe the city with her journalistic prowess, was humiliating.

"I was out of New York almost as definitely as if I were working in China," she commented.

Though the job wasn't the kind she'd dreamed about, it wasn't unpleasant. She wrote well and quickly received a raise for what didn't seem like much work. Her mother, out for a visit, was pleased to see that her daughter's life consisted of sampling resort after resort. And then, a meaty story fell into this idyllic beat and she resolved to use it to prove her mettle. President Harrison's family was vacationing at an ocean-side cottage at Cape May. The cottage stirred controversy because it was a $10,000 gift to Harrison's wife from a syndicate owned by a Philadelphia department store magnate. Some suspected it was a bribe. If the whiff of criminality wasn't enough, the nation was obsessed with Harrison's toddler grandson, Baby McKee, and clamored for news of him. No reporters had been able to get in. Jordan showed up at the door in a white linen suit and charmed Mrs. Harrison into inviting her for a conversation in the cool cottage rooms, simply appointed with cane furniture and throw rugs. Jordan emerged with columns full of house details and the antics of Baby McKee, in a report both lighthearted and rigorous. (Mrs. Harrison claimed not to know who had paid for the house, but Jordan interviewed donors in Philadelphia who seemed to view it as much more than a token of affection.) After this scoop, Jordan was called back to the *World*'s main office. And the president paid back the $10,000.

Back to the jostling, the cursing, the cigar smoking, the company of the best reporters the country had to offer. Legendary editors pushed her prose; she learned by reading the stories selected for praise and posted on the wall, by seeing which papers sold many copies, by reading recommended authors, by watching what phrases or sentences lit a fire in the editor's eyes.

A letter from the *Sunday World* editorial department to Commander Robert Peary, the polar explorer, showed the kind of articles they prized. The paper had hired Peary's wife, Josephine, for $1,000 to write a series about going north as her husband made another attempt to reach the North Pole. Peary suggested topics like features of the country and lives of the inhabitants. But an editor wrote back detailing how it should be done:

"The first story should deal with Mrs. Peary's own feelings regarding the upcoming trip." It should be told in her unique voice. Her confidence compared with the last journey north. Her thoughts about her husband's polar ambitions. Her clothes. Her planned meals. In short: "every little detail calculated particularly to interest women." Articles should include enough facts about the sweep of the expedition to be newsworthy but, the editor stressed, the whole thing should be "distinctly from Mrs. Peary's own point of view and expressed in her own way."

Though she insisted she wanted no part of stunt reporting, Jordan leaped at the chance to go on horseback into the mountains of Virginia and Tennessee and report on what she found there. The framing—warnings of the danger that she cheerfully ignored, the stress on her being a woman doing something unconventional—was very similar to the setup of a stunt, but she saw it as something distinct but still thrilling: "To me the southern mountain assignment was merely a high adventure; and a high adventure it remained from start to finish."

Jordan took the train to Bristol in Virginia. In the city, everyone told her not to venture into the long, narrow mountains that rippled across the state. Hiring a guide and ignoring the advice, she pressed beyond Big Stone Gap, a small town clustered at the side of the Powell River, crossing streams and tramping through muddy ravines on horseback. Good thing the horses have more sense than the riders, her guide commented. Finally, they arrived at the rustic, one-room log cabin of the Baptist preacher Joseph C. Wells, surrounded by a rail fence. Again relying on her ability to put strangers at ease, whether wives of presidents or backwoods preachers, Jordan was invited in.

The intense quiet and slow pace was far from the pressure of New York and the rush for the newest, most entertaining, most shocking thing. The stars felt near; animal cries echoed in the dark. Newspapers existed as an illustration to be tacked to the wall, a bit of art to brighten the room, along with the red calico curtains. Here was a man living not far from where he was born, on $30 a year, spending his days walking over mountains to marry, bury, and preach. There seemed a bit of regret for the prayer-filler road not taken when Jordan mused: "In the nineteenth century there are comparatively few of us who are laying all our treasures up above."

The piece was more than a quaint sketch. It was a eulogy for this way of life. Coal and iron deposits drew outsiders to the area; meadows and forests were being turned into mining camps. Prospectors squinted, and in the narrow valley and dirt roads could make out a new Pittsburgh. Train routes competed to pass through town. None had reached it yet, but they were coming.

And the preacher, whose life to this point had such a small radius, whose birthplace might be turned into a hotel, was going to have to move. Maybe to Tennessee, he said. This portrait, her gameness in going after it, and her general stamina cemented her place on the staff.

But the *World* wasn't all literary heaven. Lewd suggestions and abusive treatment by sources, editors, and fellow reporters could wear a writer down. Newspaper offices weren't immune from the kind of harassment Nelson documented in factories. Men made passes, winked, said degrading things that hollowed out Jordan's confidence. She felt that "the comments not only smirched one but that, in a way, I might be responsible for them. Possibly something in me drew them out!" It wasn't until Jordan had lunch with older writers, heard their stories of harassment and saw how it distressed them, that she began to think it wasn't her fault.

Jordan started to write short stories about newspaper life in which she puzzled out some of these thoughts. In one a young, naive, convent-educated reporter, Miss Van Dyke, aware that a new editor found her stories colorless, volunteered to go to a rowdy neighborhood to report on a post-election victory celebration, despite the fact that she was bound to be jostled in the streets and witness bad behavior. When she returned, colleagues back at the office who had always treated her with care taunted her and dropped liquor bottles and cigarettes on her desk. She garnered no more respect than the brassy-haired, heavily made-up woman who "did sensational stories." The cruel teasing didn't let up until she finally quit and got married to a fellow reporter to save her reputation.

Nights were their own challenge. Newspaper Row, with its posh editors' offices, was adjacent to the Bowery, with its brothels and bars. The staff stayed late to get the freshest news for the morning papers, often finishing up past midnight. At some point, the typewriters stopped and the rooms fell silent. Generally unmarried, with families (if they had them) far away, female reporters faced the question every day: How were they going to get safely home?

The streets were often lit—where they were lit—by gas lamps that didn't do much to illuminate shapes in darkened doorways. The walk to the elevated train, or streetcar, or horse carriage was marked by uncertainty. Was that noise the suck of mud on carriage wheels or something more sinister?

Once, at her first job in St. Paul, Elizabeth Banks had stayed so late that the cable cars stopped running. When her editor asked for a male reporter to get her to her house safely, the one who grudgingly volunteered commented that female reporters were "nothing but nuisances in a place like this at midnight. While I'm walking home with her, I'll ask the young lady to marry me, and that'll put an end to all our troubles." Accepting help clearly meant submitting to humiliation. Banks rejected the offer and started walking by herself, terrified, until she met a policeman who escorted her. It became a pleasant routine, until he asked to marry her, too.

And Jordan worked later than most. At times, she wouldn't be done until three or four in the morning. One night, she got off at the elevated railroad near Midtown and started walking fast, as was her habit. On an isolated, ill-lit street, the driver of a cab gestured to her. A man was already inside.

"Get in, Miss," the driver said. "It'll be worth while." Flooded with foreboding, she sprinted toward Broadway, the cab following, until she reached the blazing electric streetlamps of the large street and made her way home, "safely inside, with that door barred against the universe."

But, unlike her short-story heroine, she persisted. Jordan neither quit nor got married. The moral of the story was not her moral. (And Miss Van Dyke's realization at the end—"After all, a woman's place is in a home!"—was not something Jordan believed.) Ballard Smith and her male colleagues gradually came around to accepting her—to the point of staging a formal ceremony to urge her to throw off the habit of the nunnery, the good manners and politeness, the "I beg your pardons." It was a marriage to words and grime and scandal, the inverse of the ritual she'd admired where novices took vows to enter the cloistered order. Would she, they asked, "drop the damned formality and the convent polish and be a regular fellow like the rest of them?" Jordan agreed she would, and they all went out to celebrate at a French restaurant known for fine wines.

By December 1890, the Pulitzer Building was complete. Dwarfing competitors on either side, like a broad-shouldered soldier in a gold helmet looming over the peasants, it was the tallest office building in the world. At an opening celebration, politicians flooded in to offer congratulations. Dozens of carrier pigeons were released from the dome, clapping blue-gray wings and bearing the paper's messages of self-congratulation wired to their tails. Lights at the crest ensured the towering structure was visible for miles. The *World* touted the building's superlatives, not overlooking the smallest details: 375 feet tall! 26 stories! 16 miles of steel beams! 1,000 windows! 15,650 feet of water pipes! 57 urinals!

The Pulitzer Building

Unable to attend, Pulitzer sent a telegram from Germany, read by Cockerill at the ceremony: "God grant that this structure be the enduring home of a newspaper forever unsatisfied with merely printing news—forever fighting every form of Wrong—forever Independent—forever advancing in Enlightenment and Progress—forever wedded to truly Democratic ideas—forever aspiring to be a Moral Force—forever rising to a higher plane of perfection as a public institution."

His influence announced itself, as well, in a sign posted in the offices: "Accuracy! Terseness! Accuracy!"

And Jordan felt complete, too. After months of striving, she had finally arrived, able to walk through the high-arch entrance of the *World*, under a balcony with four statues representing "Art," "Literature," "Science," and "Invention" and a gilt sign declaring PULITZER BUILDING, into a rotunda with a floor of white marble, past the windows for dropping off payments and buying newspapers, and into the publication office. Underneath it all, the dragon in the lair, the presses roared and shuddered in the basement, printing up to three hundred thousand copies an hour. The public could watch the long strips of white paper be stamped with the day's news from a special viewing gallery.

From the high observation deck on top of the building, rather than contemplating God in a walled convent, Jordan could survey the entire city, the sharp spires, the stacks puffing smoke, the tenements leaning tiredly into one another, the elevated train reaching deep into the nest of uptown, the post office, the people, the rooms all squirming with secret lives, the Brooklyn Bridge over the ship-packed East River, the distant Hudson, and as far beyond as a hungry eye could go.

The *World*'s audacity continued to spread across the country. Out in San Francisco, Winifred Sweet had none of Jordan's reservations about sensational reporting. She slipped into the stunt-girl costume with ease, diving into oceans of trouble and gleefully paddling around. In the months since fainting at Market and Kearny, "Annie Laurie" visited a leper colony in Hawaii, sought a divorce from unscrupulous lawyers and testified in the resulting libel trial, interviewed a murderer, and canned fruit for low wages.

Later, writing about her affection for the city, she highlighted quiet pleasures: the hummingbirds that visited her garden, fig trees, and the view of Mount Tamalpais across the bay. But she savored the chaos, too.

In a single day, Sweet later recalled, she reported on "a minister's meeting from ten to twelve; interviewed Lottie Collins, the famous ta-ra-ra-boom-de-ay dancer; went to see a Russian Bishop of the Greek Church and asked him if it were true that he burned an orphan asylum full of children to get rid of some incriminating papers; and went down to the morgue to try to help identify a poor girl who had found the sweet delirium of youth suddenly turning into somber tragedy."

Throughout 1890 and 1891, the paper trumpeted her name, building the brand. The *Examiner* reprinted a column by Arthur McEwen that referred to her as "the 'Nelly Bly' of San Francisco" but insisted she was even better: "I have not met Nellie Bly, but my impression of her, from what I have read and heard, is that she is a chipper, kittenish and perhaps somewhat hoodlumesque young person—just the sort of newspaper female you'd rather not know. Annie Laurie is not of this variety at all." McEwen praised Laurie for being unobtrusive, wearing subdued clothing, and needing days to recover her nerves after one of her courageous feats.* He suggested she turn her skills to novel writing—"a womanly book and a pure one." The message was clear to aspiring female journalists: be

"WHY DON'T YOU TRY CANNING!"

Winifred Sweet as "Annie Laurie" in the *San Francisco Examiner*, August 17, 1890

---

* One wonders if he had actually met her.

anything but "hoodlumesque." It was, confoundingly, the opposite of the advice Jordan received—that she needed to lighten up and forget her convent ways.

Though she got her start echoing a Nora Marks stunt, Sweet also experimented with new material, exposing false advertising aimed at women. In one report, she described an acquaintance, her nose an odd tint of white, her cheeks smeared with purple, who happily showed off her $7 haul of bottles and tins labeled "Face Bleach," "Freckle Lotion," and "Wrinkle Unguent."

"Just wait till you read about 'em," the young woman crowed and handed Sweet the pamphlet "How to Be Beautiful" by Gervaise Graham, the "Beauty Doctor."

Sweet sent the collection to a chemist, then published the products' extravagant promises alongside his analysis (including an illustration of his letter, giving the piece a documentary feel). The Wrinkle Unguent was lard and wax scented with almond oil. The Freckle Lotion and Face Bleach contained corrosive sublimate (now known as mercury chloride, which the expert called "a most virulent poison"; modern chemists would agree). The Cucumber and Elder Flower Cream was cottonseed oil and almond oil. The value of each, he estimated, was less than 2 cents. Sweet's friend deflated as she listened to the report and finally tore the booklet to shreds. The title of the article was "Valueless and Poisonous," with the subhead "'Annie Laurie' Exposes the Dangers of Quack Cosmetics." With this, Sweet risked offending advertisers and the whole beauty industry that propped up the women's pages.*

As Sweet expanded her range, she caught the eye of one of her *Examiner* coworkers. He was not physically overbearing, but handsome and chivalrous. On nights when everyone had to stay late, he would put on his hat and coat and escort female colleagues to their cab or

---

* After the 1906 Food and Drugs Act, the Bureau of Chemistry analyzed a sample of Gervaise Graham's "Cactico Hair Grower," guaranteed to grow hair on bald heads, and found the tincture contained mostly water with a little alcohol, borax, glycerin, and pepper, and determined it wouldn't work. Graham paid a $50 fine.

streetcar. A writer himself, he traveled with hobos and worked along-side fruit pickers, but he was more known as an encouraging editor. Despite the many warnings about the dangers awaiting young women leading public lives, Winifred apparently responded to his attention. And despite the admonishments that office flirtation would lead to dismissal of a female reporter as being "pretty and coquettish" and having a reputation as a "fool," Winifred married Orlow Black in June 1891. Her son was born seven months later.

EXERCISING JUDGMENT

From the eagerness of woman's nature competitive brain-work among gifted girls can hardly but be excessive, especially if the competition be against the superior brain-weight and brain-strength of man.

—William Withers Moore, *The Lancet*, 1886

In the tiny jail cell, in Taunton, Massachusetts, in the fall of 1892, reporter Kate Swan McGuirk perched on a provided chair, prepared to interview the inmate, and took in the room. Friends of the prisoner had attempted to decorate; a table held flowers, books, and a fruit dish. But these small reminders of the prisoner's wealth and status couldn't erase the stark white paint; the narrow bed; the bucket; the high, barred window that offered a glimpse of trees on the jail's manicured grounds and ivy that smothered the walls.

Even outside the prison, the area could feel claustrophobic. Nearby Fall River, McGuirk's hometown, was dominated by textile mills, powered by eight waterfalls on the Quequechan River, and ruled by rigid New England social hierarchies that made the distance between the mill workers' tenements by the water and owners' houses on the hill seem greater than it was. A reporter for the local paper described Fall River residents as "families who lived, all of them, drab, narrow, and dreary lives, apparently deriving nothing from their rapidly increasingly wealth but the pleasure of mere possession and the joy of keeping expenses down." The city was near the ocean, but perhaps not near enough for a salty breeze to stir the heavy air.

McGuirk, twenty-six, had just escaped the stifling environment the year before, moving to Washington DC to further her journalistic career. Her witty articles, syndicated all over the country, offered an insider's view of the Capitol and humanizing details about politicians. She traveled to Vermont to document President Benjamin Harrison's vacation. In another article she reversed the usual scrutiny of women's clothes by commenting dryly on the attire of male senators: "It is very hard to have any veneration for a body of men costumed with the lack of care displayed by the senate for the last few weeks."

Her work was eminently respected and respectable. The *St. Paul Globe* lauded her as "clever Mrs. McGuirk, who knows the ins and outs of Washington life better than any woman in the country." A *Boston Globe* columnist declared, "'Kate,' as her numerous friends call her, is, in my opinion, a rare journalist for a woman." Despite the casual affection of the *Globe* writer, and the fact that her husband stayed behind when she moved south, her signed articles always referred to her as "Mrs. McGuirk," wielding the "Mrs." like a shield.

How strange to be back in this sleepy part of Massachusetts as an out-of-town reporter for the *New York Recorder*, pencil and notepad at the ready, evaluating familiar landmarks with a journalist's eye. But here she was, waiting to interview an acquaintance from her Fall River days, accused of hacking her father and stepmother to death with a hatchet.

"How do you get along here, Miss Borden?" she asked.

A few weeks before, on a hot day in early August, someone had killed Lizzie Borden's father, leaving him slumped on the sofa in the parlor, his skull crushed, blood arcing over the walls. The multiple wounds appeared to have been made by a heavy, sharp, tool.

Upstairs, Borden's stepmother lay crumpled on the floor in the guest room. When the dead body was turned over, it was clear she had also been hit many, many times. Maybe with an ax.

The crime was mystifying. The doors to the house, on a busy

street, were locked. Nothing had been stolen; Mr. Borden's watch and cash were undisturbed. The killing took place in the middle of the day when both Lizzie Borden and the maid were home. And where was the weapon? Where were the blood-covered clothes of the killer? Surely such brutal murders, accompanied by screams and falling bodies, must have made some noise, some disturbance.

Suspicion quickly turned to Lizzie, rumored to hate her stepmother, whose alibi was that she'd stepped outside to the barn for a few minutes to look for sinkers for an upcoming fishing trip, then lingered, eating pears. A few days after the crime and after a series of contradictory accounts of her actions, she was arrested. At a preliminary hearing, the judge determined she was likely guilty. Now she sat in the Taunton Jail, awaiting the grand jury.

Her sister, lawyers, and ministers visited, but Borden had no use for reporters. Every twitch of her eyebrow triggered an avalanche of criticism. The cruelty and forceful violence of the crime was such a repudiation of femininity, as upper-middle-class white women were supposed to perform it, the papers and their mostly male reporters were beside themselves. The *New York Herald* described her as a "masculine looking woman, with a strong, resolute, unsympathetic face" and a voice with a "peculiar guttural harshness." The *Boston Post* noted, "Her hands and arms are as muscular as a man's." Indiana's *Logansport Reporter* suggested that Lizzie had "a repellent disposition, at times sulky, at other times haughty and domineering." She wasn't distraught enough. Descriptions of the crime scene left her unmoved. Her mourning outfits were insufficiently somber. She laughed at odd times. In short, she was a perversion of nature, a monster.

As a result, Lizzie refused all interviews, except this one. She knew Kate Swan McGuirk from their work with Fall River Fruit and Flower Mission, bringing bouquets to hospitals, food to sick families, picture books to orphanages.

Of course, they were distinct from each other, particularly in the light of New England's rigid class rules. Both came from longtime Fall River families, but Swan edited her high school newspaper, married local journalist Arthur McGuirk at nineteen, went to work first as a proofreader and then, fired with determination, as a stringer for outlets in Boston, New York, and, eventually, Washington DC. A photo shows a long face, dark eyes under peaked brows, and a mischievous look behind a black speckled veil. A newspaper friend described Kate as "the embodiment of laughter and fun."

Borden, five years older, had been a listless student, eventually dropping out of high school. She never married and had no need to scramble for money. Her father had owned a bank, sat on the board of two mills, and was rumored to be worth half a million dollars. In contrast, Kate Swan McGuirk's father was a bookbinder, and her grandfather had been a mill watchman into his late sixties.

But still, they knew each other outside this bloody business, and McGuirk remembered Borden piling turkey on the plates of poor children during charity holiday dinners. Now, sitting across from each other, one asked the other how she was finding life in jail and wondered whether she was really facing some sort of demon.

"To tell the truth, I am afraid it is beginning to tell on my health," Borden said. "This lack of fresh air and exercise is hard for me. I have always been out of doors a great deal." Insomnia plagued her, maybe because of the enforced stillness, maybe because of the dark nights, not even relieved by a candle. Looking at the prisoner, pale and drawn, with red eyes protected by a "shade" from the glare of the whitewashed brick walls, McGuirk felt for her.

"I know I am innocent" is the first line of the September 19 interview, published in the *Recorder*. McGuirk gave the opening to Lizzie, and what follows is a meticulous defense, including an evaluation of the evidence, under the headline "A Persecuted Woman's Plea."

McGuirk used investigative skills to formulate her rebuttal to prosecutors and other journalists. A rival paper mentioned an unknown woman "whose card has taken her into the Bordens' inner circle. She is a detective for a New-York paper, or a stenographer from Boston, or an every-day spectator from Providence." Though she's never named, odds are high that this person poking her way into the funeral home and crime scene was McGuirk.

One of the critics' complaints about Borden was that she didn't cry, proof of her monstrous nature, so McGuirk tallied the tears. When Borden viewed the cleaned-up body of her father the night after the murders, she burst out crying with a vehemence almost frightening, according to the undertaker's assistant. The prisoner's letters documented the many nights she cried herself to sleep. The matron at Fall River witnessed Borden crying so much she (almost) couldn't eat supper before she was taken to Taunton Jail. "When the State comes to argue its case again it will have to give Lizzie Borden credit for every tear that she has shed," McGuirk wrote.

One suggested motive for the crime was Borden's desire to wrest her inheritance from her infamously tight-fisted father. She resented living in a spartan house in the unfashionable section of town, people said, near the tenements (just a few blocks from the McGuirks) and not perched on the hill with other mill owner's daughters. But Lizzie Borden didn't lack for money, as the reporter showed by giving the balance of the Borden sisters' bank accounts and the annual dividends on mill stocks they owned. Exploring the Borden home, McGuirk recorded pretty blue carpets and other decorative touches. If a bathtub and running water on the second story were missing, she reasoned, it was because the family was planning a move, the father finally yielding to his daughter's desires. The reporter prowled the house, gauging angles, trying the soundness of locks, looking for hiding places for any murderous stranger who might have crept in.

Hatred for the stepmother? They could often be found sharing a church pew. The letter, whispered to exist, where Borden told friends that when she joined them on a vacation to a Connecticut cottage, she'd bring a hatchet? Just a joke. Piece by piece, McGuirk addressed the evidence in a lawyerly effort to explain it away.

Throughout, the reporter stressed that the prisoner, despite her physical strength and lack of emotion, was a woman. True, she's strong,

McGuirk argued, but she used her muscles for good purposes—running the sewing machine when her stepmother was too weak, offering to chop wood for those who needed it.

Leaning on the authority of an insider, McGuirk presented Lizzie as representative of regional stoicism: "To let her stand before the world as the prosecution has pictured her would be unjust to Miss Borden, to all her family and to all New England women." She questioned whether the animosity against Lizzie was a result of her not playing the expected role of emotional female and "because she does not wave a tear-wet handkerchief in public."

McGuirk's interview was dismissed by local reporters as "a magnificent 'fake,'" but elsewhere she was lauded as "Mrs. McGuirk, that able and enthusiastic newspaper woman."

This defense, of a woman, by a woman, was significant as women didn't serve as jurors in the early 1890s.* The Sixth Amendment, which required criminal defendants face "an impartial jury of the state and district wherein the crime shall have been committed," hadn't been interpreted to mean the pool could or should include women. Female jurors had been tried in Washington and Wyoming but the experiments were short-lived, and now the concept was more of a joke, the snickering, for example, about one female juror being "sequestered" with eleven people of the opposite sex. Borden's guilt or innocence would be argued by male lawyers, in front of a male judge, and determined by a panel of twelve men.

The jury question, similar to that posed by journalism, came down to objectivity. Could women—given their fundamental nature—be unbiased and impartial? Or did the fact of their bodies mar their ability to reason? Historian Francis Parkman didn't think they were fit.

---

* It wasn't until 1975 that the Supreme Court ruled states couldn't create laws that discouraged women from participation on juries, and 1994 when peremptory challenges based solely on sex were outlawed.

The government had enough problems with hasty decisions that ignored consequences. "This danger would be increased immeasurably
if the most impulsive and excitable half of humanity had an equal voice
in the making of laws," he wrote in the *North American Review*. And
it would be impossible for a man to argue with a woman because he
couldn't strike back, "literally or figuratively." This made women's
speech particularly dangerous: "A man's tongue is strong only as the
organ of reason or eloquence; but a woman's is a power in itself." Dividing up qualities between the sexes, he listed "the essentially masculine one of justice."

The entire legal system was hostile to women's participation. When
a female lawyer applied to try a case before the Wisconsin Supreme
Court, in 1876, the chief justice argued against her, saying he wanted
to protect those of her sex from hearing about "indecencies" such as
"sodomy, incest, rape, seduction, fornication, adultery, pregnancy;
bastardy, legitimacy; prostitution, lascivious cohabitation, abortion,
infanticide, obscene publication, libel and slander of sex, impotence,
divorce. . . ." He glossed over the fact that almost every one of the listed
activities required a woman's involvement.

Those in favor of women on juries pushed back in a variety of
ways. No one should be barred from participation in the government
of the society in which she lives, one argument went. A second suggested that women offered some quality currently missing from an
all-male jury box, maybe a particularly feminine sympathy. A third
proposed that perhaps just by moving through the world in a female
body, women had some needed perspective on seduction (gaining sex
with a promise of marriage that is then revoked) or rape, or abortion.

And Borden's trial in particular, where the nature of womanhood
was a central theme, made people question banning one sex from the
jury box. Suffragist Lucy Stone saw the Borden case as a turning point:
"Slowly, perhaps, but surely, the idea is growing that a jury ought to
be composed of men and women, and that a woman especially should
have a jury of her peers, not her sovereigns, as in the case of Lizzie
Borden."

A PLACE TO SPEAK FREELY

Woman in stepping from the pedestal of statue-like inactivity in the domestic shrine, and daring to think and move and speak,—to undertake to help shape, mold, and direct the thought of her age, is merely completing the circle of the world's vision.

—Anna Julia Cooper, *A Voice from the South*, 1892

The same summer when the press would convulse over the Fall River murders, major papers were ignoring a multistate crime wave. Lynching was on the rise, growing more ornate and cruel, incorporating elaborate torture—burning, shaming, mutilation—a display of dominance that perpetrators celebrated by taking photos and souvenirs. By one count, lynchers killed 150 in the first nine months of 1892.

The initial years after the Civil War had been filled with optimism for a new society, as the Fourteenth and Fifteenth Amendments made formerly enslaved men and women full citizens and gave Black men the right to vote. Initially, federal troops stationed in the South protected these rights. But after the end of Reconstruction in 1877, when these troops left, much of the optimism left with them. The newly formed Ku Klux Klan terrorized Black citizens, uprooting them from their homes, stealing or destroying their belongings. Legislatures passed Jim Crow laws separating Black rail cars and schools from their white counterparts. Literacy tests and poll taxes frustrated attempts to vote. And in 1892, more men and women, mostly Black, would be lynched than ever before. Despite the growing violence, northern papers rarely reported the murders. Or if they did, they painted them as something far away and irrelevant to life in Boston or New York, or justified by claims of rape.

One reporter paying close attention, though, was Ida B. Wells. Though only twenty-nine, Wells already had a lengthy and varied writing career by the summer of 1892. As early as 1889, the *Journalist* profiled Wells, who wrote for papers like *The Living Way* in Memphis, the *New York Age*, and the *Little Rock Sun*, as part of a feature on African American female reporters. The *Journalist* highlighted her nerve, her appeal to readers of both sexes, her advocacy for her race, and her nickname—"Princess of the Press."

Ida B. Wells

Though stunt reporting was on the upswing, Wells and the other writers featured by the *Journalist* were not stunt reporters. The tightrope the stunt reporters walked—an ostensibly respectable woman dipping into disreputable waters, only to resurface unscathed!—wasn't available to Black women. The genre was tied to white-owned newspapers that rarely hired Black reporters or covered their communities. And when Black subjects did appear, they were often depicted as destitute or criminals rather than artists, intellectuals, or activists. These papers, and the way they wrote about Black people, were the target of frequent criticism of Wells and writers in her circle.

Though not a stunt journalist, Wells actively experimented with voice and persona. This is clear from the diaries she kept between 1885 and 1887. Diarists, especially young ones, write themselves into being, playing with handwriting styles, turns of phrase. In her journal, Wells tried on roles, literally and figuratively, aware that none quite fit. She wanted to be better—spending less money on clothes, writing wonderful sentences, wasting less time looking for lost keys—but she also took pleasure in a rich social life. Despite teaching and taking care of younger siblings (they had all been orphaned by yellow fever when Wells was sixteen), she played a scene as Lady Macbeth for a literary society, attended baseball games, chatted and corresponded with a bevy of suitors. Noting that she enjoyed the company of men but didn't want to get married, she wrote: "I am an anomaly to myself as well as to others."

At the same time as she explored different perspectives, she had a sense of how the world should be, what justice looked like. In 1883, at only twenty-one, she defied the Chesapeake & Ohio Railway Company that sold her a first-class ticket but expected her to ride in the "colored" car. When a drunk white man entered Wells's carriage, she got up and moved into the one designated for "ladies." When asked to leave, because to the railroad "ladies" meant "whites," Wells stood up for herself to the point of gripping the seat as the conductor dragged her out the door, ripping her sleeve. Then she sued.

One day in September 1886, just as she wondered whether a plot for a novel she wanted to write might be too sensational, she read a newspaper article that ignited a rage so powerful it tore through her diary's often lighthearted tone. In Jackson, Tennessee, about eighty-five miles from Wells's home in Memphis, a white woman had died of arsenic poisoning. When her Black cook was found to have rat poison in the house, the cook was arrested, dragged from jail, and murdered. Her naked body was hung up for everyone to see. "O my God!" Wells wrote. "Can such things be and no justice for it?" Outrage undergirded an account she wrote for the *Gate City Press*. And then, almost immediately, she feared punishment for voicing these thoughts, for unleashing her anger. But her need to write outweighed her worry about consequences. "It may be unwise to express myself so strongly but I cannot help it," she wrote in her journal. The article might be used against her, she concluded, "but I trust in God."

In early 1889, after her lawsuit, which she'd won in the lower court, had been overturned by the Tennessee Supreme Court; after the husband confessed that he'd been the one who poisoned his wife and that the Black cook was innocent; after she'd put away the diary, Wells decided to take a concrete step toward forging the future she wanted— both personally and politically. She invested in the *Free Speech and Headlight* newspaper in Memphis, becoming editor and part owner. This would, she thought, give her the freedom to speak her mind. And it did, at least for a while.

In Memphis in March 1892, three men were lynched on the outskirts of town, and Wells covered it for her paper. One of the murdered men was her friend, the congenial postal carrier and grocery store owner Thomas Moss, father of her goddaughter. It was clear to Wells that the killers were prompted by economic interest—they wanted to shut down a competing grocery store. Out of her grief, Wells used her newspaper, the *Free Speech*, to suggest Black Memphis citizens should abandon the city, turning their backs on "a town which will neither protect our lives and property, nor give us a fair trial in the courts, but takes us out and murders us in cold blood when accused by white persons." Many agreed and moved to Oklahoma, leaving white business owners with lost revenue and resentment. Aware of the swirling anger, hers and others', she bought a gun.

Two months later, she wrote an even more forceful *Free Speech* editorial that detailed eight additional lynchings and called the repeated claims of Black men raping white women a "thread-bare lie." While some in Lizzie Borden's community couldn't imagine a Christian white woman stepping outside the bounds of the law, Wells suggested that southern white women often slept with Black men willingly, because they desired them, and then lied about it. Interracial marriage was illegal, so when these women suspected a neighbor might have spotted their lover at the door or worried their child would have dark skin, they said they had been raped. Wells's unsigned editorial warned that if white men kept obsessing about sex between Black men and white women, "a conclusion will then be reached which will be very damaging to the moral reputation of their women."

The day the article ran, in the early summer of 1892, Wells was vacationing on the East Coast. Alarming reports from Memphis began to trickle in. A rival newspaper, the *Scimitar*, said the author of the *Free Speech* editorial should be tied to a stake, branded, and mutilated. She'd said what it was absolutely forbidden to say. Her business manager, warned of a gathering mob, had fled. Men were watching the train and her house, waiting, murderous, for her return. Her newspaper office had been destroyed—type smashed, chairs broken, a threatening note left in the wreckage. Telegrams and letters sent to her in New York carried the same message: if she valued her life, she shouldn't come back. And these were the notes from friends. She was stranded.

Thomas Fortune, editor of the *New York Age*, who had been publishing her work for several years, told her: "Well, we've been a long time getting you to New York, but now you are here I am afraid you will have to stay."

So she did, writing for the *New York Age*, at first smaller pieces, and then, on June 25, 1892, putting together a lengthy article called "The Truth About Lynching," elaborating on her claim that miscegenation laws and prejudice made it impossible for unions of mutual passion to be acknowledged. Based on extensive investigations of individual lynchings, Wells marshaled story after story to support her argument that, in many cases of supposed rape, white women were sleeping with Black men willingly. In one case, a woman said the man in her bedroom was only putting up curtains; in another, the woman insisted it wasn't an interracial affair as she, too, was Black. In another, a minister's wife declared her lover was actually her rapist. The offence lay not in the crime but in the race and sex of the participants, Wells argued. White men raped Black women with impunity. In addition: "They could and did fall in love with the pretty mulatto and quadroon girls as well as black ones, but they professed an inability to imagine white women doing the same thing with Negro and mulatto men."

From her May editorial onward, Wells discussed women's bodies, capable of interracial lust and affection, in a way her opponents found intolerable. Her banishment from Memphis was devastating, exiling her from those she loved. But it was also liberating: "I felt that I owed it to myself and to my race to tell the whole truth now that I was where I could do so freely."

Victoria Earle Matthews, a Brooklyn-based reporter who had been profiled along with Ida B. Wells in the *Journalist*'s 1889 feature on African American women, recognized Wells as a talented writer in desperate need of money and support. Matthews's own work, to this point, had been in a different vein. She wrote, mostly under pseudonyms, for white-owned papers like the *New York Times*, the *Herald*, the *Mail and Express*, as well as Black-owned papers like the *New York Age* and the *Washington Bee*. Born into slavery to an enslaved mother, Matthews was roughly four years old at the end of the Civil War. Her mother fled north and arranged to bring her children after her, so she had grown up in New York. At nineteen, she married a coachman who, according to the census, couldn't write. She sought out education wherever she found it. Peers described her as a "zealous, watchful spirit," and there was no doubt she could get things done. "No writer of the race is kept busier," noted the *Journalist*.

One of her earliest journalistic efforts was modesty itself. As "editress" for the "Home Circle" feature of the *Washington Bee*, she

**Victoria Earle Matthews in
the *Journalist*, January 26, 1889**

filled her columns with housekeeping tips. Silk scarves placed on the
mantel or a Japanese scrap basket decorated with a ribbon brighten
the home. Reinforcing sock heels will mean they need less darning.
But, unlike Bly or Banks, Matthews saw writing about domesticity
as significant—a way for Black women to build a family home—
something destroyed by generations of slavery. She hoped, too, these
kinds of articles might lead to something else, both for her and others
of her race. In her inaugural column, she urged women to overcome
their reluctance to write: "I do not think our women will object when
I say comparatively speaking, very little journalistic work has been
done by us in the past; not due to a lack of ability, but a natural timidity, which I hope is dying out." Like other women stepping into this
new territory, she was wary to appear to be asking too much.

But she'd begun to expand her scope, writing a "New York Letter"
for the *National Leader*. She used her column to advocate for Black
men to run for office, encourage the Empire Women's Republican
Club to discuss political issues, question why all the speakers at the

unveiling of Boston's Crispus Attucks monument had been white. "Peace and security are very good things to have," she wrote, "but there are other things quite as necessary to the proper enjoyment of life." What would happen, she wondered, if African Americans were given a platform, or took one?

Seeing an opportunity to build just this kind of platform, Matthews gathered friends and acquaintances and organized a benefit for Ida B. Wells in October 1892.

At Lyric Hall in Manhattan, Wells entered a room where every detail seemed crafted to demonstrate good feeling. Event programs looked like copies of her *Free Speech* newspaper, now defunct. Her pen name "Iola" was projected in lights on the stage platform. Organizers presented her with flowers, a pin in the shape of a pen, and $500 to underwrite a book of her lynching reporting: *Southern Horrors, Lynch Law in All Its Phases*.*

After songs and speeches, it was her turn to speak. Wells left her handkerchief on her chair on the stage and rose to stand in front of the hundreds of supporters, mostly women, many very accomplished. Doctors, writers, assistant principals crowded the hall. It was a sea of strangers, welcoming in white sashes but strangers nonetheless. Wells had taught and written, but she hadn't given a lot of lectures. Nervous, she kept the text of her speech in front of her, though she knew it by heart.

She started in on the story of her friend, Thomas Moss, who owned the thriving People's Grocery Company outside of Memphis, and the fight among boys playing marbles that turned into a fight among men, including the white owner of a rival store. After several days of threats, fearing an attack on the People's Grocery, Moss and his co-owners posted guards at the back of the building, and the guards shot and wounded white men creeping in. The three grocery owners were arrested, along with many other Black men in town, alleged to be

---

* She would dedicate the book to "the Afro-American women of New York and Brooklyn, whose race love, earnest zeal and unselfish effort at Lyric Hall, in the City of New York, on the night of October 5,1892—made possible its publication."

part of a conspiracy. As the men sat in jail, white-owned papers stoked anger, describing the store as full of criminals and gamblers. Just as it was announced that all the injured men would live, Moss, the grocery store manager, and a clerk, were torn out of jail, put on a train a mile out of town, and shot to death.

As Wells talked, sadness overwhelmed her. Her Tennessee life had been yanked out from under her so suddenly. Relationships forged through time, over long evening walks and lively conversation, were gone. So was the printing press that had enabled her to publish her own thoughts on her own terms. Letters, type, cherished belongings, left behind, broken, or scattered. And there was no looping back. The only path was forward.

Tears dripped down her face, though she kept her voice even. It was embarrassing—she wanted to do well by these esteemed women who went to all this effort to celebrate her—and here she was, weak.

Without stopping, she reached behind her and gestured for help. Victoria Earle Matthews put a handkerchief in her hand. And Wells kept speaking.

GUILT AND INNOCENCE

"Put a good woman on this!" shouts out the head editor to his assistant dozens of times a day.

—The Living Age, 1898

Through the rest of 1892 and into 1893, as Grover Cleveland won his rematch with Benjamin Harrison to take the presidency again, Nell Nelson reported from Europe on factory conditions in Berlin and Nuremberg, Winifred Sweet (now Winifred Black) solicited reader opinions on "Who Is the Greatest Woman Alive?," and as Lizzie Borden paced in jail, awaiting trial, Elizabeth Jordan flourished at the *World*.

She stayed up late nights, going into all kinds of New York City neighborhoods, undoing the good work of her convent education. The *World* still felt like the center of a bustling universe. In the paper's tenth anniversary issue in 1893, an illustration touted "Public Services Rendered by *The World*." These included: "Equal rights for poor and rich," "Relief for the oppressed," "Anti-Monopoly," and "Exposure of Fraud." Jordan's reporting on a medical student who'd poisoned his secret wife and Nelson's advocacy for female factory inspectors were also listed among the *World*'s decade of accomplishments, though neither woman was mentioned by name. But Pulitzer wasn't resting on his laurels; the paper continued to innovate, installing a color printing press and publishing one of the first Sunday comics supplements, popping with scrappy characters in bright reds and blues.

Jordan had proven her value as an editor as well as a writer but was still relatively new, garnering only the rare byline. So the assignment to cover the Borden murder trial was a coup; reporters all wanted to be on the train to New England in June 1893.

In the months since the crime, the mystery had only deepened. However you looked at the case, Jordan wrote in one of her early articles, "you have to make up your mind to accept things which are wildly improbable on the basis of any past experience of human action." It was impossible to imagine Lizzie Borden had committed the murders. It was impossible to imagine she hadn't.

The *World*, in a weekend feature, asked notable figures whether they thought Borden was innocent, revealing the depths of disagreement. Journalist Helen Watterson said she was guilty. Borden's sex, and its relative powerlessness, was a motive, she suggested: "Many women—faithful daughters and wives—have lived out long lives of utter soul and mind starvation in so-called comfortable homes and in surroundings that outsiders might envy, simply because the unimaginative, sordid man who held the purse-strings did not think it necessary to countenance any display of 'foolishness' on the part of his women at the expense of his cash-box." And Borden's womanhood didn't offer any defense: "The one thing to be said in rebuttal of the argument drawn from her character is that she is a woman. Which is really no defense at all. Because there may be an entire lack of moral fibre in a woman quite as certainly as in a man." This contention, though not flattering, insisted that women were full, flawed, human beings rather members of some separate category.

In contrast, Rev. Charles Parkhurst, head of New York's Society for the Prevention of Crime, who had been conducting a campaign against police corruption and prostitution in the Tenderloin, came to Borden's defense. He declared her upbringing—her environment and "Christian attributes"—incompatible with such viciousness, writing, "Angels, my friends say, do not become Frankenstein in an instant."

Like all the other reporters except Kate Swan McGuirk, Elizabeth Jordan couldn't get an interview with the defendant. But there was plenty to observe in the courtroom as the Borden trial got underway. Bright sunshine streamed through courthouse windows on either side of the audience, bringing unbearable heat. The attorneys heaped their tables with evidence: a valise containing the skulls of the two murdered Bordens, a dress Lizzie might have worn, a bloody bandanna, a large selection of hatchets. Dozens of reporters perched on stools in front of the long wood shelves installed as communal desks, alongside sketch artists flecked with ink. Women from New Bedford and Fall River, fans in hand and lunches in their pockets, glowered at the defendant. Jordan found these women, who attended every day and formed "a self-constituted jury," disconcerting, writing, "They sit and look at her with ghoulish eyes, and they have openly exulted with the prosecution on the rare occasions when a point has seemed to be scored." Of course, she hoped her readers would exhibit the same lust for every gory detail, never missing a day, though at further remove.

In full-page articles with ample pictures, she brought the courtroom as close as she could, occasionally slipping into the intimate tone of second person: "To-day, as yesterday, you squeezed your way when you entered the court-room past a blood-soaked sofa on which an old man sleeping securely in his own house at 11 o'clock in the morning, with members of his own family about him, was chopped to death by a murderer."

And, though she found the audience's glares at Borden unseemly, no one observed Borden more closely than Elizabeth Jordan.

Descriptions of women's bodies and appearance were influential, Jordan knew, and she considered how to do it. To call a woman "pretty" was one way to create sympathy, deserved or not. And ugliness may be deemed to reflect sin. Jordan clearly found Borden unattractive, with sickly skin, doughy cheeks, a double chin, lips that she licked constantly, but she struggled not to make this a judgment. The defendant's face, "plain to the point of homeliness" viewed straight on, was "not without womanly gentleness" in profile, Jordan wrote. The

Elizabeth Jordan

nape of her neck had a nice curve. And clutching a bouquet, a black fan in her black-gloved hands, with freshly curled bangs, Borden was at least very tidy. "She radiated cleanliness like an atmosphere," Jordan concluded.

But trial testimony about Borden's body kept getting in the way of efforts to portray her as feminine. A bucket of bloody rags found in the cellar was explained away by the claim that Borden was menstruating. A spot of blood on her petticoat might have been from a fleabite. The prosecutor suggested she committed the murders naked, and that's why her clothes remained clean. Her arms looked suspiciously strong. This all made her seem more bestial than angelic.

On a good day for Borden (the headlines of Jordan's articles were all from the perspective of the accused, like "Lizzie Borden Fatigued," and "Going Lizzie's Way," implying a sympathy with her) the police contradicted themselves about where they'd found a hatchet handle. Maybe it was on the box in the cellar, next to the hatchet head. Or maybe it was in the stove, where someone might have attempted to burn it. On a second day, her doctor described giving her morphine to calm her, a possible cause of her confused and contradictory testimony at the coroner's inquest. On still a third day, the judge banned evidence from a drugstore clerk who said Borden tried to buy prussic acid, a poison, from him several days before the murders.

But not everything went her way. On a bad day, a neighbor mentioned that she'd seen Borden burning a dress not long after the killings, one Borden claimed was ruined by paint.

"I would not be seen doing that, Lizzie," the neighbor had cautioned. She knew this was damning but didn't go to the police for months. In another setback, the matron of the Fall River Central Police Station reported a fight between the Borden sisters.

"You have given me away, but I will not yield an inch," Lizzie Borden allegedly said.

Nights, after Borden climbed into the carriage for the trip back to jail, and the lawyers returned to their desks to refine the next day's orations, Jordan and other reporters gathered on the balcony of one of their hotel rooms, looking for a little relief from the humid air, and tried to make sense of what they'd heard. Perhaps the only logical explanation was some grim twist, like one might read in a Poe tale: a murder in a room with no escape route, a clue hidden in plain sight. The male reporters in her circle all considered Borden innocent, but Jordan felt the power of her words to sway readers one way or another. She kept her thoughts to herself.

As the evidence unfurled, though, Jordan let her mask of impartiality slip. The police clearly conspired against the defendant, making even innocuous actions seem suspicious. The evidence was all circumstantial. When the jaw of Mr. Borden's skull, waved around by the prosecution, fell open, like something out of a horror story, Jordan told a reporter friend from *The Sun*:

"The old man is trying to testify."

"What's he saying? What's he saying," asked the *Sun* reporter.

"He's saying that she's innocent," Jordan replied.

As the trial wound down, the fact of Borden's sex took center stage, both for the defense and prosecution. In the final days, crowds gathered on the verandas of surrounding houses, not wanting to miss the verdict. In closing arguments, a prosecuting attorney said, "A woman's cunning devised how to cover up that dress." In response, the defense concluded, "I ask you to consider this defendant as a woman, and to say to the Commonwealth, whom you represent, 'It is unjust to hold her a minute longer.'" The judge's jury instructions included the command, "you must consider the sex, size, and strength of the assailant." He emphasized the fact that even if Borden's testimony didn't explain what happened, no one else's did either: "The case is said to be mysterious; the defendant is not required to clear it up."

When the jury came in after deliberating less than two hours and declared Lizzie Borden "not guilty," Borden collapsed in her seat, almost insensible, her head against the rail in front of her. Amid the applause and cheering, a reporter for the *New Bedford Evening Journal* recalled that during the announcement of the verdict, Kate Swan McGuirk was sitting behind him. The reporters knew one another as editors of rival high school newspapers, and when he turned to marvel with McGuirk at the outcome, he found her overcome with joy, weeping.

Jordan, too, felt justice had been done. "Miss Borden's vindication was clear, complete, and absolute," she wrote in her report of the trial's final day.

But at least in her imagination, Jordan allowed for a different outcome. At the time of Borden's arrest, Jordan continued to venture into fiction. In her short story "Ruth Herrick's Assignment" a bold young reporter at the *New York Searchlight*, eager to prove herself with a scoop, is sent to get an exclusive interview with Helen Brandow, accused of poisoning her husband. Gossip declared Brandow—young, good-looking, and from a respected family—certain to be acquitted. But she refused to talk with the press. Ruth, though, impressed the warden with her credentials. He had read her articles and had seen the illustration of her face in the paper—and he let her in.

Ruth Herrick was struck, almost immediately (as was McGuirk) by the distorted media image of the person in front of her. Brandow wasn't beautiful. Had the male reporters even looked at her, or had they been describing a woman of their imagination? And she was composed to the point of coldness. The prisoner told the reporter she trusted her to represent her accurately—not overwrought and sobbing. Yet through their conversation, her composure began to crack.

Her marriage, Brandow said, had been miserable. Within a month of the ceremony, she realized her mistake: "He spent his time devising ways of persecuting and humiliating me, and his efforts were eminently successful." Her body was still marked by his beatings; she waited in her room at night in dread of his kicking at the door. When he attacked her mother, it was too much.

"That night I killed him," she told the astonished reporter.

Jordan ably described Ruth Herrick's quandary. The prisoner had handed her a scoop beyond her editor's fantasies: a confession. The article would earn her applause and admiration. On the other hand, if she kept quiet, the woman would probably go free. As Herrick debated, she heard her internal voice as one of a lawyer: "Something within the reporter asserted itself as counsel for her and spoke and would not down." Though she couldn't serve on a jury, Ruth had the opportunity to mete out justice.

"I am going to forget this interview," the reporter told the prisoner.

In doing so, she gestured at theories that wouldn't be named until a century later, like battered woman's syndrome and jury nullification. Ruth offered the woman a defense that the courtroom, as constructed at the time, wouldn't provide.

The 1894 story published in *Cosmopolitan* raised many eyebrows. The timing seemed suspicious. People imagined Jordan, one of the most high-profile correspondents to report the Borden trial, might have heard and suppressed a similar confession.

"So, Ruth Herrick, that's the kind of reporter you are, is it?" Jordan's managing editor wrote her.

Jordan insisted she thought of the story before she'd heard of Lizzie Borden, but her imagined interview has many similarities to McGuirk's real one. And later, when Borden resolutely stayed in Fall River, instead of moving to Europe as Jordan thought she might, spent time with theater people instead of dutiful churchgoers, and seemed to revel in her newfound wealth, even Jordan experienced a whisper of doubt. Why, when her sister began to lose her mind, did Borden hold her close at home, where she could keep an eye on her? Children began to chant:

> *Lizzie Borden took an ax*
> *Gave her mother forty whacks;*
> *And when she saw what she had done,*
> *She gave her father forty-one.*[*]

And people began to wonder whether the jury hadn't been swayed by their inability to conceive that a wealthy, white Christian woman could do such a thing. Had the men been blinded by their lack of imagination? Perhaps. But no one suggested they weren't fit to serve.

If Kate Swan McGuirk wrote more about the Borden trial for one of her many employers, there is no obvious record of it. She spent at least part of the blazing June of 1893 working on a piece about "Summer Homes of the Washington Cabinet." These straitlaced topics made it all the more surprising that three years after Borden's acquittal, she would be considered the most notorious stunt reporter of them all. And she would be egged on by assignments from Elizabeth Jordan—who

---

* It's interesting that those who watched the trial unfold, the whole jury, most newspapermen (at least the ones Elizabeth Jordan talked to), Jordan herself, and even the judge, with his sympathetic jury instructions, were convinced Lizzie was innocent. While, now—at least among those who write television and movie adaptations—the consensus is that she was guilty. Did the prosecution just do a spectacularly bad job? Are modern-day interpreters more willing to consider female rage and psychosis? Or were viewers at the time, crammed into that hot courtroom, feet away from Lizzie and the police and their ax collection, able to see something that we can't?

went to New York determined to avoid stunts—in Jordan's role as editor of the *World*'s Sunday magazine.

As the Borden jury sweated in Massachusetts in the summer of 1893, the World's Columbian Exposition opened seven miles south of Chicago. The vision of Frederick Law Olmsted and architect Daniel Burnham, the fair promoted the country's triumphs in the slightly more than one hundred years of its existence. Otherworldly white buildings in the Beaux Arts style lined the Court of Honor, borrowing Grecian grandeur with their columns and arches. The vast Palace of the Mechanic Arts housed towers of electric lights, and telephones, both local (for eavesdropping on the German Village in the Midway) and long distance (for listening to conversations in New York). The thirty-acre Manufactures and Liberal Arts building showcased Japanese vases, Swiss carvings, Italian glassware, as well as clocks, embroidery, and lacquer boxes from all over the world. Water features wound their way through the grounds, and one might see a gondola floating by, or stumble on a wigwam. States and countries all had space to display their food, clothing, crafts. Cultures smashed up against one another in a disorienting yet tantalizing way. Visitors marveled at belly dancers on the "Street in Cairo" exhibit, clutched each other's hands 250 feet above the ground on the first-ever Ferris wheel, sampled Cracker Jacks, and sipped a fizzy strawberry crush. Some days they picked their way through sticky mud; other days they luxuriated in the breeze off Lake Michigan. But they came. Over the course of its six-month run, 20 million visitors attended the fair, eight hundred of them journalists.

Eva McDonald Valesh, formerly "Eva Gay" and now a union activist, lectured on "Woman Wage Workers," representing Minnesota at the fair's women's congress. Kate Swan McGuirk had visited Chicago with a delegation of senators to report on fair preparations. Victoria Earle Matthews rode the elevated railway that looped through the grounds, past the Foreign Building and the Fisheries Building, recalling it as a "dream of beauty." Ida B. Wells organized and distributed a pamphlet, "The Reason Why the Colored American Is Not in the World's Columbian Exhibition," drawing attention to the country's brutal history regarding its Black citizens, and protesting their lack of representation at the fair.

But the glitter of prosperity, like the gilded statue of a woman, arms aloft, representing the Republic, was a facade. Just as the fair opened in May, the stock market took a sickening plunge. Spooked depositors took their money out of banks, which then failed: 642 by the end of the year. Unable to get credit, farmers couldn't transport grain and cotton to market. Textile mills stopped production. Iron and steel companies locked their doors. Railroads went under. Unemployment soared. The pain rippled throughout the country. Elizabeth Jordan's father, a real estate developer in Milwaukee, lost everything, leaving her parents financially dependent on their journalist daughter. She joined the ranks of reporters supporting family with their wages. Still, people flocked to the fair.

On October 24, in the exposition's last days, a sportswriter and stable owner stumbled into the Chicago Press Club and collapsed. A doctor found him unable to speak and paralyzed on one side. At the hospital, he recovered enough to say he was exhausted, having spent the past week walking the city, looking for his wife and his three-year-old son. They'd been visiting her mother in St. Louis and, on October 16 a letter arrived, saying they were on their way to Chicago and the fair. And then he heard nothing else. He tried to trace her route from the train station but couldn't find any clues.

His wife, Elizabeth A. Tompkins, was a writer, too, specializing in knowledgeable stories about horse racing. The job had taken her to London not long before. She'd just written a glowing report about the Saratoga track, the lush lawns, the bright shirts, the holiday atmosphere. And yes, they'd fought about whether she should keep writing (her preference) or quit to take care of their son (his preference). But he was sure something had gone amiss. Like the actual cities of San Francisco and New York, Chicago's fairgrounds, dubbed the "White

City," tempted young women with promises of glamour and excitement. And sometimes they never came back, for reasons that could be quite sinister.

Or not. Her mother soon received a letter in St. Louis, saying it might be a long time before Tompkins got in touch again, but "no news is good news." Once again, the expected story—a girl lured to ruin by bright city lights—was perhaps not the real one.

In New York that winter, during a period of bitter cold, the impact of the financial panic on the poor was exacerbated by a moral crusade. In early December, police pounded on brothel doors in New York's Tenderloin and told the women living there they had one day to get out. Rev. Charles Parkhurst had been preaching against prostitution and condemning the police for turning a blind eye. Parkhurst and others from the Society for the Prevention of Crime had been visiting brothels that flourished through the city, taking notes, upping the pressure. Finally, the police conducted a raid.

Residents scrambled for trunks, stowing shawls and hairbrushes. They hired cabs to take dressing tables and sofas to storage. Then they set out to find somewhere to live, some lying to get access to "respectable" apartment buildings, others sleeping at the police station. Hard economic conditions became all the harder. The next day, the brothels were dark and empty.

And the temperature was dropping. A bitter wind raced between buildings, and New Yorkers pulled out their heaviest coats. Ice crusted the Hudson. The parade of women out on the streets, some who hadn't found a place to stay even days later, seemed a sign of viciousness rather than virtue. In a front-page cartoon in the *Evening World*, reformers and police battled each other while, overlooked, a woman lay collapsed in the snow. The caption read, "The Usual Result."

The police, Parkhurst concluded, staged the raid in this dramatic way to make him look bad, to cast blame on him for homelessness. He invited women to his house, printing his address in the paper, where he would try to find them shelter—provided, of course, they would swear to reform and "lead respectable lives." They started to show up, more than fifty a day.

Bly, back at the *World* after her attempts at fiction foundered, interviewed Parkhurst a week after the brothel closures, commenting on his youthful looks, the "merry twinkle" in his eyes. But over the course of five hours, she grilled him. Wouldn't campaigning against high prices and tainted food be a better way to help the poor? she asked. And "don't you think that if ministers were to learn a little more about life and take broader views of subjects that they would be more fitted to be preachers and leaders of congregations?" And the question that always consumed her: "Is not one of the great difficulties with the reformation of these women their lack of ability to work?" And then she signed off with a gracious nod to his perseverance.

ACROSS THE ATLANTIC

If acting the part of spy or detective in this way is considered by anybody as a dishonorable feature of journalism, the attention of such a person is directed to the fact that Charles Dickens, in order to obtain the material for "Nicholas Nickleby" assumed a character not his own, in order that he might better investigate the miserable Yorkshire schools.

—*Reading Times*, February 27, 1889

After several years writing for papers in the Midwest and the South, and a brief stint as personal secretary to the US envoy for Peru, Elizabeth Banks tried her luck in London. In England, she settled in to become the writer she imagined, following the lead of her personal heroine, Aurora Leigh, the title character of the Elizabeth Barrett Browning poem she had read obsessively during solitary days on her uncle's Wisconsin farm. If not a poet, like Aurora Leigh, Banks aimed least to be a real journalist. She didn't want to be tied to the women's page as she had been in the United States. She felt strongly, though, that she didn't want to be a do-gooder either, like many of the writers who claimed to improve society with their work. Any orthodoxy made her wince, and it was a pose that seemed like a luxury. As soon as Banks felt the embrace of an expectation of what she should write or why, she wriggled to escape.

Along with her typewriter, Banks brought a big, black poodle named Judge across the ocean. Though Banks's writing hailed the many gallant men she encountered through her reporting, from the coworkers who brought her offerings of candy and pencils to the artist who sketched a picture to accompany her story and offered it to her for free, no one compared to Judge. In childhood, reading Sunday newspaper stories, she fantasized about being "surrounded with dozens of lovers, any of whom would cut his head off at my command," but it was Judge who rescued her "from getting too lonely and thinking too much about myself."* The poodle wore a colorful scarf around his neck and could fetch newspapers by title. In a photo of the two of them, the dog perches by her side, face right next to Elizabeth's. What stands out is Banks's expression—there's heat behind it as she stares off the lower edge of the portrait, as if she's just heard a loud noise but doesn't want to show surprise. The poodle is relaxed, panting, seemingly happy, long ears covered with silky black curls.

In addition to pet and machine, she brought the lenses she'd used on American society, focused on the workings of class. One day, after she'd been in London a few months, Banks was mulling the fact that many girls she met in the city ground their lives away sewing for long hours and low pay, subsisting on boiled rice or crackers. Their situation brought to mind the hypnotic rhythm of "The Song of the Shirt" written by English poet Thomas Hood in 1843.

> Stitch! stitch! stitch!
> In poverty, hunger, and dirt,
> And still with a voice of dolorous pitch
> She sang the "Song of the Shirt."

The poem charted the life of a factory worker, wearing out her indoor days, like worn-out linen, while free-flying swallows with sun on their backs mocked her with the spring.

Pitying their discomfort, Banks wondered why the women didn't

---

* In one of Banks's many obfuscations, she presents herself as living alone (and as being sometimes lonely), but may have been staying at least part of the time with her sister.

become servants. Maids and cooks were in high demand; they earned better pay than factory employees and had room and board provided. Traditionally, in many working-class families, daughters would go into "service" for a few years between young adulthood and marriage. The arrangement provided money for their relatives and taught them wifely skills. But when Banks suggested this to one seamstress, she was met with indignation. Young women in England as well as the United States were warming to an expanded sense of possibility.

"I wear caps and aprons, those badges of slavery! No, thank you. I prefer to keep my liberty and be independent," the seamstress informed her.

Of course, the issue of what one might be willing to do to make a living may have been on Banks's mind. Before long, she had spent most of her moving-to-Europe money. In 1892, when she just arrived, she'd earned early fame as "the American Girl in London," after Rudyard Kipling wrote an article in the *London Times* critiquing Americans, and she'd replied in the same paper with a spirited defense of her country. He had interpreted all of America by his encounter with New England, she wrote in a piece subtitled "An American Girl's Reply to Rudyard Kipling." He should consider occupants of Illinois, Minnesota, and Montana as well as people from different classes: "in the city whistles are blowing for 6 o'clock, and employer and [employee], counting room clerk and day laborer, the woman journalist and the typewriter girl are hurrying home from their hard but well-paid work. And these, all these, are the Americans." The Kipling retort brought notoriety but not more assignments. In 1893, when that same seamstress told her she earned only one and sixpence a day, Banks felt a throb of pity but was brought short by the thought that she herself was not currently earning that much.

Perhaps remembering Eva McDonald's series for the *Globe* when they'd worked there together, with its descriptions of society women coddling their pugs, Banks put an unconventional ad in the Situations Wanted section of the paper, one that sounded more like the opening of a novel than a request for employment:

Elizabeth Banks

"As Housemaid, Parlourmaid, or House-Parlourmaid.—A refined and educated young woman, obliged to earn her living, and unable to find other employment, wants situation
as above. Expects only such treatment as is given to servants. Will wear caps and aprons, but would not wish to
share bed with another. Thoroughly reliable and competent.
References; town or country. Wages, f14."

But here the layers of Banks's disguise grew particularly thick.
While the premise of the articles was to chide English girls for an
obsession with class that kept them near starving for the sake of their
"independence," Banks elided her own background boiling potatoes
and feeding chickens early mornings on her uncle and aunt's Wisconsin farm, ironing and washing dishes to pay her way through college.

"For myself, I knew little or nothing about housework," she airily
declared. The one time she tried to sweep, it blistered her hands. Her
attempts to scrub a floor made up a long, comic scene of incompetence.

Her inability to darn socks would reveal her disguise, she feared.* (This is one of the few places her exploits are met with incredulity. Does "there actually breathe a woman in whom the domestic instinct is so dead as this?" wondered a newspaper columnist.) In an article where she pretended to employers to be of a lower class than she was, she simultaneously pretended to her readers to be of a higher class than her background indicated. Admitting domestic skills would be somehow shameful. But that didn't keep her from peppering her pieces with household hints: using a whisk broom on the corners, dunking dishes in hot water to better rinse them, installing a dumb waiter to keep maids from running up multiple flights of stairs.

Confessing her age would be similarly damaging. At some point she shaved five years off, claiming to be born in 1870 rather than 1865, making the "American Girl" twenty-three in London rather than pushing thirty.†

Readers talked over her articles but weren't always sure what to make of them. First, Banks seemed sympathetic to servants who worked for demanding employers; then she defended employers taken advantage of by duplicitous maids. Undercover work was traditionally linked to reform efforts. Reporters often justified their deceptions by highlighting resulting improvements: Nellie Bly mentioned that her Blackwell's Island piece prompted additional asylum funding; Winifred Black stressed the changes in hospital policy. But what reforms did Banks want?

In the hubbub after the servant series, another woman writer pulled her aside at a social gathering:

---

* This overwhelming concern with establishing class (even in Banks, who purported to critique it) brings to mind the poet Elizabeth Bishop's 1960 letter to Robert Lowell, commenting on female writers who obsessively reference their status: "They have to make quite sure that the reader is not going to mis-place them socially, first—and that nervousness interferes constantly with what they think they'd like to say."

† Lying about one's age was as common as adopting a pseudonym for stunt reporters. Men did it, too. The chapter about Charles Chapin's time at the *Chicago Times* in his autobiography is called "A City Editor at Twenty-Five." He was twenty-nine.

"Now, tell me exactly, what was your aim and object—your serious one, I mean,—in going out to service and writing about it? It is a question we are all asking."

"I did it for 'copy,'" Banks said, "to earn my living, you know. I knew it was a subject that would interest everybody."

In the face of the writer's surprise, Banks continued: "I'm not a hypocrite and won't pose as a reformer. I did it to earn my living; but, of course, if my published experience helps others to earn theirs, I shall be very glad. I have done my best with this series and have been absolutely honest and impartial. I have taken no sides. I have simply told the truth."

As much as she tried to distance herself from that Wisconsin farm girl, a certain practicality was the soil in which she was rooted. When the other writer, dismayed, said she'd had never written anything without the goal of helping someone, Banks dug in: "Perhaps you have an income aside from your writing, which I have not."

Her response spread, and afterward, she found herself alienated from the circle of philanthropic female journalists. (Of course, needing the money is another kind of justification, for stunts, for writing at all, perhaps more acceptable than "I craved exciting and meaningful work.")

Banks continued her campaign against self-congratulation. The English prided themselves on valuing breeding and nobility, as opposed to those cash-obsessed Americans who just bought whatever they needed—class, society, status. This seemed a lofty, inflated claim, ripe for puncturing. Banks wrote a new ad:

"A Young American Lady of means wishes to meet with a Chaperon of Highest Social Position, who will introduce her into the Best English Society. Liberal terms."

And then, taking care to bait the hook with a particularly juicy worm, she directed letters to be addressed to "Heiress."

Responses flooded in with offers of marriage and presentation at court, letting Banks conclude, "After all my investigations, my faith in the purchasing power of the 'Almighty Dollar' still remains unshaken."

After that, she hinted to editors that she might want to write more traditional stories. But, in the newspapers' view, her breakthrough was the introduction of American stunt reporting to London, though she was very much working in the path of W. T. Stead (of "Maiden Tribute of Modern Babylon" fame), who became a mentor and friend. She was an American girl, and American girls went undercover. Assignments to sell flowers, or sweep the streets, or pick strawberries piled up.

Before long, she was back to placing newspaper ads:

"A YOUNG WOMAN wants a situation in a large first-class Laundry, where she can learn the business. No wages."

But the laundry market was, apparently, more competitive, though she offered to work for free. She only got one reply, but that was enough.

In the one large room of Y_____ and Z_____ Sanitary Laundry, shirts boiled in vats, and about thirty women ironed, starched, and folded clothes for hundreds of clients. Backs were stooped from long hours and repetitive tasks. Surveying the scene, Banks felt she needed some boatman to ferry her across the water sloshing in a river over the floor. If so, Janie, a seventeen-year-old with a dreamy expression and hair half braided and half loose, lame from a childhood accident, was her Charon, easing her way into the damp Underworld.

"I'll help you, Miss Barnes,"* she said when Banks (who applied under the name "Lizzie Barnes") faced any of the many bewildering tasks. Janie set up an ironing board for a table and shared her bitter tea with her sister and Banks, patiently waiting for one of the two cups to be free before she drank her own. She also, perhaps with a

---

* Banks often wrote her characters' speech in Cockney dialect, but I've rendered it into standard English.

bit of glee, scared the newcomer with stories of exploding boilers and fingers crushed in the wringer. One recent case required amputation, she confided as they sewed red numbers on each garment so it could be tracked back to its owner.

It was a classic laundry stunt. Eva McDonald had done it, and then Nell Nelson. But Banks had a different take. Rather than charting the experience of the laundry girl, she positioned herself as an employer, sending out her own laundry to be cleaned at the same place she was working, cringing as the red numbers were coarsely stitched into her fine handkerchief. She had wondered about the condition of laundries where she shipped her clothes to be washed, Banks wrote. What if they were suffused with disease? (Meanwhile, her autobiography revealed that while in London she illegally did her washing in a hotel bathtub and almost got evicted for cooking in her room when the smell of her onions wafted down the hall.)

But this time she had another purpose, too. England had just passed a series of Factory Acts, covering at what age children could be employed, mandating a clean and ventilated workplace, and limiting the number of hours per week. But the acts didn't cover laundries. And some thought they shouldn't. They reasoned that since the acts applied only to women and children, under the logic that they needed special protection, laundry jobs would go to men. So part of Banks's mission was to see how the women felt about Factory Act protections, and whether they wanted them applied to their industry.

So here she was at the laundry, with wet boots and a hacking cough, taking it all down.

Though Banks's refusal to link her work to a noble cause made her unpopular at parties, it paid off on the page. Another writer might have painted poor lame Janie as a pathetic victim with the scar on her forehead from falling into a fireplace and a finger mashed by chopping wood, a tool to a reform end, but Banks let her be complicated.

Highly competent, Janie kept the laundry running, staying late, solving problems, and facing irate clients to explain mistakes. Banks found the laundry miserable, but Janie appeared to like it. Sundays are boring, Janie said. She'd rather work.

Janie is a fully fleshed-out nonfiction character, like Tillie Mayard, the sick woman Bly met at the asylum. They are nuanced, well drawn, giving their stories lasting power in a way that transcends a more straightforward news article about debates over the Factory Act or asylum funding. "I was beginning to get intensely interested in this strange species of laundry-girl," Banks told her readers. And her interest was contagious.

When Banks wanted to learn something besides stitching numerals into shirts, Janie convinced the boss to let Banks try ironing. In an effort to be chatty with the chief ironer, Mrs. Bruckerstone, known to be a prodigious gossip, Banks found herself embroidering the tapestry of her fictional life, adding in a soldier boyfriend named James, who was, alas, in Australia, her home country.

At the end of three hours of ironing, Banks's skin smarted with burns and she'd pressed only thirty-four handkerchiefs, which, at "a penny a dozen" would have earned her less than a cent an hour. She tried her hand at pinafores where she was competent but slow. One took two hours with frequent breaks.

For her part, Janie was starting to wonder what was to be done with this delicate, well-spoken, yet dismayingly uneducated (by her own account) woman who seemed so very bad at laundry work. Her incompetence worried the other women, too. If she failed at laundering, what would she do? They set to finding her a job. An accountant? A server in a coffeehouse? A barmaid? A nurse?

"Hospital patients are too cross and fidgety. I wouldn't like to be a nurse," Banks declared.

Mrs. Bruckerstone lost her temper at this, insisting that if she was too weak for the laundry and too bad at math for accounting, nursing was the only option.

Finally, Janie announced she had the perfect position for this odd, weak Australian who'd washed up on the shores of the laundry: a clerk at a candy store, pushing peppermint sticks and caramels.

After a few more days, Banks quit before she was fired, telling the owner, "I'm afraid I'm not strong enough for this sort of thing, Mrs. Morris."

"Miss Barnes is going to a confectioner's," Janie added, in an effort to make everyone feel better.

But Banks didn't bury herself in chocolate creams. She dug in and pursued all angles. To flesh out first-person experience, she dressed as a journalist again and visited Acton, nicknamed "Soap Suds Island" because it had so many laundries, and interviewed female workers about Factory Act amendments. She visited smaller establishments in the East End, where Banks found that the laundrywomen married young to keep from being old maids, but then continued working. Like Janie, they liked it, though they were eager to hear about changes that might better their situation. (Their mothers, on the other hand, often approved of long work hours as a way to keep their daughters out of trouble.)

After a meeting of the Working Girls Club, a gaggle of young women walked Banks to the train station. The lively pack offered safety in numbers that the few women in any given newspaper office weren't able to provide, along with a constant stream of conversation. When boys outside a bar threw pebbles at them, they yelled and hurled one back. It might not have been ladylike, but it was effective, and Banks admired their nerve.

As the train pulled away, one hollered after her, "Say, miss, don't forget to make them give us that Act you told us about."

There was plenty of room for improvement, Banks reflected. Water could be drained from the floor, fans could provide circulation, machinery could be fenced so it wouldn't catch skirts. Working six a.m. to nine p.m., as some did, made for a long, wearying day, even for those heartier than Banks claimed to be. She mused: "If the hours of the young girls, at least, could be reduced so that their day would commence at eight and end at six, then night-schools might be established in the neighbourhoods of the large laundries, and from eight until ten the girls could be instructed and amused."

One might have thought she was trying to do some good.

GIRL NO MORE

"She pulled out a small notebook and with a dainty pencil put down the memorandum in a rather shy way as I thought. But that is what I liked about her—nothing mannish, not the least. Though it's deuced rare among girl reporters."

"Why don't you say women reporters?" put in Bunzie, on whose fine ear "girl" grated.

"Because this one was nothing but a girl, and a slip of a girl at that. And then you never heard of a woman reporter did you?

They're all girls."

—Frank Bailey Millard, "The 'Shield's' Girl Reporter," 1892

The panic of 1893 bled into 1894, increasing unemployment, depressing wages. Back in Chicago, those who had hired on at the Columbian Exposition now paced the sidewalks looking for work or, homeless, took refuge in remnants of the glorious White City. Those who worked for the Pullman Company in Illinois—which made luxurious sleeping cars—saw their paychecks drop by as much as 35 percent, but the rent in their Pullman-owned factory town remained the same. In early May, a committee of laborers went to ask company owner George Pullman for higher pay or housing relief. When they were turned away and then fired, workers voted to strike. They were soon supported by the huge American Railway Union, headed by Eugene Debs. The ARU ultimately refused to handle any trains with

Pullman cars. This decision swept 250,000 workers into a boycott and confounded railways throughout the West. Passenger trains were stranded in the mountains. Produce rotted in freight cars left sitting on the tracks.

At the urging of the railroad companies, President Cleveland sent troops to Illinois and issued an injunction against the boycott, the first federal involvement in labor issues on this scale. Soon two thousand armed men entered Chicago with the goal of ending the strike. In response, crowds overturned trains and set them on fire; troops shot indiscriminately, killing protesters and bystanders.

Nellie Bly went to Chicago, arriving amid newspaper reports of mobs, destruction, and rioting. Labor's reputation for violence had only grown with bloody altercations at recent strikes in Homestead, Pennsylvania, and Coeur d'Alene, Idaho. But when she visited the Pullman town, she found a distinct lack of murderousness. Instead, there was mainly sadness and frustration, and a funeral was underway for a striker shot in the head by a deputy. She approached a man sitting on a porch, told him she was from New York, asked in her faux naive way when the rioting would begin.

"Do you think we're as bad as that?" he asked.

"Oh yes," she answered. "We are all frightened to death. We think you are all bent on burning down, blowing up and assassinating." Invited into the house, she talked with the man and his friend, drawing out the problems with the company town. One of the main sticking points was the lack of freedom that came from living in a place where your employer dictated every rule. A man from Rosedale, a town next to Pullman but not factory-owned, laid out the comparison:

"I have a lot of 90 feet front by 124 feet deep. I have a house of eight rooms. I have a garden, where I raise all my vegetables and I have my own chickens and eggs and I only pay $12 per month rent and $3 a year water tax. Compare that with this five-roomed house with no garden for $17 a month and 71 cents a month for water."

When Bly asked the Pullman man why he didn't move to Rosedale, he said job priority went to those in Pullman properties. If he moved, he would have been unemployed. She talked with women and children in Pullman, bringing to life complicated family dynamics, humanizing the strikers. Readers encountered the German immigrant, consumed by her rage, who declared "Curse America"; a wife who hated the union her husband needed to join; and those stretching food and keeping tiny spaces tidy, doing their best in a bad situation.

Taking another tack, Bly went to Springfield to interview the beleaguered Illinois governor. After asking him whether he was an anarchist (no) and believed in women's suffrage (dodged), to warm him up, she pressed him on the strike. Federal troops had made things worse, he said, and Pullman workers were too much at the company's mercy. "Their only hope is to stand together, but at the same time keep within the law," he told Bly.

By early August, it was clear the strike had failed. The Pullman Company reopened, only rehiring those who swore never to join a union. It was another high-profile labor defeat, an intimidating display of corporate muscle, and a cause of popular disillusionment with Grover Cleveland's Democratic Party.

For Bly, it was an eye-opening summer, leading into a fall and winter of good, intense reporting. A St. Paul newspaper editor noted, after watching her cover a northern Minnesota fire that killed more than four hundred people, her single-minded focus on journalism: "While it occupies her she hasn't room for anything else, not even a dinner." She traveled through Nebraska and South Dakota, visiting homesteaders freezing and starving in sod houses during a blizzard that followed a crop-killing summer drought. Increasingly sympathetic to the labor cause, she interviewed American Railway Union president Eugene Debs, jailed in Illinois for violating a court injunction against the Pullman strike, and defended striking streetcar operators in Brooklyn, documenting their bandages from ill treatment by police. Socialists began sending her letters, hoping to recruit her.

The start of 1895, though, found Bly in an increasingly bleak frame of mind. Sidewalks filled with trash caught her eye, as did the slush that soaked women's skirts as they climbed the stairs to the elevated railway. Her dog—a favorite—had recently died. Liars and frauds seemed to dominate society. Even organizations bent on doing good just seemed to talk and talk, never getting anything done. These thoughts unspooled in her *Evening World* column, "Nellie Bly Says," offering a glimpse behind the chipper facade of most of her first-person reporting. One essay began simply: "Life is growing worse every day."

S till, Nellie Bly continued to inspire. A racehorse, a steamer, and a gold mine had all been named after her. Young women continued to show up to newspaper offices, make their pitch to editors, and use stunt reporting for their own ends.

The magazine publisher Mrs. Frank Leslie-Wilde sometimes received a dozen letters a day from aspiring journalists, queries she tried to answer, offering help and encouragement. So when a young woman calling herself Mary Martin asked to tour her home for a piece about houses of the wealthy, Leslie-Wilde agreed. It was only when she found two checks missing, along with a $500 crescent-shaped jewel-crusted pin, that she became suspicious. Martin was arrested in Brooklyn. She may have been the "Ethel Townsend" who had been passing bad checks and posing as a reporter two years before in the Midwest, or she may have been someone else who settled on the same scheme. Sometimes being a reporter was the disguise.

Other recruits were more legitimate. Bly's career also caught the attention of Caroline Lockhart, a woman in her early twenties, raised in Kansas and sent to boarding school in Boston because she didn't get along with her stepmother. She was soon mired in trouble for getting drunk at her uncle's hotel. At first Lockhart thought becoming the next Sarah Bernhardt would offer a life of excitement, free from pieties she found oppressive. Bernhardt, the renowned French dramatic actress, traveled the world, hunted crocodiles, and stormed across the stage as Joan of Arc and Cleopatra. But when Lockhart found her bit parts unsatisfying, she cast about for other ideas. "Why couldn't I write for a newspaper," she thought to herself. "Nellie Bly was making history at the time so why couldn't I?" She joined the *Boston Post*.

The *Boston Post* was experimenting with journalism in the Pulitzer mold. The owner, Edwin Grozier, had worked as an editor at the *World* when Bly went into the asylum, before buying the *Post* in 1891. One of the lessons he learned from his time there was the benefit of appealing to women.

In February 1894, the *Post* produced an issue written and edited entirely by women, a stunt of newspaper production. Much of the space was taken up with articles about female preachers, surgeons, jail wardens, lawyers, sea captains, all kinds of people the regular paper didn't have time for. But for the men's page, a mirror image of the typical women's page, editors sharpened their pencils to a particularly fine point. The top left corner displayed an illustration of a man, tipped back in his chair, feet up on the table, reading the *Sunday Post*, under the caption "This Page for the Lords of Creation." Articles written in the cheery, infantilizing tone of those aimed at female readers offered advice on "Ambrosial Locks" (Young men take note: long hair in the style of Beethoven, Sampson, and Byron is all the rage); "Pointed Shoes for Men" (These are painful but those men, what they won't sacrifice for vanity); "Bachelors' Buttons" (Studies show men are shrinking. This is clearly something they should be concerned about, rather than fretting over their "rights").

Nell Nelson contributed a lengthy piece on the premise that behind every great woman is a helpful man. Her article "Useful Husbands" had the wry subhead, "Nell Nelson's Opinions of the Convenience of Having a Masculine Attachment to a Clever Woman's Career." Actresses, authors, doctors, teachers, all benefit from a supportive man in the background, she wrote. The tone was mocking, but took a serious turn as she mentioned that a woman, no matter how financially sound, could rarely rent property in her own name. Nelson offered an example of a novelist who wrote constantly, compromising her health, but never got ahead until she married, and her husband took over the marketing.

In other efforts to engage female readers, the *Boston Post* developed
a character just for stunts, punningly named the "Post Woman," and
Lockhart took up the part. And that is how she found herself on a
boat in Boston Harbor, stepping into a rubber suit, pulling a heavy
metal breastplate and collar over her head. A man tightened the bolts
with a wrench, securing the collar to the rubber. A handkerchief tied
over her head kept her hair out of the way. Diving shoes encased her
feet, then weighted overshoes, so she could barely lift her own legs.
While she leaned over the rail, sailors buckled her into a diving belt,
adding even more pounds. Attempts to scare her hadn't worked—all
the talk about the sound of a roar like cannon and the sensation of
knitting needles through the brain. She had confidence in her grit.
She hadn't fainted when the doctor set her arm after she'd tried to

THE POST WOMAN HAS A CONFIDENTIAL LITTLE CHAT WITH MR.
M'GINTY.

**Caroline Lockhart in a diving suit for
the *Boston Post*, June 2, 1895**

break a mustang, and stunt reporting for the past six months already tested her nerve. "Have I not been drinking moxie all this spring?" She asked herself. But when the helmet descended, cutting off what felt like all but a few gasps of air, despite the hissing of the oxygen, a shiver did course through her. Then she plunged over the side into the blue-black water.

Nudging stunt reporting into new territory, Lockhart's exploits were often outdoor adventures instead of undercover exposés. Rather than stressing her fear, she dwelt on the pleasure of walking on seaweed, almost weightless, thirty feet underwater. She would later write a vivid story about getting lost in the fog off the Maine coast in a rowboat, spotting whales, landing on a strange island and gathering wood for a signal fire, a bit chilled, a bit exuberant. These escapades, sometimes written as the "Post Woman," sometimes under her own name, embraced stunt reporting's new direction. Where could a woman's body go—up in the air, underwater, across the ocean?

But at the same time as Lockhart explored this physical freedom, more established reporters were beginning to discover the limitations of their situation. By March 1895, Bly had abandoned New York for Chicago, taking a job with the newly formed *Chicago Times-Herald* and staying at the lavish Auditorium Hotel, a few steps away from the wind and beauty of Lake Michigan. The exterior with its massive, gray stones had an almost prehistoric feel, belying the sleek modern interior, brilliant with electric lights, housing a theater for the Chicago Symphony along with rooms for posh guests. One of the hotel clerks noticed that the famous reporter spent almost every day for two weeks in the company of another New York guest—Robert Seaman. Seaman, though in his early seventies with thin white hair, was a natty dresser with good posture, a confirmed bachelor with a reputation as a man about town. And as president of the Ironclad Manufacturing Company, he was reputed to be worth millions. Finally, on April 6, after reporters interviewed the clerk and unearthed a license made out to Robert Seaman and Elizabeth Cochran, headlines asked, incredulous, "Is 'Nellie Bly' Married?"

Perhaps it was another stunt, maybe a piece on the nature of honeymoons, or an exposé of May–December marriages to be followed by a first-person account the following Sunday of divorce? But none was forthcoming. For once, Bly seemed in dead earnest. On April 5, at the rectory of the Church of the Epiphany, a small structure of ruddy stones and heavy arches to the west of the city, with a lawyer as a witness, she married Seaman who, apparently, she had met several weeks before at a hotel dinner. In an interview, Bly said they'd kept it quiet because of their business affairs and illness in her family. And then she headed back to Manhattan, this time to her new husband's fancy Midtown Manhattan mansion, a long way from her old cramped rooms in Harlem.

Some papers tried to frame it as a kind of fairy tale, but most were deeply cynical. Hearst's *San Francisco Examiner* commented: "The marriage of Nellie Bly doubtless resulted from love at first sight of the groom's bank account." The *Weekly Pioneer Times* of Deadwood, South Dakota, suggested a moral: "And thus is refuted the theory that if girls were educated to support themselves they would not marry for money, for position, for a home, anything but love." Of Mr. Seaman, the *Buffalo Morning Express*, said, "He is very old and a millionaire. What better luck could befall a young woman of Nellie's cast of mind?"

Bly's younger self would have been cynical, too, the one who counseled in her second-ever published article, "Mad Marriages," that couples should enter into marriage slowly, deliberatively, with consultation from friends and investigation into their prospective spouse's personal history. Urging lovers to be upfront about their faults, the twenty-year old had written solemnly that lying about one's past should be a crime. Maybe she forgot those concerns; maybe other concerns overrode them. There was no time for the leisurely confessions the young Nellie demanded.

Just a few months before her wedding, she'd been riding in a decorated coach in a seaside parade with editor James Stetson Metcalfe. Their names had been linked for years. He'd taken the train to Philadelphia to travel at her side for the final miles of her round-the-globe trip. But that December, as reflected in her column for the *Evening World*, loneliness was on her mind. A friend, Walt McDougall, a cartoonist at the *World* who'd drawn her liberation from the asylum and spent long nights with her in haunted houses, recalled that, despite Bly's fame, she was intensely private: "Everybody knew her but she had very few familiars."

Here was just another mystery, though McDougall offered a clue to her Chicago move and to her marital leap: "Nellie was deeply attached to a friend of mine, and when he suddenly married another she abandoned New York. I never knew, nor does anybody, I suspect, what her intentions were."

Maybe something was in the air. Two months later, in June 1895, Nell Nelson returned from Europe on the steamship *Brittanic* from Liverpool. She'd been traveling with her ailing mother, sending dispatches from Paris and contributing a chapter to a serialized "composite novel." The next day, barely having had time to unpack, she ducked into the modest Church of the Transfiguration, a bright spot in the Manhattan landscape with its redbrick tower, golden wood doors, lush green garden. And there, under a fanciful ceiling painted with stylized clover and morning glory, with only a few friends to witness—she married S. S. Carvalho, the publisher of the *World*.

At this point, Carvalho was deeply involved in the day-to-day operation of the paper, with Pulitzer leaning on him increasingly heavily. He'd apparently been scheduled to come to Europe to meet her but hadn't made it, possibly because of yet another upheaval in the *World*'s staff. The wedding caught many off guard: "It is a genuine surprise to all his friends, and they are legion," wrote a *Boston Post* columnist about Carvalho. But the writer declared himself "delighted." Carvalho was known to be serious-minded, well paid, vigorous despite a limp, and dogged in pursuit of the paper's interests. A *World* staffer described him as "a small man with muscles of iron gained by driving a fast horse every evening" and "the most energetic, resource-ful and original of all of J.P.'s finds." Many who knew Nelson also commented on her work ethic, the way she'd taken care of her invalid mother, looked after two sisters, and written article after article. Eliz-abeth Jordan, who'd been awed by Nelson as she paced through the *World*'s offices, wrote, of all the hard labor that culminated in this marriage: "Her reward was great." Nelson never wrote again.*

The same day as Nelson's nuptials, Ida B. Wells lectured at St. John's Church in Kansas, describing for her audience, in detail, the violence of lynching, explaining the cruel economic calculations be-hind it, then continuing to press her message over punch at the re-ception after. With the publication of *Southern Horrors*, Wells had become an acknowledged leader of the anti-lynching movement. The revered Frederick Douglass contributed the introduction to the book, thanking her for writing it ("Brave woman!") and lauding her methods: "You have dealt with the facts with cool, painstaking fidelity and left those naked and uncontradicted facts to speak for themselves." The book launched her career as a public speaker and resulted in an invita-tion to take her message to England and Scotland.

Wells took two trips abroad, in the spring of 1893 and again in the spring 1894. In churches, drawing rooms, and YMCA halls, she urged listeners to start anti-lynching societies and shower the United States with moral condemnation. On her second visit, the *Chicago In-ter Ocean* printed her dispatches from abroad. In one, she marveled that even in Liverpool, which had been deeply invested in the Atlantic slave trade, citizens showed up to her lectures, in venues that held up to a thousand people. After giving up its dependence on slavery, the city had been able to prosper, she noted, and also commented that for a Black person raised in America, time spent in Liverpool was a revelation: "It is like being born into another world, to be welcomed among persons of the highest intellectual and social culture as if one were one of themselves." Her talks received positive English press in

---

*   Under this pseudonym. That we know of.

venues ranging from the *Birmingham Daily Post* to the *Ladies Pictorial*.

After returning from England, Wells had been traveling the United States, from Santa Cruz, California, to Rochester, New York, making similar speeches. She'd also published a second book—*A Red Record: Tabulated Statistics and Alleged Causes of Lynchings in the United States, 1892–1893–1894*. If possible, it was even more unblinking than *Southern Horrors*. One illustration showed a naked man hanged by a chain, well-dressed people clustered around him, pointing to the corpse. A photograph captured another crowd around another dead man, his clothes torn, body mutilated. Lists, all narrative stripped away, detailed people murdered by mobs each year under headings of their alleged crimes: "attempted robbery," "well poisoning," "asking white woman to marry him." These were followed by stories of particular cases, tortures detailed remorselessly, at length.

While many reporters of the age experimented with including their own subjective impressions, Wells underscored the subjectivity of institutions supposed to be most objective—police and the courts—and the savagery of those supposed to be most civilized—white men. She put side by side the killings of Black men accused of raping white women and the acquittals of white men accused of raping Black women. The book also took on the selective nature of the South's vaunted chivalry. The most chivalrous men seemed impervious to Black women and even to the white teachers who came from the North to educate the formerly enslaved: "The peculiar sensitiveness of the southern white men for women never shed its protecting influence about them." Wells critiqued, at length, Frances Willard, head of the Woman's Christian Temperance Union, who courted southern support for her causes by condemning the "great dark-faced mobs," writing sympathetically of the need to restrict voting by uneducated Black men.

Despite the importance of her advocacy and the fact that several southern states had passed anti-lynching laws as a result, Wells's campaign was taking a personal toll. It must have been emotionally draining and it depleted her financially. Her writing was too frank for some.

There was nothing nice or polite or exalting of womanhood about her prose, no rhetorical batting of an eye. *A Red Record* sold few copies. Others saw her eagerness to make her case abroad as a betrayal. A *New York Times* columnist complained that Wells, an "octaroon evangel," fired up the English, who already tended to be reform-minded and "meddlesome." And even those she thought she could count on for backing were wavering. In Europe, she struggled to get a statement of unequivocal support from Frederick Douglass and had to reuse his flattering introduction from *Southern Horrors* for *A Red Record*. She told the truth. And she paid for it.

And then, a few weeks after her talk at St. John's Church, on June 27, at the AME Bethel Church in Chicago, in front of almost a thousand people and wearing a dress trimmed with orange blossoms, Ida B. Wells married Ferdinand Barnett, a lawyer and founder of the *Chicago Conservator*, an African American newspaper. He was notable for his commitment to equality, not just for men of his own race but for everyone, writing against the Chinese Exclusion Act and in favor of women's suffrage. He had gone out of his way to help Wells as early as 1891, before they were romantically involved, when she instigated a lawsuit to protect her reputation. And still, Wells was torn about what marriage might mean for her writing and advocacy. People weren't shy about expressing their fears that the anti-lynching campaigns would suffer in her absence. She herself delayed the wedding a number of times, taking every lecture opportunity. With marriage, though, she declared herself "retired to what I thought was the privacy of a home." (Her retirement didn't last long. The Monday after the ceremony, she went to work as editor of the *Conservator*.)

This cluster of weddings in spring and summer 1895, as distinct as they were, demonstrates the power of demographics. Most of the women who burst into journalism in the late 1880s and early 1890s were born during or just after the Civil War.* This meant Bly, Nelson,

---

* And most were from the Midwest, where eastern notions of propriety didn't have as much weight. Back in 1887, when Nellie Bly interviewed New York newspaper

and Wells were in their early thirties. All had been writing for ten years and supporting family members with their wages. Maybe they weren't where they wanted to be professionally and financially. Journalism had let them travel only so far. The economy was still struggling to recover after the crash of 1893. Marriage might be a last bid for a more conventional kind of happiness. Nelson's comment in the previous year's all women's issue of the *Boston Post* echoed through those churches and chapels, in perhaps a less scornful tone than it seemed at the time: "Next to a great, big bank account the best thing a woman could have is the strong right arm of a good man."

In addition, Nelson and Bly, at least, were aging out of the "girl reporter" role they had helped create. What models were there for midlife career women except the spinsterism of reformers like Susan B. Anthony, a lifestyle that newspapers routinely mocked? A number of stunt reporters expressed ambiguity in print about the woman's suffrage cause, at the same time as their actions flaunted self-sufficiency. Stunt reporters were often young women, reacting to an older generation they found stuffy and unfashionable. By mid-1895, Anthony and Elizabeth Cady Stanton, high-profile movement representatives, were in their seventies. And the suffragists seemed to have little power: the movement suffered loss after loss at the state and the national levels. In 1894, a pro-suffrage petition with more than half a million signatures went nowhere in New York; shortly after, the New York State Association Opposed to Woman's Suffrage was launched. Stunt journalists tended to have less formal education and, as a result, be less erudite than writers like Anthony or Margaret Fuller, a journalist of an earlier generation. In the newspaper offices where they were trying to fit in, they were surrounded by the attitude that suffragists were to be made fun of, to be treated lightly. And their jobs depended on their spritely good nature, on being one of the boys.

---

editors about female journalists, many stressed that attitudes toward the role of women were more liberal in "the West." Wisconsin alone contributed Banks, Jordan, and Sweet, with Valesh coming from nearby Minnesota.

Beatrice Webb, an English social reformer who went undercover in 1888 sewing trousers and wrote about it for *Nineteenth Century*, tried to articulate this internal conflict as she reflected (embarrassed) on her attitudes toward suffrage when she was young. The suffragists were off-putting with their repeated demands and grievances, she remembered feeling. Webb was thriving personally, so it was hard to see the larger argument for systemic change: "In the craft I had chosen, a woman was privileged. As an investigator she aroused less suspicion than a man, and, through making the proceedings more agreeable to the persons concerned, she gained better information. Further, in those days, a competent female writer on economic questions had, to an enterprising editor, actually a scarcity value. Thus she secured immediate publication and, to judge from my own experience, was paid a higher rate than male competitors of equal standing."

Another one who felt this ambiguity about the source of a woman's power was Winifred Black. Still a *San Francisco Examiner* star, though married and a mother, she had covered the Woman's Congress in the summer of 1895 and found the speakers distasteful. Their stridency and zealous focus on voting excluded things she felt were more important. Black hoped the "new woman" with her suffrage obsession was a passing phase: "She deals only with ballot boxes and conventions and grievances. She can't touch the real things of life, and we shall go on loving and suffering and being happy quite as if she didn't exist."

Though she expressed reservations about the suffragists' demands, Winifred Black did, however, take particular care to investigate lecturer Anna Shaw's claims that women owned nothing in a marriage—not their children, not money they'd earned, not their own bonnet. In fact, she went so far as to consult a lawyer, who assured her that under California law a woman had the right to all of these in case of a divorce.

A few months later, Black's musings on the subject of "the real things in life" would be put to the test. One sunny morning in fall 1895, as Black tended the roses, heliotrope, and calla lilies in her San Francisco garden and kept an eye on her three-year-old son, a messenger handed her a telegram. It was from Hearst, commanding her to come to New York right away. As she later commented in her memoir, "There are certain moments in life that stand out in your memory as if they had been etched upon your brain." The lanky, blue-uniformed boy showing up with this explosive note was one.

Despite her fond words about family, while she doted on her boy and relished quiet moments in front of a homey eucalyptus fire, when Winifred's career hauled her out of the blooming garden, she didn't hesitate. She packed her bags, hugged her son, and told him good-bye. At the docks, where limes from Mexico arrived, and cranberries, pomegranates, oranges passed through, though melons were almost gone, Winifred caught the ferry that would take her across the bay to the train that would send her hurtling three thousand miles toward Hearst's unknown whim. In the station and then on board, she met the *Examiner*'s star cartoonist and sportswriter. They were in Omaha before they learned that Hearst had bought the *New York Journal*, the eight-page, rather tame paper formerly owned by Albert Pulitzer, Joseph's brother.

Hearst had spent eight years as a publisher, honing his sense of the market and readers' tastes. Now he was returning to Newspaper Row, where he'd been so awed and inspired. He'd tried before, angling for the *New York Times*, the *Record*, and the *Herald*, but no sales had gone through. The *Journal* offices were located in the *Tribune* building, in the shadow of the *World*'s showy tower. But not for long. He was ready to challenge Pulitzer on his own turf. And he needed his prize woman reporter by his side.

FULL SPEED AHEAD

When [the *Examiner*'s] manager detailed women reporters to attend prize
fights, to explore the slums, to exploit the inner depravities of society,
and to interview convicts and thugs, we omitted comment on the subject,
leaving to the tongue of public opinion the administration of a merited
rebuke."

—*San Francisco Call*, December 12, 1896

Hearst entered New York in his usual style—like a runaway
freight train. And any obstacle in his way was dynamited with
cash. Flush with a portion of the $3 million* from his mother's sale of
her share of the Anaconda Mining Company, Hearst set out to build
the best paper he could, regardless of cost and at blistering speed.

Building on what had worked in San Francisco, he imported the
chaos of the *Examiner* to the *Journal*. One editor found himself final-
izing his contract to oversee the *Journal*'s editorial page on Saturday,
only to show up to work on Monday to an office where no one knew
who he was. His only contact was gone, and Hearst was out of town.
The man was at a loss, until he remembered the name of an acquaintance at the paper who led him to the compositing room and told him
to get to it. No one seemed to acknowledge or care he was there, but
he made up the pages and the paper came out. As he wrote a friend
back home, "I had secured very remunerative employment in a lunatic

---

* About $30 million today.

asylum." It was more than the organizational structure that gave him this impression. Though Hearst himself didn't drink, several of his best reporters drank heavily and occasionally disappeared, needing to be hauled back from Europe or South America to write their sparkling prose. Hearst, still in his early thirties, liked to get up late, go to the opera, then saunter into the newspaper offices well after midnight and change headlines and rewrite editorials.

And, as it had in San Francisco, his method worked. One of his editors commented, "It seemed to some of us who day after day inhaled the fumes of his burning money, that he was mad, but he was only, as a matter of fact, shrewd and daring." In the first weeks of 1896, he hired away almost the entire staff of the *Sunday World* at stupendous salaries. Pulitzer had done the exact same thing to his brother, Albert (to Albert's astonishment and pain), when he entered the New York newspaper market a little over a decade before, but the knowledge didn't ease the sting. Pulitzer and Carvalho schemed to lure the reporters and editors back, but the moment it seemed like they had, Hearst countered with even more money, and prevailed. Hearst's entry into the New York market ended up boosting salaries at all the newspapers. It was a good time to be in the business.

The *World* was left reeling, facing the loss of many of the creative minds that fueled a decade of journalistic invention and market dominance. In an attempt to rebuild his depleted staff, Pulitzer promoted Arthur Brisbane to editor of the *Sunday World*. As London correspondent for the *Sun*, Brisbane made his name with his coverage of Jack the Ripper—an in-depth investigation that included a memorable tour through the poverty of Whitechapel, interviews with doctors about the criminal mind, and visits to the morgue that resulted in detailed, stomach-turning descriptions of the dead. He had been working at the *World* for a number of years, but now was his chance to shine. The ever-competent Elizabeth Jordan stepped in as assistant editor.

She'd already been overseeing artists and writers and editing copy for the Sunday edition in an unofficial capacity, but the new title gave her the chance to shape the direction of the paper. And Jordan found that, for her, the real adventure was in the newsroom. Writers rushed in, scribbled sentences longhand or clattered them out on typewriters. Editors ripped out paragraphs and stitched together a narrative with a slashing blue pencil. Illustrators sketched tiger snarls, a fraught glance on the face of an interview subject, gears of a pioneering machine. Crumpled drafts littered the floor. Rooms smelled of sweat, tobacco, and ink.

As an editor, she was responsible for not just the content but the look of the pages. Before the *World* adopted linotype machines, Jordan spent hours in the composing room. Brisbane, though smart and energetic, didn't know much about typesetting, as quickly became apparent.

"Can I help you with the make-up, Mr. Brisbane," she recalled asking him when he took the job.

"Yes."

"How much?"

"All of it."

Alongside a hundred compositors, she set type into wooden frames by hand, working off dummy sheets that showed article placement, the dominant headline. Fingers moved as fast as they could, then swapped type out and started again when a reporter with new information plummeted in and the story evolved. Past midnight, exhaustion crept in. Metal plates were cast of each full page, curved to fit over printer rollers. Down in the *World*'s basement, the press gobbled paper and sped it through wheels with raised words on them. One plate rolled the news onto the front of the paper. Then the next stamped the news on the back. The machine cut the sheets and folded them. Stacks landed with a thump in front of newsboys, who spread the latest edition to all corners of the city.

The hypnotic rhythm of late nights; the job that changed from day to day with the news; language, whittled to its sharpest and most compact: she loved it. Jordan, warm and charismatic, made friends easily. The *World* was now large enough that she wasn't the only woman in the office, as might be the case at a smaller paper in a smaller city. An

1890s photo shows her at her desk, surrounded by female colleagues, one of whom cradles a kitten. One of her newspaper-room short stories showcased the bond of these women, making their own way. In "A Point of Ethics," female writers and editors relaxed at an apartment. One idly played the piano. Another stretched out on a rug in front of the fire. A third sprawled in an easy chair.

Jordan liked her male coworkers, too. Brisbane was a charmer with fine features and ruddy hair.

Arthur Brisbane

A noted ladies' man, he was rumored to have had an affair with Bly. (He denied it, saying their relationship was entirely professional, though he would prove to be a great friend when she needed it most.) And he did have a not particularly secret affair with Pulitzer's wife, Katherine. Brilliant and mercurial, enthusiastic then depressed, friendly then mean, he was described by Jordan as "by turns fire and ice." Jordan denied a crush—"I have sometimes wondered why I did not fall in love with him"*—though she gave him an entire chapter in her memoir and recalled fondly coming in each morning to find a blizzard of notes on scraps of envelopes and scratch paper, suggestions about reporting and editing that he'd pinned to the roll top of her desk. They were very good at their jobs.

Together, Brisbane and Jordan redesigned the Sunday paper, paying particular attention to the stand-alone *Sunday Magazine*. They added more pages, and then even more. The section was crafted explicitly for women, though not in the bonnet-and-frock way of the women's pages (which still existed at many papers). Instead, interviews featured suffragists and women in unconventional careers, like cowboys. A "bicycle department" covered races and new designs. Ample, sprawling illustrations often showed men with their shirts off, including a large feature on modern athletes mimicking Greek statues of wrestlers. The journalistic purpose was unclear, though it was a fine display of muscles.

This era is supposed to be the beginning of the end of Pulitzer's dream, as his paper was sucked into Hearst's vortex of disrepute. But at least to this reader, the *World* of 1896, full of sea snakes, and X-rays, and arctic voyages, is enchanting. The world, as reflected in the pages of the *World*, seems rich and exciting. It is also beautiful. Illustrations had evolved since the coarse sketches that accompanied Bly's asylum writing in 1887. In one article, wind pushes a hot-air balloon across the page. In another, a skyscraper stretches from top to bottom. Five baby lions, recently born at the zoo, huddle at the top of a third. Reproductions of sheet music and handwritten notes enliven the text. Other images bear the marks of the recent invention of the motion picture, with its rapid series of photos capturing second-by-second shifts in a hand or face. The narrow columns crammed with small type of less than a decade before were only a gray smear of memory.

As part of their efforts to build circulation in the face of the

---

* Jordan never married and lived with other women for most of her adult life.

Bold illustration in the *World*, February 16, 1896

Journal's competition, Brisbane and Jordan brought back Bly. Bly had become part of the paper's mythology of itself. The edition commemorating the *World*'s ten-year anniversary with Pulitzer at the helm included illustrations of Bly in the asylum, exposing Edward Phelps's corruption, going around the world—stories not just notable because of the subject matter but because they were written by Nellie Bly. They needed her, and she needed them.

Married life wasn't all she might have imagined. Late one night, in an unseasonably warm November marked by dense fogs, Bly sensed someone tracking her movements. She'd tried to lose the tail at the Imperial Hotel, to no avail. Riding in a hansom cab at Thirty-Fourth near Broadway, she leaped out, confronted a police officer, and pointed to a vehicle across the street. "Officer, there is a man in that cab who has been following my cab about all day. . . . I want you to arrest him." At the police station, the man, Henry Hanson, said he'd been hired by her husband.

"Oh, that is all I wanted to know," Bly said.

Her husband, Robert Seaman, bailed out the private detective, who had been the manager of his Catskills property.

In court the next day, Bly told the judge that men had been following her for weeks, even rattling the doorknob of her private chamber in her house. Her jealous husband didn't trust her. But since no one ever talked with her or touched her, the judge said there was nothing he could do. After court, in the lobby, Hanson approached Bly.

"If I have done anything wrong, I want to apologize. I did not try to break in your door and I never followed you before last night," he said.

"You have followed me before and you know it," Bly responded. "I see that I can get no redress from the court for this shameful piece of business, but I give you fair warning that it will not be tolerated by me any longer. If you continue in your despicable spying you will find that I will take the law into my own hands."

Over the next few days, Seaman claimed to reporters that Bly no longer dined at the house and that he had just wanted to see where she was eating. Bly, in turn, said he'd refused to honor the pre-marital pact where he agreed to support her mother and sister. (Since the early days of the break with her stepfather, Bly had looked after her mother. Letters between them showed a close, protective relationship, with Bly urging her mother to buy warm winter clothes and take care of her own needs before anyone else's: "Learn to think only of yourself. Selfishness is the only thing which gains in this world." She still signed with her childhood nickname, "Pink.") Both Bly and Seaman denied wanting a divorce, but things were not going well. Tensions weren't eased by the revelation printed in the papers two weeks later:

Seaman had paid a hefty settlement to a woman who claimed to be his common-law wife.

So, maybe to control her own finances, or maybe to splash something on the front page besides her marital troubles, Bly signed onto the *World* once again.

Her resulting coverage was all over the map, sometimes infused with the humor and spirit linked to the character of "Nellie Bly," sometimes hampered by blinkers of money and a new social status. In late January, Bly covered the National Woman Suffrage Association convention in Washington DC. After the high-profile defeat in New York, the suffrage movement was scrambling for purchase, celebrating smaller victories: Utah's admission to the union with suffrage for women; four recently elected female members to the Board of Education in Lexington, Kentucky. But Bly's take on the significance of the meeting was an odd one. Her keen observation skills didn't fail her; she noted the lack of young women and the fact that there was only one Black delegate. Bly spent most of her space, though, running down the suffragists' clothes, charting out-of-date styles and ill-fitting skirts she found "frightful," dinging them for speaking with their hats on. "I really believe women will never be emancipated until they abolish the handkerchief from sight," Bly wrote, brittle and cranky.

But then, she found her way back to the insightful questions and human connections that had always characterized her reporting. With her irreverence and instinct for the compelling detail, she set out to interview the seventy-five-year-old Susan B. Anthony. The reporter drew out Anthony's past, concerns about women being paid less than men, her blossoming public profile. But then she changed tactics, giving in to the fact that, as Bly said of herself: "I adore the little peculiarities of people." She asked Anthony whether she feared death. And then,

"Do you pray?"

"I pray every single second of my life," Anthony answered. "I never get on my knees or anything like that, but I pray with my work. My prayer is to lift women to equality with men."

Cautiously, Bly pressed on.

"Were you ever in love?" asked the reporter. At the time, Bly knew how tangled these passions could be. She was still dodging detectives sent to spy on her and James Metcalfe, her rumored suitor.

"Bless you, Nellie! I've been in love a thousand times!"

"Really!" The reporter said, looking at the white-haired woman in her rocking chair.

"Yes, really. But I never loved anyone so much that I thought it would last. In fact, I never felt I could give up my life of freedom to become a man's housekeeper."

On Sunday, February 9, 1896, Bly had the lead story in the *World*'s Sunday magazine. Theodore Roosevelt, the recently appointed police commissioner, had been swept into office on a wave of reform after an investigation revealed the deep corruption of the force. Roosevelt had decided to clean up New York's Oak Street Station House and stop allowing homeless women to sleep there. In the guise of a representative of a charitable association, Bly went to investigate the impact. Wood boards rested against the walls so women could take them and lay them on an iron grate on the floor for their beds. Water dripped constantly; it smelled terrible. The ground was covered with slush, and the women had barely enough clothes to cover themselves.

But again, as in the suffrage meeting article, Bly didn't seem to know what point she wanted to make. The ostensible purpose was to learn where the women would go when kicked out in a few days, but she focused more closely on their addiction to whiskey and willingness to trade everything—job prospects, family—for another sip. They were disheveled and didn't seem to care. The reporter recoiled. Bly might have been particularly unsympathetic to alcoholism because of her violent stepfather, but here, too, was the echo of the wife of a rich industrialist rather than the open-minded reporter on the boat to the asylum.

The piece ended, though, with a glimpse of one final woman who stumbled in late. In her fifties, from Philadelphia, she seemed sober enough, just miserable. She said she'd never slept at the station house before and hoped never to do it again, but she'd lost everything. The final image was of this unhappy woman hunched on the board that would be her bed, sobbing, while the others, splayed around her, snored.

And one week later Bly interviewed Elizabeth Cady Stanton and focused on her ideas rather than the cut of her sleeves. Playing the piano when Bly arrived, the eighty-year-old Stanton had just published a *Woman's Bible*, a translation by a female scholar with commentary about the role of women. Interpretations of Eve had long been used to define women as flawed and deserving of a subordinate role because she was only Adam's rib. Stanton felt it was important to offer another view (though the National Woman Suffrage Association didn't agree with this radical perspective and refused to endorse the *Woman's Bible* at the convention).

"You know every time women wish to make any advance in the world the Bible is quoted against us," Stanton said, adding that, in addition to seeking out improved versions of Genesis, women should also be taught about evolution. It was an alternate, more equal, origin story. As Bly was leaving, Stanton inscribed her a copy of the Bible: "Man and woman a simultaneous creation."

Lest things get too slow, the next week, Bly trained an elephant at the circus. Her descriptions almost seemed to lampoon her more serious work. Of baby elephant Alice, rolling a barrel and crying, Bly wrote, "She fell from the see-saw the other day and sprained her ankle. It was never a slender, willowy ankle, but now it reminds one of dropsical patients I have seen in hospitals and tenement houses." Alice followed her in the ring, and then Bly, characteristically, asked to command the adult elephants and ride one.

The article wrapped around a full-page illustration of Bly perched on an elephant's back in a striped dress with enormous puffed sleeves and a wry expression.

Though ample, realistic images of Bly existed, this one showed a generic Gibson girl. Stunt reporters were being paid more than ever before, but they were becoming interchangeable.

"Nellie Bly as an Elephant Trainer"
in the *World*, February 23, 1896

Pulitzer, rarely in the office, sent letters from across the globe, scrambling to keep a handle on the *World* from Maine, Germany, Barbados. In the spring, the *World* launched a midnight edition and cast about for other ways to check Hearst's momentum, regardless of cost. It dropped the price to one cent, matching the *Journal*. While Pulitzer was impatient to crush his nemesis, he also had his doubts about the paper's direction, sensitive to criticism that the sensationalism went too far. Rival papers began to grumble about the larger headlines, the focus on crime, the showy illustrations, the breathless tone. Comics increasingly included racial stereotypes. Articles detailed very dubious scientific theories, like the existence of butterfly women on the planet

Venus. Pulitzer kept after Brisbane to chase Hearst without falling to his level. Avoid "freaks" and "froth," he urged, "your old energy on new lines will assure you brilliant success & higher reputation." Pulitzer requested a portrait of recently retired General O. O. Howard, who'd lost an arm fighting for the Union in the Civil War and helped found Howard University, on the front page of the *Sunday World*. But Brisbane, who feared the general would mouth clichés—very decent, very boring—wrote back: "Sorry we did not have that O. O. Howard picture and interview. Instead, on the front page, I had a wonderful picture of Kate Swan in the electric chair and circulation is up 15,000."

Brisbane had tracked down Kate Swan McGuirk, the astute Washington DC reporter who'd made such a notable scoop with her Lizzie Borden interview. Or she had volunteered herself. Either way, the *World* hired her, and she became a key element of the publication's reimagining.

One of McGuirk's first stunts for the paper tied in with the story of Maria Barbella (also called Barberi), who was on death row for slitting the throat of a man who promised, then refused, to marry her. She was scheduled to be the first woman to die in the electric chair. Brisbane, who had fainted when he witnessed an execution several years before, had taken a sympathetic interest in the Barbella case. Continuing to pursue questions, launched in the Borden trial, about the way a predominantly male justice system treated female criminals, McGuirk visited the prison and went through the experience of being walked from a cell to the electric chair and buckled in, aiming to show what it felt like to be a woman encountering the death penalty.

McGuirk dwelt on facing death surrounded by men, who would dress her, walk with her, and watch. She emphasized that to attach the electrode, the criminal would need to bare a knee. Talking with New York State's head executioner afterward, she extracted from him the promise that he would never execute a woman. Having achieved this tangible result, she wrote, "I am not sorry that I endured all the strange agonies I did during my experience in the death chair."

"Kate Swan in the Death Chair"
in the *World*, February 16, 1896

A huge illustration, the one Brisbane gloated over, showed a woman shackled to the electric chair at wrists and ankles, leather strap over her eyes and across her chin, and a helmet with wires on her head. The paper had commissioned a noted fashion designer to create a dress that allowed for the electrode to be attached to her leg while the woman retained as much dignity as possible. Showing an execution itself would be taboo, and this toed right up to the line. It sold a lot of copies.

After the story ran, Pulitzer was gracious in defeat (and always happy about a circulation bump): "You know perfectly well I am blind, and must rely on you. Congratulations," he wrote Brisbane.*

---

* It's interesting to note where Pulitzer would balk. Several years later, a female reporter wrote a piece that mentioned a prominent socialite readying a nursery, implying she was pregnant. For Pulitzer, whose paper interviewed prostitutes, illustrated X-rays of hands, and showed a woman on the verge of electrocution, an article

Though she'd always signed her pieces "Mrs. McGuirk," the reporter now developed a second persona: Kate Swan. She was nothing like the upright Mrs. McGuirk, with her arch commentary on senatorial outfits. Kate Swan was youthful. Adventurous. Risqué. And, apparently, inexhaustible.

Over the course of a year, Kate Swan jumped into the surf from a rowboat at Coney Island to test the rescue capabilities of the Volunteer Life Saving Corps, wrapped herself in a boa constrictor, pedaled a $3,000 bicycle built for six, swung on a flying trapeze, had her heart X-rayed, drove a carriage in a horse race, floated the East River in an inflatable "Merman life-saving suit," shoveled coal into a ferry-boat furnace, visited a burial vault at night, explored the inside of a whale skeleton to prove the impossibility of the literal truth of the story of Jonah and the whale, and judged a contest for the best-looking baby.

One night she stayed on Ellis Island, with those scheduled to be deported. This article worked in the sly way of some of the other stunt reporting pieces. Even though the reporter here was not in disguise, the opening proposed one kind of tale that turned out to cloak another one. Here her role was not that of a participant but of an active mind able to see things beyond the way they were usually framed. Guards detailed the dangers of these masses of immigrants: the knives they carried, the anger and restlessness in the crowds of men—most from Italy—waiting to be sent back across the Atlantic, the probability that some were escaped criminals. Wide-eyed, the reporter documented her fear for the first few paragraphs.

But the reader's understanding shifted as the reporter detailed the "cages" where the deportees were kept, the 250 beds for a population of five hundred, the lack of ventilation. (Officials assured Swan that renovations were planned, but it would be months.) At some point in the evening, a man started to play a concertina and the music lured

---

suggesting pregnancy was too far. This oblique hint at "an interesting condition" was "disgusting and sickening" he wrote to his staff, and he demanded the writer—Zona Gale—be fired.

some of the dangerous deportees to waltz. After they settled down to sleep, many still in their boots, Swan (whose in-laws emigrated from Ireland; whose immigrant employer had devoted all the resources of his newspaper to raising money for the base of the Statue of Liberty) noted, pointedly: "The light from Liberty's torch streams across the water and shines on the sleepers. That is the nearest some of them will ever get to the liberty they have come to seek."

Still another episode found her leaning, close to midnight, over the railing of the elevated train station in the Tenderloin, watching customers stream in and out of the Internationale Apotheke, a pharmacy. A small round box smudged with opium sat in her jacket pocket. Opium addiction was rampant in 1896. The anarchist Emma Goldman, writing of a time when she was in charge of the jail dispensary at Blackwell's Island, reported that most of the prostitutes she met there were suffering withdrawal. Finally, after watching a handful of women come up with boxes that seemed similar to hers, McGuirk walked down the stairs and went inside.

She started with a perfectly legal request for a disinfectant.

"Give me two ounces of a 4 percent solution of carbolic acid."

When the pharmacist obliged, she flashed the box and a half dollar.

"Can I get that filled here?" she asked.

He took the box, went into the back, then returned:

"Who told you?" When she offered a name she had at the ready, he handed her the opium. She didn't have a prescription, he didn't record her identity, as the law required, and the box didn't bear the mandatory poison label. Story complete, she turned the evidence over to the assistant district attorney and ended up testifying about illegal opium sales in front of a grand jury.

While some of Kate Swan's articles, like those on illegal drugs and immigration policy, had a serious purpose, what lingered in some readers' minds were the half-page illustrations of the reporter at work, hair billowing, eyes ablaze. These lodged the character of the "daring journalist" in the public imagination and set the stage for comic-book female reporters like Lois Lane and Brenda Starr. Meanwhile, the more proper "Mrs. McGuirk" kept writing, too. On the page, Mrs. McGuirk was the opposite of Kate Swan, keeping her distance, cool and skeptical, never illustrated. The two sides of Kate Swan McGuirk were so distinct, the paper had room for them both, and they often competed for space on the same page.

McGuirk, with her Washington DC savvy, covered the upcoming 1896 presidential election between big-city, big-business William McKinley and William Jennings Bryan, the young populist hero of western farmers. After the low-key election of 1892, the contest gripped the politically minded: New York broke records on the first day of voter registration. McGuirk interviewed McKinley's campaign manager, Mark Hanna, a wealthy Ohio businessman, with wariness. Burnishing his importance, he kept her waiting then settled into a leather couch, a gold nugget dangling from his watch chain. Her interview revealed that his investments stood to benefit from government policies, that he wasn't interested in China, didn't care for travel, and, rich as he was, had never been to Europe. Could this really be the next ambassador to England? she wondered.

Bryan, too, she met with a raised eyebrow, highlighting his manufactured appeal to women, with his collar rolled down in a "Byronic fashion" and his constant references to his dear mother. He has a "profound respect for womanhood," she commented, one that seemed based in a certain vagueness. And his western women supporters in turn were similarly vague on his policies. The whole piece appeared complimentary, about his warmth, his storytelling, his smile, yet not. Her conclusion: "Bryan would make a good dress-suit figure."

McGuirk did have the occasional adventure. The much-hyped "Thrilling Hunt for a Wild Woman" took McGuirk into unaccustomed scenery, but she still represented a decent lady looking at the oddities of those beyond her sphere. Kate Swan would likely have played the wild woman herself, tramping through the trees, bedding down in the swamp, branches tearing at her hair. In fact, the same issue had her driving an electric engine through a tunnel at seventy-five miles per hour.

"Kate Swan Drives the Electric Engine"
in the *World*, May 31, 1896

Hearst continued his assault. Pulitzer tried to keep his distance from the day-to-day workings of the paper, but he couldn't help himself. Particularly after the loss of so many of his staff, he worried about spies. Ideas dreamed up at the *World* seemed to appear in the *Journal* the next day. Pulitzer increasingly relied on a complex code to keep his moves secret from telegraph operators and others who might glimpse his communications. Codebooks helped staff decipher and encode messages. "Semaphore" meant that the previous communication had been read and understood. "Geranium" meant *"The Morning Journal,"* "Hearst" was "Gush" or, perhaps grudgingly, "Magnetic." Pulitzer himself was "Sedentary."

In one typical letter to his business manager, Pulitzer started, "I hope you are satisfied with my abstention from business and general non interference," then offered a list of suggestions, labeled "a" through "e," and then three more pages of notes, numbered 1 through 10. The *World* should be an entertaining paper that is still truthful, not all pictures and horror stories: "freedom of thought and public interest would make up for any lack of features of size or splash." And then,

written in pencil "—let us hope." In another letter, he warned staffers
not to underestimate their adversary: "Geranium has brains and genius beyond any question, not only brains for news and features, but
genius for the self advertising acts which have no parallel."

The Hearst-Pulitzer battle could be exhilarating, brainstorm
upon brainstorm. In early summer, the *World* empaneled a "jury" of
all women, including a lawyer, a principal, and a Tolstoy translator, to
mull over a case where a woman was accused of poisoning her mother
by putting arsenic in her clam chowder. It was likely the brainchild
of Elizabeth Jordan, who was one of the "jurors." The female jury
weighed in over the course of the trial, and the series had a specific
political purpose: "to prove a conspicuous experimental illustration of
the theory that a woman should be tried by a 'jury of her peers.'"

It could also be exhausting for those watching from the outside.
Charles Dana's *Sun* editorialized: "There was never before anywhere
on earth such a rivalry, and, God willing, there never will be again
after Mr. Pulitzer is dead or has gone mad, or after Mr. Hearst is tired
out or has reluctantly come to his senses."

Though she didn't object to a little vicious competition, Winifred Black wasn't relishing her time in Manhattan writing for
Hearst's *Journal*. Life in the city seemed relentlessly grim, peopled
by those grinding out their lives in utmost poverty, packed into dark
tenements, standing in soup kitchen lines, shivering out on strike in
thin shawls. The scorching summers and freezing winters exacerbated
the misery. Those with money spent their energy fretting over clothes
and social status. There was no natural beauty like the moon over the
Pacific or wild roses or crates of oranges at the dock to blunt the bleak-
ness. Like Kate Swan McGuirk, she developed two literary characters,
in order to cover the maximum number of stories in multiple styles.
When the *San Francisco Examiner* ran her articles, they appeared under
the established name "Annie Laurie." In the *New York Journal*, she
wrote under her own name: "Winifred Black," chasing human interest

stories from police station to the alcohol-soaked Bowery, with little time to do anything but report and type. "I used to go to my hotel at night absolutely dizzy with the pressure of life that beat and surged up and down those dark and narrow streets like a tidal wave rising to engulf us all," she wrote. A few days after she settled into a New York routine in the fall of 1895, her husband and son came to join her.

As happy as she was to see her little boy, her feelings about her domestic life were mixed. Back in 1892, when she'd been married for a year, she'd hidden in a wooden box with a slit in it so she could watch a boxing match and not be observed. The men, some acquaintances, were transformed, howling like beasts. A doctor she knew gave a "guttural snarl" and a lawyer followed the fight blow by blow with his fists. Her article read like anthropological fieldwork. "I saw that I was looking on a race of beings I had never seen before." The race was men. She wrote, of the faces in the crowd, "They told a wonderful story of repression, of dissimulation. Since I saw them I know that women never see men as they are. Women do not know anything about men. They see them, they talk with them, they love them, they fear them, they laugh at them, but they do not know them."

Perhaps it goes without saying that her husband was not what she'd hoped for. For a number of years, paid generously by Hearst, a big draw for both of his papers, she supported their family. Her husband had been withdrawing her money without telling her, breeding mistrust. Something would have to give.

While Winifred Black buttressed the *Journal* in New York, readers of the *San Francisco Examiner* who craved adventure followed the exploits of "Helen Dare." Stunting with a particular California flair, she rode forty miles down a log flume in the Sierra mountains, a feat her paper called the "Wildest Ride Ever Made by a Woman." (These flumes inspired amusement park "log rides.") As with many of these reporters, though her name was dashing, she did other kinds of journalism, too. As well as picking hops with migrant workers, she wrote about threats to California forests—highlighting human-caused fires—on the same page that featured an interview with John Muir, who blamed sheep and poor logging practices. She also conducted a humanizing series of interviews with prisoners in San Quentin.

Helen Dare promotion in the
San Francisco Examiner, July 25, 1896

Then in October, a reporter from a rival paper revealed that Helen Dare was actually Elizabeth Tompkins, the noted horse-race writer who'd vanished on the way to the Chicago World's Fair with her son and left her husband temporarily paralyzed with worry. She'd met a dashing representative of the California Jockey Club at Saratoga and had run off with him to San Francisco. But she was bored and lonely, even in the Pacific Heights apartment with the view and her now five-year-old boy. The pseudonym had allowed her to do the work she loved, while staying in hiding. And she kept doing it, false identity stripped away, exposed to public view and condemnation.

Back on Park Row, stunt reporters continued to multiply. Throughout 1896, the *World* had so many, its Sunday magazine could barely contain the thrills. "Daring Deeds by the Sunday World's Intrepid Woman Reporters": the headline of March 8 spanned two pages of heart-stopping adventure. Dorothy Dare headed out in a pilot ship in a storm, another reporter (perhaps less daringly) took up shears as a barber, while Kate Swan McGuirk lived a childhood dream of balancing on a moving horse as a circus "fairy bareback rider." Nellie Bly declared she would raise an all-female regiment to fight for Cuba. Since 1895, when Cubans had rebelled against Spanish control of the island, both the *World* and the *Journal* followed developments—the torching of the countryside by both rebel and Spanish armies, the relocation of rural people into urban concentration camps, the resulting disease and starvation—and agitated for United States intervention. And Bly, pictured sword in hand at the head of an army, was ready to lead the charge.

Hearst's answer to this flood of female reporters was the "Journal Woman." It was an umbrella term covering several reporters, but the one who dominated the *Journal*'s Sunday pages was Kate Masterson. She profiled a Michigan town where women wore the trousers, literally and figuratively, conducted an interview with Edison, took a trip on a haunted schooner. Bly's military bravado may have been inspired by reports of Cuban "Amazons" fighting with the rebels. Kate Masterson did her one better, traveling to Havana to interview Spanish military leader General Valeriano Weyler in the palace hung with red velvet curtains. Weyler, called "the Butcher," denied her requests to visit the battlefield and prison but gave her a tour of his elaborate bathroom and bedroom. She asked him specifically about the stories of female soldiers, and he said they were true. In fact, one had been captured, wearing men's clothes and holding a machete. "These women are fiercer than the men," he told her.

Circulation numbers spiraled up, but the sheer volume of stunt stories blurred the boundaries between one reporter and the next, flattened individual writers and their styles. When Nellie Bly first started writing for the *World* in 1887, the selling point was her voice. That was why headlines featured her name. But nine years later, the value of uniqueness was slipping away. Like the "Journal Woman," the pseudonym "Meg Merrillies" covered more than one reporter. The way stunts and their performers became indistinguishable was underscored by the play *Very Little Red Riding Hood*, a show by the Mask and Wig Club at the University of Pennsylvania. In a tumultuous burlesque that included seventy-five student performers and a "Shakespearean ballet," the show featured "a chorus of women reporters," including actors dressed as Nellie Bly, Dorothy Dare, and Kate Swan.

Besides the rare solo, a chorus contains few distinct voices. "Stunt reporters" was a more invigorating cliché than "domestic angels," but it became a cliché nonetheless.

"Dorothy Dare's Wild Ride on the Snow Plough" in the *World*, March 22, 1896

And as the popularity of stunt reporters grew, so did the objections. The *Chicago Times-Herald* (a merger of the *Chicago Times* and the *Herald*) railed against the contest between the *World* and the *New York Journal*, deploring "the furious exploitation of crime, vulgarity and squalid enterprises of women reporters." Did New York contain multitudes of morbid readers who demanded this kind of thing? "The only alternative is that the directors of these papers are insane," the *Times-Herald* concluded.

Critics included women writers. Frances Willard, head of the Woman's Christian Temperance Union, warned against reputation-ruining assignments in her book *Occupations for Women*: "If any girl who reads this is ever tempted to make her entrance into newspaper work through this unclean path, let her put aside the temptation and give up her fondest hopes of becoming a newspaper woman if they are to be obtained at such a cost."

A column in the *New Orleans Times-Democrat* by playwright Lucile Rutland was a long howl of protest.

Rutland particularly objected to the reliance on the first person, an unseemly bid for attention. She decried the way these reporters were "intruding their individuality on the public," deploying "the first person singular." In contrast, she praised a southern woman who'd written anonymously, displaying "an innate shrinking from public notice." She saw it as a contest between the "New Woman" and the "True Woman." She also disliked the way the writing was marked specifically as female: "If women have to do men's work (and it seems inevitable), why, in the name of decency, can't they do it like men? Why must they label everything with the vagaries of their sex?" She singled out, as egregious examples, Bly ("clever enough to know better") and Kate Swan McGuirk ("short skirts, crocheted slippers, disheveled locks").

Did the editors who assigned these stories even care about the plight of female writers? Rutland wondered. She told the story of a New York woman who, like so many others, felt called to "Write!" But no one saw the value of her work, and she met only rejection. Unwilling to give up and accept her failure, she kept at it until she starved. "The paper that recorded her death, with a few paragraphs of post mortem justice, had a full-page illustration of Kate Swan exposing her shapely body to the revolting rites of electrocution, for the sake of new sensations to work up into several columns of hysteria and capital I's," Rutland wrote.

Unlike most other stunt reporters, Kate Swan McGuirk used her real name, though she played with variants. For good or ill, that name, and her face (and calves and ankles), which graced so many Sunday magazine front pages, became a symbol of the *World* and this moment of its history.

It was a risky move, rather like taking a turn as a fairy bareback rider, sweating in the glare of hot stage lights, wearing an itchy yet shiny costume, slowly rising on the spine of an unpredictable animal, toes clinging for balance.

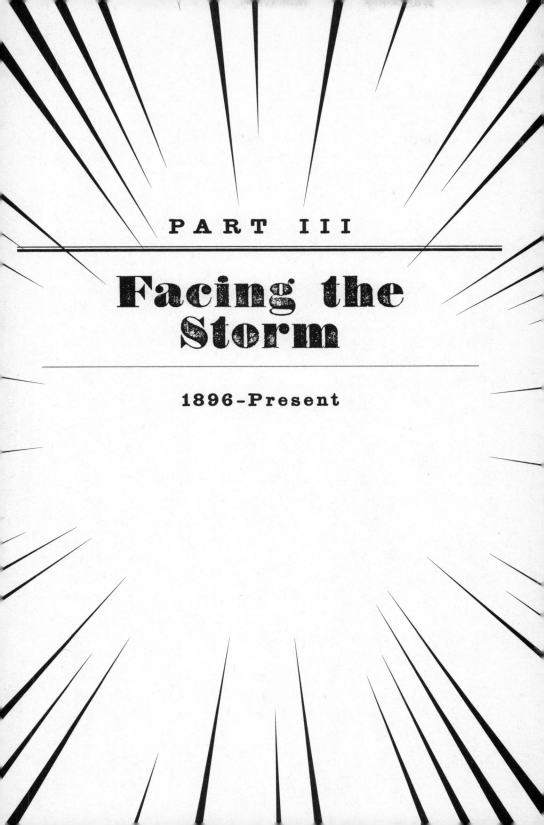

PART III

Facing the Storm

1896–Present

A SMEAR OF YELLOW

The yellow journals incite them to do the things that get them into jails, though they do sympathize with them a great deal afterward and send their oldest girl reporters to draw touching pictures of how much they suffer in confinement after they have battered in somebody's head or carved a man into pieces and thrown him around two counties.

—*Brooklyn Daily Eagle*, September 12, 1897

In fall 1896, Elizabeth Banks disembarked the steamship *St. Louis*, back in New York City after four years in London. Accompanied by her big black dog,* she stepped onto the pavement of a shifted country, a shifted city, a shifted journalism landscape. The Vitascope allowed moving pictures to be projected on a screen, and audiences marveled at images of heaving surf. Bicyclists flew through the streets, on the cutting edge, but in peril: one had just died when hit by a train, another suffered internal injuries after being run over by a carriage. Hearst and Pulitzer's frenzied competition continued unabated, with newsboys hawking dozens of "Extra" editions per day. Several weeks before, Kate Swan visited North Brother Island, New York's leper colony, and a Journal Woman joined the hunt for alleged murderers in the New Jersey Pine Barrens. A flock of reporters awaited Banks's arrival.

---

* Reporters called the dog "Senator," but in her books, Jordan referred to him as "Judge." Did she give her pet a pseudonym, too?

She was a big name in Europe, with her undercover jaunts inspiring plays and poems* and, even better, a fair amount of controversy and scorching editorial commentary. *Campaigns of Curiosity: Journalistic Adventures of an American Girl in London*, her book filled with photographs of Banks in various disguises and details of her exploits, sold well enough in England to require multiple printings and was pirated in the United States. She'd covered a coal strike and conducted a rare and high-profile interview with the Chinese diplomat Li Hung Chang. One of Hearst's reporters was among the first to approach her when she arrived in the States.

But when the interviewer asked about her undercover reporting plans in America—hiring out as a servant? Advertising as an heiress angling for an introduction to high society?—Banks demurred.

"Oh, no; I am not going to do any sensational work here," she said.

That was all in her past, she insisted, touching the bracelet of coins she earned as a housemaid. She'd paid her dues, and now she'd gone straight. Her heroine, Aurora Leigh, dreamed of being a poet, not a stunt girl. With visions of respect and safety (no more fear of losing fingers in the mangle), she'd written one essay for the journal *Nineteenth Century* and hoped to do more, delving into what she considered legitimate topics of intellectual inquiry.

"I am merely going to write up the curiosities of a political campaign in America," she told the *Journal* reporter.

Assignments came easy at first. Telegrams wafted in with requests for interviews and features. She spent a few months writing inoffensive (and dull) articles about the English man versus the American man. After McKinley won the battle with Bryan, she featured his family in "The Home Life of the American President." But though writing as a special correspondent paid up to four times the usual amount, it was

---

* See Sir Walter Besant's "The Lady Housemaid," marveling at Banks dressing up as a servant:
"And behold a Transformation! A Fairy tale in variation!
A housemaid, meek and mild, once lady fair!"

still freelance work: feast and famine. Before long, suffering a "financial catastrophe" that made her London poverty pale in comparison, Banks once again found herself broke.

On Newspaper Row, "sunlight, sparkling on a dome of gold" kept catching her eye. The sensational papers seemed to be printing money along with their front pages. Both owners were conspicuously wealthy and paid more than anyone else. As a result, the smartest, most talented reporters worked there. A staff position could provide the $40 a week she needed.

And they offered genuine opportunity for those of her sex. Under the *World*'s glittering roof, in the Hearst office pandemonium, Banks knew that "the most difficult, the most enterprising, the most sensational and the most original work on this class of papers is done by women." Hearst, though he didn't pontificate about women in journalism, would do whatever it took to win. Female writers equaled sales. As a result, he hired a lot of them. As a journalist wrote years later, of Hearst and women: "Hundreds of them passed through his doorways, some to lose their jobs with staggering swiftness; others to build up big syndicate names and draw down the highest salaries in the profession." But that style of journalism still left a bad taste in Banks's mouth. Stunt reporting and writing about the body had been a liberating choice for many, but it was becoming an imprisoning expectation. Banks had a hard time finding a well-paying assignment that didn't involve, for example, getting arrested as a prostitute in the Tenderloin and spending the night in jail. At the beginning, stunt reporters often came up with their own ideas, but now that the demand was so great, did they have the chance to say no? At what point did opportunity become exploitation?

From its earliest days in the late 1880s, one strain of stunt reporting had been more sexual than public-spirited. Some of Nora Marks's first ventures for the *Chicago Tribune* involved applying to work for a publisher of pornographic books and then as an artist's model for a man who turned out to want to take and sell seminude photographs. An aspiring writer who arrived in Chicago as early as 1881 (she hoped to write literary essays until a magazine editor said she'd never make a living that way: "You'll have to write about something you have seen, can describe, something no one else has done"), she was assigned to interview a train full of prostitutes and found herself mistaken for one. Female journalists whispered among themselves the story of a Chicago editor who requested that a new reporter marry a Mormon and send dispatches from Salt Lake City.

Banks wasn't the only reporter who thought this kind of work risked damaging, not furthering, women's careers. Florence Finch Kelly, who'd reported for the *San Francisco Examiner*, found the stunts embarrassing. The "clamour of the stunting sisterhood" and the headlines that shrieked "its daring and unsavory exploits to be everywhere talked about" made established writers pause before recommending journalism as a profession. She worried these antics would cause male editors to think twice before hiring women at all.*

And then there was the lack of originality. To be a stunt reporter seemed more and more to be one of a troupe of anonymous women performing the same tired tricks, and Banks felt her value as a writer was her unique perspective. Later, when discussing her autobiography with her agent, Banks insisted her individuality was a selling point. When he positioned the book as one about the tough lives of newspaperwomen in general, she reminded him that the manuscript's significance was that it told the story of "the American Girl in London" who had lit the Thames on fire:

"My book will not go because it is by a woman journalist but because it is by ME!"

Banks also wondered about the cost of these adventures to the women who performed them. Some of the assignments risked physical harm. The peril was genuine. As one aspiring reporter asked her editor, when he suggested she sail from Europe to New York and let

---

* But Florence Finch Kelly didn't view men's exploits in the same light. Her husband was the *Examiner* reporter who brought a grizzly bear out of the mountains at Hearst's request.

herself be taken in by one of the gangs that preyed on immigrant girls: "But one thing troubles me. Won't there be real danger in it?"

The larger culture echoed her unease. Banks had been in town only a few months when the *New York Press* coined the term "yellow-kid journalism" in January 1897. The phrase referred to a comic-strip character popular in the *World* then scooped up by the *Journal* (while the *World* continued to run an imitation). The term implied cartoon-ish, accessible, vulgar, like the slang-speaking Yellow Kid himself. It may have had roots in the dismissive phrase "yellow-covered litera-ture": cheaply printed adventure novels marked by, not surprisingly, their yellow covers. Beyond the Kid's bright shirt, the color also brought to mind diseases like yellow fever. The *Indianapolis Journal* in February 1897 quoted the *Press* under the title: "Gotham's Great Ep-idemic." It continued, "After an attack of yellow-kid journalism, New Yorkers are not going to worry about the Bombay plague." Certainly, there seemed something feverish in the approach.

This then became "yellow journalism," meaning everything out-rageous, crowd pleasing, colorful and—the implication was—false. Other terms clung to "yellow journalism" like flies to fly paper: "lu-rid," and "prurient" and "sensational." "Lurid," with its roots in the Latin color "luridus," means a pale yellow, like the skin of someone who is ill, a sickly slice of sky before a storm. Or reddish, like a flame against darkness or smoke. Metaphorically, it means to look at some-thing in this unsettling light, a tint that distorts. "Prurient" refers to itching with lust or curiosity, particularly that "dangerous curios-ity" mentioned by clergyman Josiah Tucker as "that prurient desire of knowing where lies the exact Boundary between Virtue and Vice." "Sensational," unsurprisingly, is knowledge rooted in the senses, which brings readers back to their troublesome bodies.[*]

---

[*] While "sensationalism" is derogatory, concrete details that can be seen, touched, or tasted remain the best way to engage a reader. In Mary Beard's book *Women & Power*, she commented on the discomfort with these effective strategies: "The smart-est ancient rhetorical theorists were prepared to acknowledge that the best male techniques of rhetorical persuasion were uncomfortably close to the techniques (as

By March, the categorization "yellow journalism" was being used to boot the *World* and the *Journal* from libraries. The Newark Public Library led the charge. When the Union Club voted to eliminate the papers as well, the *Sun* commented, approvingly, "In many institutions where the *World* and *Journal* are still admitted they are and have been for some time excluded from the libraries and reading rooms, and are kept under lock and key, to be brought out on the express demand of adults only." Other libraries followed suit, including the Ansonia Public Library in Connecticut, which banned "yellow journalism" from the reading room to limit access to "pernicious and unclean newspapers."

Pulitzer struggled to maintain control, impeded by his distance and blindness. It must have been hard to feel the pulse of events without being able to see the excitement or indifference when a given edition hit the streets. Did commuters miss a train to read the headlines, or use the front page to wipe mud off their boots? Circulation numbers were the only way to track this, so he pressed for them, endlessly. Writing to his business manager, he stressed that the *World* needed to recover "the respect and confidence of the public" and destroy "the notion that we are in the same class with the *Journal* with recklessness & unreliability." He worried the code had been cracked.

The criticism didn't bother Hearst at all.

Other New York papers sought to distance themselves from the yellow stain, advertising their unsoiled brands. The *New York Times* moved its newly minted, rather prim, slogan to the front page: "All the News That's Fit to Print." If simply reading these papers was indecent, what did it mean to edit one, as the convent-educated Elizabeth Jordan did? Or to write for one?

But still, the *World* beckoned. Eventually, Banks went in.

It was as she feared. After she refused to be arrested as a prostitute, the editor assigned her to take a train, then a mule, into "the wilds of

---

they saw it) of female seduction. Was oratory really then so safely masculine, they worried."

Virginia," where a group of whiskey distillers had recently attacked government officers trying to arrest them. It was an echo of Elizabeth Jordan's journey to the South, where she interviewed a backwoods preacher years earlier, but with much higher stakes. If Banks pretended to be lost, with her delicate appearance, she could get access to their headquarters. An interview with the gang leader would be quite the tale. Could she leave in half an hour?

When Banks asked which male reporter would be sent along to keep her safe, the editor replied, "Men! . . . why, if I sent a man along with you, both he and you would be shot! Your only safety lies in your going by yourself." Chivalry would protect her, he suggested.

Banks's faith in the chivalry of the American man had its limits. She declined that assignment, too.

But she couldn't continue saying no and keep her job. She had to come up with an alternate plan. Increasing concern over Cuba spurred interest in military technology. An inventor named John Holland was working on a boat that could attack an enemy from underwater: a submarine. Banks's editor ordered her to be sure to be in it for the first test. Imagining plummeting to the bottom in a large metal coffin, without even time to type up a first-person piece on this novel kind of death, Banks tried a new strategy. As she had way back in St. Paul, she disguised herself as a "womanly woman," shunning her usual practical skirt for a dress, frilly and white. Perfecting her "delicate, feminine appearance" in the mirror before she left, admiring the way the pale outfit made her face green and sickly, she set off for the Holland Torpedo Boat Company at the shipyards in Elizabeth, New Jersey. Looking at the fifty-foot tube lurking under the water's surface, armed with not just a torpedo but two dynamite guns, Banks let fear play across her face. Ruffles trembling, she timidly asked Holland to let her step in the vessel and be submerged. Though Holland had full confidence in his invention, she got the refusal she wanted.

"You would not die of the going down, but you would die of the fear! You would be actually and literally frightened to death!" he said.

Then she got him to promise he wouldn't let any other reporters go down either, and fluttered away.

Even with these tactics, Banks stayed busy and employed. In between bringing stray kittens and injured dogs to the Society for the Prevention of Cruelty to Animals, she chased stories into the hospital, the jail, the morgue, smelling salts at the ready. She worked in a sweatshop, slept in a 15-cent-per-night lodging house, X-rayed her foot, interviewed a murderess.

Though usually, as fit the genre, the writing featured a light touch, Banks's chipperness could gloss over real turmoil. While in London, isolated, plagued with insomnia, in a state she later described as "breaking down under a very great mental strain," she'd befriended journalist and reformer W. T. Stead, who let her recuperate at his property. And sometime during her stint at Pulitzer's paper, a story unfolded that cut through the gloss to rage. A friend had introduced her to a girl from England who had come to America looking for employment. The woman had a child but no husband. She seemed pleasant and competent, and Banks found her a job as a governess with someone known for her charitable works. Then, one day, the employer burst into the newspaper office. She had discovered the out-of-wedlock child and kicked her governess out on the street at night. Did Banks know about this? she demanded. Banks demanded in turn where she thought her employee would go so late in a city that was strange to her.

A Rescue Home, the woman answered. Banks exploded, all her feelings about hypocrisy, religion, charitable poses pouring out.

I had forgotten that you were interested in those pathetically funny institutions—those places where they herd women together and tell them the story of Mary Magdalen, and pray over them, giving them to understand that the crime they have committed is the one that takes the largest amount of the blood of Christ to wash out, if it can be washed out at all, and then, branding them with a mark, send them out to work at such odds as few women can combat.

The philanthropist, in turn, sneered that she should have reminded herself about the trashy publication where Banks worked. Then she left. No longer able to focus on her writing, "bitter hatred in my face and in my heart," Banks stepped into the street to look for her friend. But she had no luck. Manhattan itself, sometimes so invigorating, set itself against her: "The great skyscrapers, the crowds of people, the loud jingle of the cable cars greeted me and seemed to laugh, in all their bigness, at me in my littleness and powerlessness."

The incident became a chapter in her autobiography called, in the English edition, "In the Name of Christ." Perhaps daunted by the tone, the New York publishers requested she cut it from the American version, and she did.

Hearst continued to needle the *World*. He'd hired away S. S. Carvalho, Pulitzer's trusted publisher (and Nell Nelson's husband), a few months after arriving in New York, and followed up by taking Arthur Brisbane, one of the *World*'s most dynamic editors, a year later.* He also doubled down on exuberant, pricy experimentation. Bringing *Examiner* successes to New York, Hearst ran endless contests. *Journal* readers could win prizes for the best hat design, the best breakfast menu, the best limerick, the best composition praising the *Journal*, the best name for a baby hippo at the Central Park Zoo. (Winner: "Iris.") The paper offered $50 for deciphering a code in the Want Ads, $1,000 for the best solution to the serialized mystery "The Mill of Silence."

The *Journal* continued to push its nascent form of activist journalism into new realms. In the summer of 1897, when three boys swimming in the East River brought to shore a package wrapped in red and gold fabric that turned out to contain a man's torso and arms, the

---

* Unlike other Hearst hires, Brisbane did not get a gargantuan salary increase; his motive might have been, instead, that his relationship with Katherine Pulitzer was over, and he needed some distance between him and the Pulitzers.

city editor wondered whether it was a joke. But the next day, when a father hunting berries with his young sons found another piece of the man near the Washington Bridge over the Harlem River, and the two pieces fit together, the *Journal* assembled a team of thirty reporters (and one novelist), a "Murder Squad" devoted to solving the crime. Some members tested the tides of the Harlem River to see where a package thrown from the Washington Bridge might end up, some looked for stores that might have sold the cloth, one found a palm reader to interpret the severed hands, one consulted with a surgeon. Others rented a boat to drag the river for the head. The novelist wrote up possible scenarios.

At one a.m., on June 29, a *Journal* reporter interviewed staff at a Turkish bath with a missing masseuse. After hearing a description of the man, and learning that a rival for his mistress's affections had beat him not long before, the reporter went right then to interview the mistress. She seemed unconcerned about her lover's disappearance. Employees of the bath identified the body at the morgue—that damaged index finger, the flesh removed from the chest just where his tattoo would have been. The next morning, the reporter visited the mistress again and found her packing her apartment, having told the landlord she was leaving immediately for Europe. The police arrested her later that day and her lover not long after.

The solving of the mystery, played out over the course of a week, allowed the *Journal* to brag: "When the educated man of special training and habits of thought competes with the detective who graduated from a lazy life of patrol duty he wins easily."

Now that his reporters had mastered the role of detective, Hearst pushed them into another—revolutionary hero. The *Journal* was firmly on the side of the Cuban rebels and had been advocating for the United States to declare war against Spain. Now it had discovered a potent symbol of Spanish outrages in Cuba: an innocent maiden in the form of the dark-haired Evangelina Cisneros, locked in the tower of a Havana jail. Daughter of a rebel leader deported to an island off mainland Cuba, she'd caught the eye of a high-ranking Spanish official.

Coordinating with insurgents, she agreed to invite him to her house, under the pretense that she returned his affections. According to the plan, the rebels would be waiting and, while his guard was down, capture him and take control of the garrison. She did her part, luring the official into her house, then shouting, "You, men, take care of the situation." But her coconspirators were distracted by distant gunfire and missed their cue. She was arrested for treason and thrown into jail.

Hearst launched a letter-writing campaign, gathering signatures from prominent women to plead with the pope and the queen regent in Spain for Cisneros's release. Then, in October, using funds in part from the Cuban businessman Carlos Carbonell, he sent reporter Karl Decker to stage a rescue. Decker was well cast: strapping frame, bristling mustache. After secreting Cisneros a message about his plans, he rented a room next to the prison and sawed through the bars at her window. She drugged her fellow prisoners with laudanum in their coffee, then climbed through the window and over the roof. A few days later, disguised as a sailor, she boarded a ship to New York. Hearst was ecstatic, reveling in the celebration that greeted her arrival. His paper lauded the "shy, dark-eyed Cuban maiden, concerning whose beauty no dissenting voice has yet been heard." She met with the president, while the *World* grumbled and suggested the guards might have been bribed to let her go. There seemed no limit to what a paper could do.

In addition to solving murders and rescuing maidens, the *New York Journal* in 1897 profiled Victoria Earle Matthews in the haphazard way it often jumbled together items considered of interest to women. Her photo with the caption "Mrs. Victoria Earle Matthews who was once a slave, is now the chief organizer of the National Association of Colored Women, and is a clever writer" appeared on a page with pictures from a play and the article "The Real Swell Girl Wears Ten Pairs of Shoes in One Day."

Matthews's life had taken a dramatic turn, leaving her searching for her own kind of purpose. Through the early 1890s, her career continued to bloom; she'd written well-received short stories and a play; a biographical sketch said that, among African American female journalists, "none are more popular than Victoria Earle." She was deeply literary, both in her writing, which showed evidence of wide and careful reading, and her sense of the importance of including stories from Black Americans in the country's canon. In a profile of Frederick Douglass, she described his life as "America's great epic." She defended reading novels (often scorned as a trivial pursuit), and her lecture at the First Congress of Colored Women in Boston impressed listeners with its meticulously detailed case for "The Value of Race Literature."

"We cannot afford any more than any other people to be indifferent to the fact, that the surest road to real fame is through literature," she told the gathered crowd. "Who knows or can judge of our intrinsic worth without actual evidence of our breadth of mind, our boundless humanity."

Many of her nonliterary hopes were tied up in her son. When she'd met Frederick Douglass at the Chicago World's Columbian Exposition, where he was the representative of Haiti, they rode the railway through the grounds together. In a later letter, reminding him of that encounter, she asked if she could bring her son to visit him for a jolt of inspiration. She imagined the fourteen-year-old as a grown man, saying, "Yes I had seen The Hon. Frederick Douglass—heard him speak—his hand has rested upon my head."

But her son didn't get a chance to grow into that man. He died in September 1895, at fifteen. At a loss for something to do with her grief, a state she described as "torn and disordered," Matthews traveled to the South. She watched brickmaking at the Tuskegee Institute; she chaired the Resolutions Committee of the Congress of Colored Women of America during the Cotton States and International Exposition in Atlanta. Resolutions condemned lynching and railcars that separated passengers by race. Others praised the elevation of "motherhood and womanhood of the race" and requested "the same standards of morality for men as for women."

And based on disturbing observations, she channeled her grief into an investigation of the conditions of those who remained in rural areas of the South. Matthews had deep-set dark eyes, strong features, thick bangs. With her light skin and straight hair, many thought she was white—a notion she took pains to dispel, often announcing her background at the start of lectures: "When I speak of the colored people, I speak of people of whom I have my maternal origin. I speak of my brother, or my sister." In letters she implied her father might have been the man who enslaved her mother. But in this instance, she may have taken advantage of the ability to disguise herself as a different race.* In Alabama and Georgia, the state where she'd been born, Black women and children mired in poverty languished on plantations, eager for any education that could help them. Prison reform was essential: the lack of any juvenile justice system meant that children labored on chain gangs alongside adults.

Matthews's first impulse was to stay in the South, where she seemed so badly needed, to create a model home where she could teach life skills, but a minister urged her to use her energies to help young Black women drawn to New York under false pretenses. So she turned her attention to fraudulent employment agencies, based in Richmond, Norfolk, and other southern cities, those that tempted inexperienced young women with the lure of jobs in the North. The agencies promised to loan recruits money for boat fare, meet them at the dock, and provide housing until they found work. All the girls needed to do was to sign a contract giving an agency their wages until the debts were paid. It was, essentially, indentured servitude.

---

* I couldn't find any sources from Matthews's lifetime that described her passing as white to ferret out additional information in the South. She doesn't mention it in any available lectures or letters. But the 1933 book on the Black Women's Club movement, *Lifting as They Climb*, describes her as traveling "fearlessly and unobserved through the black belt of the South" and suggests that she was able to discover so much about the exploitation of young women because of "her personality and natural endowment, physically, which gave her entree to places, and conditions in the South not accessible to many of our women."

The southern women found themselves sleeping on the floor in filthy boardinghouses, racking up more debt as time ticked by. The situation of Black women looking for work was complicated by discrimination. They were barred from some factories because white employees refused to work with them. Nursing schools were closed to them. So when they were offered employment, finally, it was often the kind that would bar them from polite society (like Bly, like all the others, Matthews understood the importance of staying on the right side of the line, the safe side)—serving beer in bars and gambling houses, working as prostitutes.

Matthews had a very different sense of New York and its dangers than that reflected in the *World* and the *New York Journal*. The major charities at the time focused more on the needs of Eastern European immigrants than on those of Black Americans migrating north. For Matthews, concrete activism, beyond airy conference resolutions, was becoming more appealing than writing articles or short stories. Helping these girls and publicizing their plight was something she could do.

As 1897 came to an end, a little girl wrote to Santa requesting the *Round the World with Nellie Bly* board game. Ida Wells-Barnett debated a preacher in Boston who thought lynching was sometimes justifiable. Helen Dare went to the Yukon for the *Examiner*. Winifred Black filed for divorce. At the *Journal*, she'd been her husband's boss, which he resented. When she corrected his work, he assaulted her, and it wasn't the first time. Things had gotten very ugly, with Orlow Black claiming their son wasn't his. The divorce was granted.

And Elizabeth Banks took a different tack on the working-girl stunt. Rather than charting the conditions of employees in the factory, she would experience their lives at home. Like so many did, she would live on $3 a week. When she announced her plans in the paper, a dour note arrived from a working girl, predicting her demise: "If you are going to try to exist on $3 a week I advise you to leave your order with the undertaker in advance."

The first day, Banks worried over making her rental apartment cheerful and comfortable, priding herself on creating a shelf from a box top, wishing she could sew a calico cushion for her chair. But soon, her focus shifted entirely to food. She thought about it all the time. By the end of the second day, she was already down to $1 and hungry, needing another loaf of bread. She spent three hours looking for a chicken within her budget, and when she tried to cook it, it was painfully tough. Like so many stunt reporters, her body offered proof of her claims: "My head aches and my eyes ache with poor food and worrying over it." Meager breakfasts sapped her energy and, when she got home from work, she was often tempted to go to bed rather than cook a meal. By the fifth day, she declared, "No working girl can live comfortably on $3 a week. . . . It is a shame to ask a girl to do it." By the end of her experiment, all but two cents of her money was gone, leaving her nothing for an emergency doctor visit, a new plate to replace the one she'd cracked, or more oil for the stove if a cold wind blew in. On the final day, she accepted an invitation to dinner with a "girl bachelor" who bought a more expensive chicken that tasted much better. In addition, the paper held a contest with the prize being Banks's humble apartment, the one she'd obtained and furnished for the story, with three months' rent paid.

Banks insisted she hated this kind of reporting, found it "loathsome." Certainly, it would be hard to admit you liked something so universally condemned. And yet.

This life was more free than almost any other option. In the morning, a reporter might put on a corset, pull on stockings, lace up practical boots that could take her from Central Park to City Hall, step into a wide-bottomed cotton skirt that allowed for jumping on streetcars or chasing down an interview and wouldn't be ruined by contact with a little dirt. A short jacket went over an unfussy striped shirtwaist. A silk tie, like a man would wear, could be tied around the neck. She might put her hair up and back, and pin on a straw sailor hat that could provide shade and take a battering. Then she'd be ready to take off, like a tennis player, or a bicyclist, or the other modern women who peppered the *World*'s pages.

As she wrote in *Autobiography of a "Newspaper Girl"* about her New York reporting:

> As the days and the weeks went on I could even feel myself growing, growing in grace, growing in charity, putting aside such narrow creeds and prejudices as had been a part of my up-bringing, and were, perhaps, in their place and time, good and wholesome for the girl, but cramping, distorting, warping to the woman. Life! Life! Seething life was all about me. The life of a great city, its riches, its poverty, its sin, its virtue, its sorrows. . . . I entered it and, while I studied, became a part of it, learning how akin was all humanity, after all, and how large a place had environment and circumstance in the making a character and the molding of destiny.

It was the answer to those cold mornings on the Wisconsin farm, the monotonous existence she feared more than death by submarine: "A quiet life which was not life at all."

Banks, a savvy adult woman who calculated risks, made her own decisions, and lived with the results, belied the constant worry over naive young girls taken advantage of by unscrupulous assigning editors. In many fictional short stories of the time, heroines like Jordan's Miss Van Dyke abandon reporting for love of a man or family, but hundreds of flesh-and-blood women were making the opposite choice.

Proud of navigating the perilous yellow waters that lapped at her ankles, of standing up for herself (an ability she credited to her "self-assertive and combative disposition"), Banks finished up her series on $3 a week with satisfaction. Her next assignment seemed right up her alley, both meaty and decent. But it would threaten to drag her under.

O n New Year's Eve, 1897, the *Journal* funded a massive celebration. On January 1, all five boroughs would be joined together as one city: Greater New York. Flags, fireworks, clowns, horns, Chinese lanterns on sticks would pack the streets around City Hall and Newspaper Row. Searchlights and hot-air balloons would embellish the sky. As many as eight hundred singers would belt out songs. A 120-piece band would blare "The Star Spangled Banner," "Auld Lang Syne," and "Ode to Greater New York."

On its editorial page, the *Journal* metaphorically rubbed its hands in glee. On December 3, the paper trumpeted its accomplishments, along with its philosophy: "Above the boards and councils and commissions stand the courts, and by the side of the courts stands the New Journalism, ready to touch the button that sets their ponderous machinery in motion." It highlighted the paper's mottoes: "While others talk the *Journal* acts," and "What is everybody's business is the *Journal's* business." Then, days later, it taunted Pulitzer. The *World's* accomplishments were all in the past. The paper had become "timid and dull, as bankrupt in enterprise as it is in talent." The editorial writer, clearly channeling Hearst if not Hearst himself, imagined that in the *World's* shining dome "a sad and reminiscent and beaten lonely man will be sitting, listening to the *Journal's* triumphant music and the applauding shouts of the city far below, in the world of the present." It was personal. It was always personal.

Despite the *Journal's* glowing predictions of clear skies and moonlight, New Year's Eve was cold and rainy. The fireworks and colored lights lit up the clouds and reflected off the damp pavement. Gaps yawned in the parade where groups had dropped out. Some celebrants, drinking to keep off the chill, stumbled into the parade route, only to be herded back by police. The singing societies were hard to hear, but there was no lack of noise, with whistles and horns, and the bells of Trinity Church over it all. At midnight on the East Coast, the mayor of San Francisco, standing in California, pressed a button that unfurled the flag of Greater New York, marking the new city, but also the stretch of Hearst's empire, from West to East.

But Pulitzer was not up in the dome, pulling out his hair at the sight of the *Journal*'s glory, wincing at every firework explosion, watching the parade with churning envy. He was in Bar Harbor, Maine, with his teenage daughter, Lucille, who had been battling typhoid fever. She seemed to be making a recovery, but at 6:16 p.m., just as crowds gathered and organizers were debating whether to call the whole thing off because of bad weather, Pulitzer's secretary sent a telegram to the *World*'s manager. "Chief much broken," he wrote. Lucille had died, and for once her father's mind was not on the newspaper business.

ALL TOGETHER IN NEW BEDFORD

Do you believe that "woman is the weaker sex"?

Do you believe that the Fates intended that woman's scheme of life should be worked out in a place called Home, where she should rest secure from the hubbub and turbulent hurry of the working world?

If that is your idea of woman's existence, pay a visit to New Bedford.

—*Boston Post*, January 23, 1898

January 1898 found Eva Valesh (formerly Eva McDonald, pseudonym Eva Gay) on her way north to New Bedford, Massachusetts. The city had a rich history as a lively whaling port. In *Moby-Dick*, New Bedford appeared as a prosperous town built on whale oil. The mansions "came from the Atlantic, Pacific, and Indian Oceans. One and all they were harpooned and dragged up hither from the bottom of the sea," according to Melville. With the decline of the shipping industry and the move away from whale-oil lamps, though, the city turned to textiles along with nearby Fall River. Massive stone factories lined the waterfront along Buzzard's Bay, churning out fine cotton cloth. Nearby, ramshackle buildings housed immigrant mill workers. The bay shore bristled with piers, and, this time of year, ice crusted the water's edge.

But after declining profits prompted a 10 percent wage cut, almost ten thousand textile workers had walked out—a strike that some feared would spread throughout New England. On the first day, as strikers jostled outside the shuttered mills, boys threw rocks at one of the factories, breaking windows. Rumors swirled that the owners might bring in Pinkerton detectives to act as private security, that a riot was imminent. And just as in her very first reporting job in Minneapolis, Valesh, now on assignment for Hearst's *New York Journal*, was headed toward the heart of it.

As she braced herself for the tumult on the streets, Valesh was coming off her own tumultuous year. For one thing, her marriage of seven years was failing.

She had met Frank Valesh back in the Twin Cities, organizing for the eight-hour-day campaign. Frank, who had emigrated from Europe when he was nine, had drooping light eyes, a drooping mustache. A portrait showed him in a white hat and a bow tie, giving the impression of a clerk pressed into cattle-roping duty. There was no East Coast slickness about him.

And at the start, all this appealed. They shared political convictions, a love for books; they critiqued each other's lecture style. Eva Valesh wrote giddy newlywed letters to her reporter colleague Albert Dollenmayer, also a newlywed. She addressed him as "Friend Doll," saying that "marriage opened so full and new a life to me" and describing the "utter wretchedness" at being apart from her husband. Even though Dollenmayer seemed similarly happy, she wondered whether he could truly understand as, she noted, "I hardly think marriage makes the difference to a man that it does to a woman."

But even then, she could sense domestic life might conflict with other desires. With her marriage only a month old, she was already far away, in western New York on a lecture tour to promote the formation of a third political party. The People's Party aimed to support farmers and laborers and wrest power from large corporations, and she was the state lecturer for the Farmer's Alliance. Building her skills, speaking alongside senators, rallying the crowd, the work grew more fascinating all the time.

"It is a hard struggle," she wrote to Dollenmayer. "I hate to leave him and I'm unhappy all the time away, yet I can't bear to let slip the opportunities to get to the front." Her companions were impressive but not overshadowing: "I think without egotism that I could stand side by side with them and hold my own. Of course my ambitions are confidential."

Her ambitions may have been confidential, but they were, in fact, clear to everyone around her. She and Frank fought over whether she should return to the lecture circuit after giving birth to her son in the spring of 1892, a pregnancy that almost killed her. When Dollenmayer planned to stop by to offer congratulations, Frank wrote to say that she wasn't well enough to come downstairs. Would he mind postponing several weeks? (By then, he added, not only might his wife be better but the "baby being then considerably older will appear more intelligent hence more of a credit to this family.") As soon as Valesh was able, she arranged for her mother-in-law to help with childcare and went back to writing and politics.

They also clashed about where to live. She loved the East and missed the landscapes of her Maine childhood, the green lushness, the buttercups. While in New York State, she wrote to Dollenmayer, "I don't think I shall ever be content to live in the prairies again." But Frank seemed perfectly happy with Minnesota life. Like other journalists of her generation, Eva married young with one set of expectations of what life might offer, and then grew into another, more expansive, reality.

Finally, after years as a labor activist, in the summer of 1897, against the advice of many, including colleague and American Federation of Labor leader Samuel Gompers, she took her son, Frank, with her younger sister to look after him,* and moved back East to

---

* Fights over childcare in Valesh's family were intergenerational. She resented looking after younger siblings; Eva Valesh's sister resented dropping out of high school and moving to New York to look after little Frank. The sting lingered. "She was the most selfish and self-absorbed person I have ever known," her sister wrote in a letter after Valesh's death.

seek work as a reporter. Friends warned that some of these jobs were perilous for women. Assignments required haunting criminal courts. Subject matter might cause a "loss of self respect." But New York journalism once again dangled its lure, and she wanted to give it a try. She'd started to tell people her husband was dead, though he was alive and well, making cigars in the Midwest.

Now she was a reporter for Hearst.

The circulation battle between the *World* and the *New York Journal* was growing more heated, but the life wasn't as bad as people had said. Rather than dangerous and degrading tasks, she found, like other hopeful women before her, a lack of good assignments. Her stack of *St. Paul Globe* columns didn't have much weight. The *Journal* hired her as a "space" writer, paid by the article rather than a staff salary, the kind of position that left Elizabeth Banks broke before she signed on at the *World*. Colleagues poked fun at her unfashionable black lambskin coat. She worked from noon to midnight and found herself scrambling, always with the threat of being fired, under an editor who didn't have much use for women in the newsroom.

One day, after struggling at the *Journal* for months, she was sent to uncover the identity of a woman who killed herself by drinking carbolic acid on the sidewalk along Fourteenth Street. Unidentified bodies often had absorbing stories behind them, but they were hard to get. Young women drawn to the city (as she had been) often didn't have nearby families to claim them. Valesh considered it "an impossible assignment," designed to get rid of her. On viewing the corpse at the morgue, she got sick and, stomach roiling, sped back to her apartment. But after she recovered and tidied up, her luck broke.

On her way back to the street, she—always up to talk—chatted with the boy selling papers. She mentioned her hopeless task, adding, bleakly, "I'm getting nowhere."

"Oh," the boy said, "I know something about that girl. Go in and ask the druggist at the corner here. She tried to buy the carbolic there, but he wouldn't sell it to her. I'm sure that's the girl. Then she got it at a drug store down the street."

Not only did the druggist know her—Mamie Donahue—he knew where she was from. Donahue was one of a group of young women who hung out at the Florence Crittenton Mission, a house on Bleecker Street that held night religious services and offered rooms to young women, many of them prostitutes. Tired of a life Valesh characterized as filled with a "terror of work, of monotony, of subjection to authority, of the hospital, of waning beauty, of hunger, of contempt" and covetous of the flower- and hymn-filled funerals the mission provided, about a dozen girls, after a night of drinking, had cooked up the idea for a "Suicide Club." They drew lots, and the one who got the skull and crossbones had to kill herself by drinking carbolic acid before the next meeting. Two had already died.

At the mission, Valesh confirmed the woman's identity with the assistant matron then accompanied her to the morgue. If it's Mamie Donahue, Valesh told her, pinch me, but don't say the name out loud.

"I want an exclusive story," she said.

A Suicide Club, featuring a dead girl on a slab, body displayed for the writer and reader to peer at without shame, was just the thing to please the *Journal*. "She has good looks to recommend her. Even her dead face, showing as it does the burns of acid on lips and chin, is handsome. The features are regular and feminine, without conspicuous marks of dissipation, the hair is thick and the eyebrows are superbly arched," wrote Valesh.

She didn't receive a byline, but she established her worth, kept her job, and earned a reputation as the "suicide editor," a regular beat, though a far cry from the labor journalism she loved. As she commented later of *Journal* reporting: "It was gruesome work."

She weighed the pros and cons of staying. On the one hand, perhaps the constant emphasis on crime promoted crime, including copycats for particularly gory acts. Unlike in the Twin Cities, where reporters would wait for stories to land on their office desks, the cutthroat nature of New York journalism demanded going out and finding a story even when there was no obvious news. Reflecting on her experience later, Valesh wrote that readers expected the kind of drama that happened only in novels, so she and her peers faked details of clothing and facial expressions, keeping in mind that "these things must be done artistically."* On the other hand, the *Journal*'s motto, "Journalism that acts," echoed Valesh's own philosophy: "a great paper has a duty toward the country in critical times." Such a paper "may wield an enormous influence if the proprietor desires to spend the money and take the trouble to do so." For someone who shifted between journalist and activist from her very first assignment, it was a perfect fit.

But then in January 1898, she faced a new opportunity. Hearst himself called Valesh into his office to say he was sending her to cover the textile strike in New Bedford.

The summer before, more than one hundred thousand coal miners in Pennsylvania, West Virginia, Ohio, Indiana, and Illinois, frustrated by eroding wages, struck in dramatic fashion. A group of miners near Hazelton, Pennsylvania, protested, in particular, a new tax of 3 cents per day on employers hiring immigrants, a fee the owners passed on to the workers. The men walked out and marched from mine to mine, urging others to join them. A sheriff and his men opened fire on the strikers, killing at least nineteen men, all unarmed immigrants from Eastern Europe. The *Journal*, eager to align with sympathies of its readers and to support labor, reported on the dire poverty of the workers, the violent suppression of their protest, and the union's ultimate (rare) victory in extracting concessions from the owners. Perhaps things were changing for labor. New Bedford had the potential to be similarly explosive.

"Of course, we are a bit sensational," the soft-voiced, yet intimidating editor said. At thirty-four, he was still youthful, still with the center part in his hair, though his dandyism had been tempered by

---

* Though this goes against modern journalistic ethics, it is an aesthetic embraced by John D'Agata, a noted nonfiction writer. The debate over whether artistic license allows making up details in creative nonfiction is the subject of his book and the Broadway play based on it, *Lifespan of a Fact*. He told a reporter, about fabricating statistics and place names, "By taking these liberties, I'm making a better work of art—a truer experience for the reader—than if I stuck to the facts." I don't agree.

time. "Do you understand enough of the way we run our papers to be able to give us the sort of a story we want?"

She certainly did. She had been racing from Harlem to Jersey City to Brooklyn for months, tracking down details of contentious divorces and ferreting out dress styles of corpses. Even though Valesh knew she got the chance only because his star reporters were off covering Cuba, where rebel forces were making headway against the Spanish with much encouragement from the *Journal*, she was not one to let any opportunity slip away.

"Yes, sir," Valesh said.

In New Bedford, Valesh rushed to find scenes and interview subjects, as her New York experience trained her to do. She quickly recruited a heroine in Harriet Pickering, a thirty-three-year-old weaver originally from Lancashire, England. She had many traits Valesh valued, including courage and a seriousness of purpose. A widow, she was raising her twelve-year-old son to be a lawyer, a career Valesh imagined for herself, if her circumstances had been different. And when Pickering wasn't weaving, she studied economics and lobbied state politicians for labor-friendly legislation, often hauling a satchel of papers to support her arguments.

Valesh saw Pickering in action at the meeting of the Weavers' Union, not long after she arrived. The central issue in the strike was the 10 percent pay cut, but some weavers wanted to include reform of the "fining" system in their demands. While weavers worked for set prices per piece, like sweatshop seamstresses, if the cloth showed any damage, the weaver would be fined, her pay drastically cut for that item: even for an oil stain that could be cleaned off and the fabric sold as perfect; even for an error that occurred before the yarn reached the weavers' looms. In theory, the practice was outlawed by an 1892 statute. In practice, the law was ignored. And women, maybe because managers thought they wouldn't object, were fined much more frequently than men. "A man, you see," explained the treasurer of the New England Federation of Weavers, "has more ways of standing up for his rights. There's the ballot-box, for one."

Pickering stood up confidently and argued that objection to fining should be part of the protest. Tall and thin, pale from hours in the mill, Pickering preferred a severe black dress with white collar and cuffs, but it didn't lace in her spirit. If there was anything Valesh prized, it was the ability to give a good speech.

"Sit down!" a man yelled at Pickering.

"Not I," she replied. "Your Executive Committee know I am right, but they have grown timid."

Ultimately, though some complained the fining issue would complicate matters, her resolution carried, and Valesh made the debate the centerpiece of her early reporting.

Pickering wasn't the only woman the *Journal* highlighted in the strike's early days. All of a sudden, after being denied so much as a byline, Valesh's identity was integral to the story. The January 19, 1898, *Journal* splashed a large illustration of Valesh on the front page, showing her strong-jawed and serious, detailing her labor past, touting her as "the Journal's special commissioner to the cotton strike." Three

Eva McDonald Valesh

smaller pictures showed her in alternate guises: "labor agitator," "shop girl," "reporter." Her background gave her authority.

The strike offered Hearst and Pulitzer another battlefield and created a new opportunity for female reporters. In addition to Valesh, the *Journal* sent Anne O'Hagan. Not to be outdone, the *World* put its own women on the job: Kate Swan McGuirk, who grew up in nearby Fall River, and labor leader Minnie Rosen, an organizer with the Women's Branch of the United Brotherhood of Tailors, a Russian Jewish immigrant who lived in a tenement. A *World* reporter heard Rosen give a talk at the YWCA and offered her a job covering the strike, rushing her to Grand Central Station to board a New Bedford–bound train. Rosen's introduction to readers emphasized that she worked long days in a sweatshop and that her family members spoke only broken English, counterbalancing Valesh's expertise. Elizabeth Banks, done with living on $3 a day, also set out for New Bedford. Suddenly, instead of being the only woman covering a given story, all these reporters who'd slipped into the newsroom through the door of stunt journalism converged in one place.

The *World* would offer a female story from a female perspective, advertisements claimed: "The woes of the 4,000 women who are warring against capital strikingly told by women writers. Startling statements by labor experts. All in the great *New York Sunday World*."

Though nothing much happened, initially, Valesh made the most of it. Finding the streets quiet rather than roiling, she wrote: "Grim Silence Everywhere." Remembering the *Journal* style and her promise to Hearst, Valesh sought out examples of suffering, hoping to show the mill owners as villains. She visited a tenement with a large family short on food; the mother hadn't been able to go back to the mill after giving birth and losing the baby. In another house, suffused with anguish, the mother had died of consumption only the week before. Valesh visited an old man, fired when his eyesight got too bad for loom work, and ate pea soup with a family unable to add meat because the father was an invalid and they lived only on the mother's salary.

A follow-up on New Bedford tenement life went even further.

Valesh encountered an eighteen-year-old dying of consumption drawing "her ragged gown about her" and a four-year-old so neglected no
one had bothered to give her a name. Valesh asked for a glass of water,
only to find it had been shut off. In summary, though she'd seen the
worst of Paris and New York: "The New England mill operatives can
compass a blank despair and slow starvation not to be matched anywhere."

Other reporters offered images in a similar vein: The *Boston Post*
reported on a mill worker's pantry that contained only half a cabbage,
a handful of potatoes, and some chicory coffee; O'Hagan described a
tenement with plaster falling from the ceiling, calling the scene: "unutterable degradation—the degradation of dinginess, of forlornness,
of poverty, of absolute hopelessness"; Rosen described sickly workers,
with blue lips, in falling-down houses that "a howling wind might
blow into the river."

But this presentation of laborers as helpless victims was at odds
with much of Valesh's previous work as an organizer. Her speeches
had urged women to come together to use their power, and she always
stressed that she had been a working girl herself and kept her membership in the Typographical Union current. Her early stories built
on tips from young factory women who lived in the same boardinghouse she did. They were her friends. Like Bly, who got her first job
because of the *Pittsburg Dispatch*'s desire to add the voice of a genuine
working girl to its staff, she claimed to be the very kind of person
she wrote about. Now, in an effort to meet the *Journal*'s expectations,
Valesh faced accusations of being out of touch.*

Local reporters in New Bedford and Fall River were disturbed by
what they viewed as a New York invasion and an insult to their proud
New England community. These two clashing portrayals—workers
as victims and workers as heroes—didn't escape their notice. What

---

* Some of these expectations had been set by Bly's reporting of the Pullman strike.
Bly had asked town residents to point her to the homes of the poorest strikers, a request echoed by New York reporters' first attempts at covering New Bedford.

did this poverty have to do with the strike? they asked. The strike was only two days old. New Bedford reporters and editors pointed out that in much of the out-of-town reporting, the pictures and words didn't match. About the *Journal*, one local journalist raged, "Yesterday's story was mainly given up to women 'with blanched faces and wasted figures' who were dying here of cold and starvation. With the story was an alleged portrait of a woman who is a striking weaver. . . . The girl was superbly gowned in a walking suit which must have been made by a very skillful tailor and she wore a heavy boa of fur." The image was of Valesh's heroine, Harriet Pickering.

New Bedford was, coincidentally, also the site of the Lizzie Borden trial, and memories of the press circus lingered. One local reporter objected to the mill workers of New Bedford being portrayed as "a few degrees lower, if such a thing were possible, in the societal and intellectual scale than the wretched and semi-civilized Huns and Slavs of the mining districts of Pennsylvania and the West." New England reporters and editors were disgusted. Degradation? Worse than the slums of Paris and tenements of New York? The outrages of the *Journal* and *World* were endless.

And they had the perfect term to sum it all up and discredit the New York reporters: "yellow journalism."

The weavers and spinners also pushed back against these renderings. From the days of the Lowell Mill women's strike in 1836, factory workers had a tradition of standing up for themselves, of describing their own experiences, and they resented being painted by outsiders as pathetic victims. Alice Brierly had been profiled by the *Journal* as "the Oldest" striker, drinking cold tea, not wanting to light a fire because there was no food to cook, bemoaning her sixty years in the mills and wishing she were back home in England: "America's a cruel country to the work people." Not long after the article appeared, she and her husband arrived at the *New Bedford Evening Standard* offices, carrying the *Boston Post* and the *Journal*, which bore an unflattering illustration of an ancient crone. She was only fifty-seven, Alice pointed out, and rather than scraping the bottom of the tea canister, their home was one where her daughter played piano during the interview. Not to mention that their last name was misspelled.

Valesh, maybe stung by the criticism, maybe wanting a comprehensive overview of underlying causes, maybe tired of the sharp elbows as all the New York reporters competed for interviews with the same sources, maybe wanting to cover the story in a way that played to her strengths, left the quiet streets of New Bedford for Washington DC after only a few days. The important decisions were made far from the waterfront shacks or even the mill owners' mansions, she knew. She went to interview the president.

In her report (including a large illustration of her talking with President McKinley, which made even this journalistic triumph seem vaguely stunt-like), she recorded his approval of arbitration between management and labor, the eight-hour day, and a current bill restricting immigration (using the logic that it would provide higher wages for laborers born in the United States).

Two days later, Valesh tracked down Representative Nelson Dingley of Maine in the Hamilton Hotel. The Dingley Act, passed the previous July, hiked tariffs on many kinds of cloth, china, and sugar. In Dingley's analysis, New England mill owners had bought cotton relatively high and prices had dropped, leaving them with overstock and an inability to pay workers what they demanded. But southern competition was the real trouble, Dingley stressed, with southern weavers and spinners willing to work longer hours in worse conditions.

"Could you suggest any other plan by which the difficulty might have been tided over?" Valesh asked. Dingley proposed a reduction in hours with the mills running only a few days a week until the financial picture improved.

It was a very technical, wonky interview, and it's clear Valesh relished every minute. Suicide might have been her *Journal* beat, but labor policy was her forte.

Other reporters, though they started out following an expected script, also found their own perspectives, pulling away from the stunt reporter's increasingly generic tone. In response to Valesh championing Pickering, Anne O'Hagan offered Jane Gallagher. Gallagher, a weaver who'd also emigrated from Lancashire, demonstrated a quieter kind of resistance than Pickering, who shouted down her critics in the lecture hall. "Her bravery is not the Boadicean sort, that arms itself with sword and shield and goes out to battle with its foes. It is the rarer, more significant kind that resists oppression strenuously and steadily, and that, without any sounding of cymbals, announces its intention never to yield to injustice," O'Hagan wrote.

In O'Hagan's telling, when Gallagher handed in a piece of cotton cloth to receive the $1.17 she was due, she was fined 58.5 cents for a flaw. Rather than complaining, Gallagher declared: "I will not be fined." And when the mill's representatives laughed in her face, she walked out and then took them to court.

This offered an opportunity for the *Journal* to swoop back in. In keeping with its motto of "Journalism that acts," the paper offered to pay for Gallagher's lawsuit, previously funded by the Weavers' Union.

Ever the contrarian, Elizabeth Banks also developed her own approach. Her arrival in New Bedford met both praise and pushback. In a newspaper image announcing her assignment, Banks stared challengingly out at the audience, a set mouth softened by a cloud of wavy hair, above two smaller pictures of Banks dressed as a maid and a street sweeper. To modern eyes, it looks like a movie poster. She is touted as the correspondent with the most "interesting and unique personality," one who "roused all England by her campaigns of curiosity." Meanwhile, the New England papers looked askance at the idea that the stunting young woman "who obtained situations in the homes of the families of the English nobility that she might write up the members" would be paying them a visit.

Banks determined to provide the opposite of the expected gloom. She rebelled against the assumption that, because of the *World*'s reputation as "a friend of the poor workers," she would automatically side with the strikers. Her early articles were aggressively cheerful, going out of their way to laud positive aspects of the strikers' lives. She visited their homes and noted that, though the women might

**Illustration of Elizabeth Banks,
announcing her presence in
New Bedford**

make only $7 a week: "such clean houses they keep . . . and such an amount of comparative comfort as they manage to extract from it!" She continued, "I never saw such an intelligent looking and really pretty set of working girls as are now on strike in New Bedford."

The vice president of the Weavers' Union, William Foley, told her outright, "Write up some of the happy things in New Bedford. . . . Don't you go painting this town blacker than it is." So Banks complied, covering the church, Foley's lovely home, and his mother ("one of the happiest and brightest of old woman I have ever met"). A boy making mud pies in an alley was "Little Lord Fauntleroy." She toured some of the poorer families, taking on Valesh directly, commenting, "To compare their homes and the streets in which they reside to the slums of London and New York is to libel them and bring out their just resentment." The headline? "Jolly Strikers Who Don't Whine at Woe."

Once she put aside her boosterism, though, Banks offered some of the most valuable straight reporting on the strike; her articles are where one would turn to find out what was happening day by day. Banks also painted a nuanced portrait of New Bedford, a place where local women created a community-subsidized nursery for the babies whose mothers worked at the mill; one where the library hosted fifteen-year-old boys devouring the news from Cuba, readers demanding books on economics, and a gaunt man refining his poetry. When Banks received a letter from Staten Island offering a place as a servant for a suffering mill girl, she recorded the polite refusals of the young women who, though hungry, didn't want to leave tight-knit families. They saw such work as demeaning, just like their London counterparts.

Banks stayed at the strike longer than almost anyone else, offering increasingly complex analysis. It was the kind of reporting opportunity she'd been waiting for.

Kate Swan McGuirk, heroine of dozens of the *World*'s Sunday-page adventures, hewed to what she knew best: an undercover exposé. An advertisement for a new self-feeding loom claimed to eliminate health hazards of the traditional system where a weaver, when loading a new bobbin, put his or her mouth on the shuttle, and sucked the loose end of the thread through a small hole. The ad outlined the risks: "Weavers on all common looms choke their lungs with cotton fibre. When the filling is colored the effect is more or less poisonous, and in either case the health is undermined." McGuirk decided to see whether the old method was still in use and whether it posed a danger.

The factories in Fall River were still running, unlike those in New Bedford, so McGuirk waited outside in the cold dawn. The lit mill glowed against the dark sky. It wasn't that strange a scene; her family had been in Fall River for generations, and her grandfather had worked in the mills until late in his life. McGuirk asked one of the weavers streaming in with their lunch pails to take her inside and teach her the trade. She watched amid the clatter as a mother and two children tended sixteen looms. McGuirk tried threading the shuttle, inhaling, wondering about disease that might spread from equipment that touched multiple mouths each day. The resulting article in the *Sunday World* showed a lovely young woman, raising a shuttle to her lips, under the headline: "The Mill Weaver's Kiss of Death."

The local papers scorned the doomsday premise and the scare-mongering. They warned readers, "One newspaper woman couldn't find enough here to keep her busy, so she went to Fall River, and has secured employment in a mill where she is learning weaving."

But actually, she was right. Many women in mill families in New Bedford suffered from tuberculosis. The disease ran through weaving communities at higher rates than elsewhere. Decades later lung problems that weavers suffered from inhaling cotton fiber would be given an official name—"byssinosis." In 1911, Massachusetts banned the use of the "suction shuttle," effectively putting an end to the "Kiss of Death."

It's easy to share the frustration of the local journalists, to dismiss the New York reports as bumbling fabrications from clueless out-of-towners. And there's no doubt that New York editors sought out the angles most likely to infuriate their New England counterparts, to the point of saying the situation of textile workers in New Bedford, a city proud of its abolitionist history, was worse than plantation slavery. But the New Bedford reporters had their own reasons for wanting their town to look good. Perhaps they hadn't fully embraced the shift in their city from one with a noble whaling tradition to one where factory workers lived in substandard conditions. To call a piece of writing "yellow journalism" could be a legitimate critique. It could also be the equivalent of deeming an unflattering report to be media bias or manipulation.

The *World*'s Minnie Rosen defended her writing to a doubtful reporter's face. Against the accusations that those she profiled were perpetually drunk or lazy rather than strike victims, she said she hadn't met anyone like that: "These good people claim New Bedford's honor is smirched by its being known how bad off many operatives are. It is far worse to defame the hard-working women whom I have met by charging them with intemperance." She hadn't encountered lazy drunks; she had, however, met someone whose scalp had been badly torn by machinery and was unemployed as a result.

"There may be cases which have been exaggerated in the newspapers," she added, "but those which came under my observation are no newspaper tales, but stern realities, and in each case they are sadly in need of help, not sympathy," she added. Her articles aimed to trigger action, not emotion.

Though journalists were viewed as having clout, perhaps too much, women on the ground still struggled to marshal actual power. As the strike wore on, soup kitchen lines lengthening, daily rumors percolating either that the strike was spreading or about to collapse, Harriet Pickering's control began to slip. She wanted to organize the women whose interests—like fining—she saw as divergent from the men's. The union leaders were incompetent, she thought, to the point that mill owners refused to meet with them. She planned a meeting just for women, but on the chosen day, both sexes crowded the audience. And as she headed toward the front of the room, the janitor took her table away. She tried to talk over the yelling, catcalling, and hissing, but it was futile. The meeting was over in five minutes.

She tried again, this time at City Hall. Pickering had an idea about how to stop the fining. What if workers called the manufacturer's bluff? If an employee was bad, fire her. If not, pay her the wages she earned.

Pickering stepped on the platform and faced the restless crowd of three hundred.

"I have called you together to act upon a proposition of appointing a committee of women to wait upon the mill-owners in reference to the abolition of the fining system. I move that a committee of five be appointed," she started.

"I move we don't do nothing of the sort! It's the men's business to attend to such things. We must act in harmony with the union, and I move your motion don't be seconded, that's what I do," someone shouted from the audience.

"I am in harmony!" Pickering said. "None of you has worked so hard as me in the union. But I say if we women don't get to work and do something the men will lead us into a ditch. If the mill owners are to be approached we must approach them!"

Then, once again, her hoped-for meeting descended into chaos. Cries of "Order" and "Stop fightin'" echoed through the room. Chocolate caramels, passed out by Pickering as appeasement, didn't settle the crowd. Some threw them on the floor.

Eventually, unable to make herself heard, Pickering said, "If you don't appoint a committee, I'll go and wait upon the manufacturers myself!"

Outside the fractious meeting, a representative of silk-weaving mills in New Jersey waited. He was looking for weavers to train for positions that paid up to $20 a week, he said. This was better than chocolates. The women clustered around.

Banks, amused as she watched the whole fracas, noted, "Can one woman lead hundreds of other women? Not in New Bedford."

A while later, not far away in Boston, where girls threw snowballs at the statue of George Washington in the Common and papers reported gold in the Yukon, Valesh walked into the Massachusetts State House on Beacon Hill, a grand structure of redbrick and white columns, topped, like the World Building, with a shiny gold dome. Buildings with historic significance appealed to her. Giving a speech in an Illinois courthouse where Lincoln had spoken had been an inspiration.

Taking the notion of "journalism that acts" to heart, Valesh would be advocating for a law that she called the "*Journal*'s bill." It specified that if any pay deductions were made, the manufacturers had to give the weavers written notice. The weaver needed to see the flaw and agree to the amount of damage. Hoping to rely on legal training she'd picked up from her husband's night-school classes to argue for the *Journal*'s positions in front of the Labor Committee, Valesh entered a room full of mustached men, including AFL leader Samuel Gompers. Harriet Pickering was also there, opposing the bill.

Apparently, Pickering made good on her promise to go see the manufacturers and present her idea, one she vastly preferred to Valesh's. In her view, the fine system should be abolished, not amended. From Valesh's perspective, Pickering, the woman she'd once considered the Joan of Arc of the strike, had been reduced to a "pitiable object," doing the bidding of the mill owners by speaking out against the *Journal*'s plan.

Valesh gave her testimony, basing it on her New Bedford observations, followed up by Gompers and representatives of weavers throughout New England.

Then she turned to question Pickering, underscoring the irony of the weaver testifying for the manufacturers.

"You are out on strike in New Bedford?"

"That's none of your business," Pickering said. "Find out for your-self. We don't want you to come down to New Bedford and make it any worse and your bill here does make it worse."

A *Boston Globe* reporter wrote dryly: "The two women were evi-dently not entirely friendly."

Papers (other than her own, where articles—written by her—applauded her performance) mocked Valesh for her pushiness, her endless talking. At the end of the first day, when she suggested they close the hearing before the manufacturers had the chance to argue their side, everyone laughed. But she found her stride. On the last day, the *Globe* reported her argument straight.

In the final speeches, counsel for the manufacturers began by claiming the law was born of "sensational yellow journalism." He then lavished praise on Pickering, mentioning she'd come of her own voli-tion.

Though Valesh wasn't a politician or lawyer, lecturing was her expertise. She tied up all her questioning in the final argument, chip-ping away at the claim that workers who didn't like the fining could just leave: "We have always had the right to do that. We can leave or starve or throw ourselves into the river. We do not have to come to the manufacturers to have that privilege conferred on us."

While Valesh left the meeting optimistic, poised for success, thinking it was one of the most important things she'd ever done, Pickering had a hard time being heard anywhere after her testimony against the bill. The tone at the next union meeting turned threaten-ing as word of her appearance at the statehouse spread. "Choke her off," yelled one striker when her name came up. The Weavers' Union secretary urged female strikers to ignore Pickering and indicated that when the strike was over she'd be dealt with: "This woman carries nothing only a long tongue, and that tongue had better be shortened."

As the weeks passed with no concessions by workers or manufac-turers, some weavers left and looked for other jobs. Pickering won-dered how to get the union to listen. Eva Valesh awaited the outcome of her bill. More national labor leaders arrived, sensing publicity. Hunger and anxiety didn't soothe tempers.

The outcome was still unknown, except for this: as a result of all these reporters flooding New Bedford, each defining her own niche, the papers were full of women—far beyond aristocrats marrying in silk finery and "ruined" girls leaving beautiful corpses on the streets of New York. Paging through the New Bedford coverage, readers encountered a rare reflection of a society where both sexes contributed. There were female strike leaders and church organists, weavers who supported their entire families, volunteers who ran the childcare center for the mill workers' children, boardinghouse managers, teachers, and millionaire industrialists. And, of course, dashing journalists.

Far to the south, the *Maine* waited in the Havana harbor, moored to a buoy. The night air was hot, the sky cloudy, the whole place unsettlingly still. The armored war ship, flying the American flag, had been called to Cuba from Key West for what the Department of State termed a "friendly" naval visit. But the captain noted sullen faces in the crowd when he was on shore and ripples of tension among Spanish officers as he carried out the rituals of military etiquette. Sweltering, the captain put on a lighter jacket than usual and found, in the pocket, a letter he was supposed to have mailed for his wife ten months before. As the crew, forbidden to leave the ship, swung in their hammocks belowdecks, he penned an apology. The notes of taps, played with a flourish, echoed over the water.

Then, with sounds of gunshots and rending metal, the ship exploded.

In the falling debris, the splintered shards of the *Maine*, the deaths of 266 men, one thing became clear: Hearst would get his war. No one cared about New Bedford anymore.

REVERSAL OF FORTUNE

America is a big country; it is destined to become a great country, for there is manliness and vigor in the memorable phrases coined by celebrated Americans.

—*The Standard Union*, August 20, 1898

M aine Explosion Caused by Bomb or Torpedo?" ran the *World*'s February 17, 1898, headline. The front page announced that the paper had deployed a boat with divers to investigate the scene and floated a number of rumors—including overheard talk of a plot to destroy the *Maine*. An illustration of a ship ripped in two, bodies flung into the air and water, filled most of the space. The second page followed up with a rebuttal: "Blanco Reports to Spain That It Was an Accident" and a graphic of a cross section of the inside of the annihilated ship. (The paper also bragged of a circulation of 863,956.)

"Destruction of the War Ship Maine Was the Work of an Enemy," the *Journal* asserted, more definitively, the same day. It cited former New York police commissioner and now assistant secretary of the navy, Theodore Roosevelt, saying the explosion was no accident (Roosevelt later denied saying this). The *Journal* offered a $50,000 reward for the identity of the perpetrator. Its lead image, imagination-infused, showed a mine below the surface of the water, lurking under the unsuspecting *Maine*. Another edition the same day declared with a maniacal cheerfulness, "War! Sure!" and displayed a picture of an alleged torpedo hole in the *Maine*'s side. Both papers claimed evidence of a "suppressed" dispatch from the *Maine*'s captain to the secretary of the navy, speculating that the destruction was not an accident. (The cable didn't exist.)

Reverberations from the explosion soon reached the White House. On April 25, President McKinley issued a proclamation that war with Spain existed, and had been ongoing since April 21. The headline in the *Journal* took up a third of the front page and looked hand-drawn rather than typeset, giving the whole thing a precarious, shaky feel: "Congress Declares War."

The highly paid reporters, the ability to print lavish illustrations and bright color, the outsize type, the competitive hunger, all was unleashed. If anyone had overlooked the newspaper contest before, now it would have been unavoidable. Newsboys waved the latest edition, the word "Extra" glowing red. The *Evening Journal* printed forty editions a day, adjusting for each additional scrap of news. Headlines ballooned to cover entire front pages. Arthur Brisbane, Hearst's prize steal from Pulitzer, calculated the shortest usable words so letters could be even larger. In March, before McKinley's decision to go to war, a *World* editor, delirious with exhaustion and the stress of trying to beat the *Journal*, convinced himself that war had actually been declared and put out an Extra saying so. Copies had already hit the streets before the issue was recalled. He collapsed and died of overwork-related pneumonia not much later at age thirty-eight. The fact that information was hard to get heightened the drama. The Spanish government censored news of the island and rebel outposts were remote. One reporter, defying the news ban, was arrested by the Spanish twice, saved from execution only by American public outcry.

In some ways, even though war was deadly serious, the spirit of Hearst's time at the *Harvard Lampoon* lived on. In June, the *Journal* reported the death of the Australian "Colonel Reflipe W. Thenuz," killed in Cuba. Editors were thrilled when the *World* picked up the story—because it was a hoax. "Colonel Reflipe W. Thenuz," unscrambled, became "We Pilfer the News." But in their pleasure in the deception, editors took the wrong moral from the episode. Yes, the *World* stole from the *Journal*, but the *Journal* had made up news just to play a prank. And even for reports made in earnest, the pressure for a scoop meant inaccuracies crept in. An entrenched rivalry between two men was making it hard for readers to find an accurate picture of the war.

Opportunities for journalism and heroism abounded, but not for everyone. After a decade-long debate, in which the stunt reporters played an integral part, about what it meant to be a woman, coverage of the Spanish-American War concerned what it meant to be a man. Teddy Roosevelt—hunter, police commissioner, outdoorsman—had long been worried about American manliness and its decline. An advocate for war with Spain, he joined a regiment of young men eager to experience the first war of their lifetimes. Harvard students, Roosevelt's hunting buddies, cowboys, miners, all clamored to join up. In his self-mythologizing book about the regiment and its war experiences, *The Rough Riders*, he said applicants "possessed in common the traits of hardihood and a thirst for adventure. They were to a man born adventurers, in the old sense of the word." War made men.

Male reporters, too, took the opportunity to test their mettle. Novelist and journalist Stephen Crane, who'd imagined the plight of a Civil War soldier so vividly in *The Red Badge of Courage*, felt his lack of firsthand experience as a flaw. When the *Maine* exploded, he was in London and scrambled for funds to head back across the Atlantic to witness Cuban events. Reporters like Crane not only wrote about the war, they carried weapons, spotted the enemy, translated, and, allegedly, led a bayonet charge. The line between soldier and reporter was indistinct, like the lines between detective and reporter, factory inspector and reporter, coast guard rescuer and reporter. New Journalism had done its boundary-blurring work.

Hearst himself emerged from the editor's office and opera box to become a correspondent for his own paper. Wearing a Panama hat, he carried a gun and wrote about vultures feeding on corpses of Spanish soldiers. Never one to miss a publicity opportunity, he met with a Cuban general who presented the newspaper publisher with a tattered Cuban flag, for his paper's "services to liberty." He interviewed one of his reporters, who had been shot, and, cruising in a rented steamship, witnessed the wreckage after a Spanish naval defeat in early July. It was here that Hearst, spotting Spanish combatants waving a white flag on shore, accepted their surrender, took them prisoner, and turned them over to the military.

All these brandished weapons and troop movements produced few stories about women. The combat zones, the army camps, the brotherhood of the regiment: this was inviolable male territory. For its few female characters, papers retreated to feminine tropes. Rather than highlight rebel soldiers, medics, or spies who were women, the *Journal* touted Evangelina Cisneros, and portrayed her in the most stereotypical way possible—the beautiful girl extracted from a castle. In the *Journal*'s reporting, Cisneros was jailed for resisting a man's advances rather than for treason; it became a case of a woman protecting her chastity, not fighting for her country. In his introduction to *The Story of Evangelina Cisneros*, the book that came out immediately after the rescue, reporter Julian Hawthorne (Nathaniel Hawthorne's son) made no bones about what kind of story this was, an old-fashioned one: "We are indeed accustomed to finding truth stranger than fiction; but it is a new sensation to find it also more romantic—more in the fashion of the Arabian Nights and the Gothic fairy-tales of the Medieval Ages."

This wasn't the only story in that vein. Earlier, in February 1897, in a ship on the way back from a less-than-fruitful reporting mission to Cuba, the jaunty *Journal* reporter Richard Harding Davis* sat next to Clemencia Arango at dinner. The sister of a rebel leader, Arango had been banished from the island under suspicion of carrying messages for the Cuban fighters. In an article titled "Does Our Flag Shield Women?," Harding described Arango being undressed and searched by government officials at her house before she left, again at the Custom House, and again on the ship. In a huge second-page

---

* Son of Rebecca Harding Davis, author of the 1861 industrial exposé in short-story form, "Life in the Iron Mills."

illustration by Frederic Remington, a naked woman stands, her pale back to the viewer. Three men, fully dressed, hover ominously. One has a devilish pointy black beard. This strip search was an affront to American manhood, a letter to the *Journal* opined several days later, suggesting if "the American government declines to call Spain to account, it shows a lack of virility that ought to bring the blush of shame to the cheek of every American woman, and indignation to the heart of every American man."

But, as Arango told a *World* correspondent a few days after the article ran, the picture was wrong. She had been searched by women in a private room with closed doors, not leering men on deck. And the Spaniards' fears were entirely justified.

"It is true that I was actively engaged in the conspiracy as far as I could be," Arango gleefully confessed. She had delivered secret messages in the past and carried some on that very trip. Once in the United States, she acted as an agent for the rest of the war, supplying gunpowder and weapons to Cuban fighters, hiding bullets in the bottom of cans of milk. As in the case of the Evangelina Cisneros rescue, the damsel-in-distress narrative undermined women as drivers of their own stories—as rebels, as spies. Davis, disgusted and embarrassed, said that Remington's illustration didn't reflect what he'd written and swore off contributing to Hearst's paper. As it turned out, the only one who displayed Arango's body to prying male eyes was the *Journal*. Cuba itself became a maiden in need of rescue as Roosevelt and others emphasized the country's inability to take care of itself.

And many women writers, heroines of their own narratives months before, were pushed aside just as they were coming into their own. As Brisbane put it bluntly in an article about the *Journal*'s war coverage: "The fair young female journalist dropped utterly from sight or joined the Red Cross." He painted the scene in newspaper headquarters, emptying out as male reporters headed to the front: "Every beautiful newspaper woman declared that of all mankind she was best adapted to enter Havana in disguise, interview Blanco, get his views on the war and the enterprise of her newspaper, and return unscathed." But the editors, concerned about danger where they hadn't been before, said no. Battlefields were for men. (Brisbane may have been describing a conversation that played out in his own office, as he would have been the *Journal* editor making these decisions.)

The experience of Eva Valesh illustrates this abrupt shift in female reporters' fortunes. In early March, fresh from New Bedford, Valesh had finagled a spot on the *Anita*, a 170-foot private yacht that Hearst filled with senators, representatives, and their family members, and sent on a fact-finding trip. He called it a "Congressional Commission." At the Key West Hotel, before leaving for Cuba, the politicians toasted Hearst for his generous funds and activism. Valesh topped off the celebration with a final toast to the "New Woman in Journalism." But it was more hope than prediction.

Unlike in New Bedford, where her expertise was deemed important and her name appeared in headlines, Valesh's contributions from Cuba were strangely muted, and anonymous. It had been an honor for her to go. But back in the United States, when she slipped off a streetcar, hurt her back, and needed to take time off, the *Journal* quickly fired and replaced her.* With war as the main subject, her value to the paper had plummeted. One minute, her portrait graced the front page; the next, she was booted out the door.

At the *World*, Elizabeth Banks, once the toast of the Thames, struggled to get assignments on anything other than Cuba. War fever gripped the newspaper office. Reporters donned red, white, and blue neckties (they teased Banks when she accidentally wore a red and gold one, reflecting the Spanish flag; the men made her give it up, then lit

---

* Harriet Pickering also lost her job. A few days after the declaration of war, the Weavers' Union in New Bedford voted to return to work. Manufacturers made vague promises about restoring wages when the market improved. Then the spinners decided to go back. And in May, Pickering quit the Grinnell Mill after being fined 52 cents. "I have always advocated that weavers who do not do satisfactory work should be discharged, not fined," she said. "I did not intend to go back on my principles. I don't think the poor work was my fault. I am now looking for a situation as a double or single entry bookkeeper."

cigars with it), and editors shunned everything that wasn't a battle report or at least a colorful item about a society woman attending some
glamorous function with "To Hell with Spain" pinned on her skirt.
Banks's decision to go on salary seemed smarter than ever, especially
when she met a freelancer colleague aimlessly kicking around City
Hall Park. His salary had plunged from $150 to $7 a week.

"God pity those who could not at command turn their thoughts
warward and dip their pens in blood!" she wrote. It was particularly
hard on women, she noted, less likely to have military expertise or be
able to travel to the battlefield.

Other female reporters found themselves similarly adrift. Side-
lined, they cast around for new opportunities. Elizabeth Jordan, still
at the *World*, though eyeing her escape to an editor's post at *Harper's
Bazaar*, published a collection of short stories on newspaper life: *Tales
of the City Room*. Ida B. Wells-Barnett met with President McKinley, seeking justice for a North Carolina postmaster who had been
lynched. (She didn't get anywhere.) Kate Swan interviewed a wealthy
woman who, when her husband lost their money, launched a dress design business. Elizabeth Banks wrote a magazine story on "Sunday at
the White House." Nellie Bly, reconciled with her husband, traveled
Europe. Nell Nelson rocked her infant daughter.

Even those women who did manage to get credentials from the
US Army to cover the war struggled to do meaningful reporting. One
of these was Kathleen Coleman, a journalist for the *Toronto Mail and
Empire*, who'd emigrated from Ireland at twenty-eight, spoke with a
lilt, and wrote under the nickname "Kit." Over the course of her career, she had dressed as a man to report on seedier neighborhoods in
London, and now she was headed to Cuba. This, too, was sold to readers as a stunt, with ads that promoted "'Kit' as a War Correspondent,"
as if it were just another fanciful role.

But she found herself thwarted at every turn. The antipathy of
the male reporters was obvious—they ignored or actively discouraged
her. She understood that the presence of a woman, doing the same
work they did, devalued it. This was true even when she made herself

and her ambitions small, insisting to readers, "I am not here to detail the serious events of the war (which have not yet commenced) rather I am to write that light and airy matter which is ignominiously termed, by the trade, guff, but which is not always easy to manufacture." Coleman told one of the male reporters that she didn't want to write "in the grand style such as you boys write, but just the poor woman's side of the war, don't you see?"

But for weeks, Coleman was stuck in Tampa, the jumping-off point for soldiers headed to the battlefield, left behind when most of the male correspondents set off for Cuba in late June. She tried to get on a Red Cross boat, but they wouldn't take her either. So she wrote around the edges of the conflict, interviewing a chambermaid whose husband had enlisted and a recruit who sat on an ants' nest and stepped on an alligator his first day. In the heat of the afternoon, she retreated to her room to write. The envelopes she sent to her Toronto editors were fat with interviews and commentary, but it wasn't the war. Women writers had broken down all kinds of barriers over the previous decade, but "war correspondent" remained male terrain.

Finally, near the end of July a naval supply boat picked Coleman up with some Red Cross workers, but by then the war was virtually over. Spain had surrendered on July 17. Still, she made valuable observations about the little she was allowed to see, documenting the Spanish soldiers ill with yellow fever and typhoid in Santiago, and detailing inadequate medicine and transportation home for infected and wounded American soldiers: "one hundred and thirty-three men in every stage of sickness, living on rotten rations and apparently forgotten by the country for which they were suffering."

The Spanish-American War remade the world map and turned America into an imperial power. In the treaty following, the United States took control of Cuba, Puerto Rico, Guam, and the Philippines. McKinley had annexed the Hawaiian Islands, too. America, bold, muscled, masculine (in its own mind), took these countries behind its protective arm. The story became much more about American might than Cuban independence. Though its pages crowed about freedom and self-government for the Cubans, the *Journal* ran a headline the day after the surrender that read "Old Glory over Santiago." An anonymous reporter concluded, "The ceremony of hoisting the Stars and Stripes was worth all the blood and treasure it cost." (And the front page touted a circulation of 1,250,000.)

D espite the victory, reflecting on the Cuba coverage began to turn serious reporters' stomachs. It had been too breathless, too much flirting with panic. It was like the whole news business had been stricken with hysteria. Things clearly had been totally out of control. Whether or not Hearst actually told the artist Frederic Remington, "You provide the pictures and I'll provide the war," as he was alleged to have done, whipping up a passion for bloodshed was an unsettling way to sell papers.

The *World* staff, specifically, seemed ashamed. The publication had gone off the rails behind Pulitzer's back: "The paper is a jest, a travesty, a smear, a damnable injustice to the man that owns it and possible only for the reason that he cannot see it I should think," one editor wrote. In November, *World* editor W. Van Benthuysen served coffee and rolls and gave a speech to the staff, an effort to combat some of the slipping standards.

"We must heed it in every department, in every vocation that goes to make up this great newspaper. Absolute accuracy! Write it down! Have it ever before you!" It was supposed to rouse them to excellence, but the talk wandered, was repetitive, fell flat.

Those who felt wronged by Hearst and Pulitzer's form of yellow journalism took advantage of the pile-on to try to outlaw it. In New York, a senator proposed a bill that made it a misdemeanor to publish an indecent paper or one that "corrupts, depraves, degrades, or injures" the minds of the public, punishable by a $1,000 fine or a year in jail. California passed laws that banned publishing portraits or caricatures of anyone but a public official without their permission. One California senator suggested that the killing of a reporter be classed as justifiable homicide.

Other critiques bubbled up as well, voiced by reporters like Wells-Barnett and Matthews. Newspapers implicitly make a claim that they represent reality—the world as it is. Over the previous decade, these urban, northern papers expanded to include more single women, working-class people, and certain groups of immigrants. In another way, though, the reality portrayed was false. Concerns of Black citizens, Chinese immigrants, American Indian tribe members were almost entirely absent, except as curiosities. But these observations gained far less traction than the "yellow journalism" outrage.

A narrative began to harden that the press coverage caused the war and that *World* and *Journal* reports were marked by outrageous, deliberate fiction.*

Those who criticized the *World* and *Journal* most vociferously were, as was the case in New Bedford, rival newspapers. Yet their word was accepted as the unbiased truth. "Yellow journalism" became a cry of "fake news." Powerful people complained that negative reports were "yellow journalism." Politicians dismissed critical editorials, claiming "yellow journalism." Southern papers referred to accounts of lynchings as "yellow journalism."

At times, it seemed that objections had to do more with class (cheap newspapers aimed at the "masses") than subject matter. One writer pointed out in the *Arena* that there wasn't really much difference in the tastes of yellow journalism readers and its high-brow critics: "The latter simply prefer scandal, crime and combat that deal with imaginary or historical characters. They are indifferent to the tragedy enacted yesterday in a slum tenement; but they follow with vivid interest

---

* These claims are persuasively argued against by W. Joseph Campbell, among others. It's worth noting, too, that the worst transgressions of "yellow journalism" occurred during war reporting. But being a war correspondent remained respectable, while being a stunt reporter did not.

Caricatures of Pulitzer and Hearst in *Puck*, surrounded by readers devouring headlines like "Nellie Spy as a Flower Girl" and articles by "Fanny Fake"

the investigations of Sherlock Holmes; and thrill with the horror of Poe's tales or Balzac's gruesome stories or Stevenson's morbid, ghoulish, dual creature, Dr. Jekyll and Mr. Hyde." What was Boswell's *Life of Johnson*, she said, but gossip?

Even Hearst, who had seemed impervious to arrows of scorn, began to feel the sting. For the first time in years, he turned down stunt suggestions. And when, in 1901, the anarchist Leon Czolgosz shot and killed President McKinley, and the *Journal* was blamed (two *Journal* editorials several months before had hinted that political assassination could be justified), the paper defended itself but sounded chastened. Of its critics, the often-raging editorial page commented sedately, "The *Journal* has too sincere a sympathy for the President, too much self-respect, to reply to such men now." And in a rebuke in the language Hearst would most understand, circulation declined. He changed the *Journal*'s name to the *American*. In the early years of the twentieth century, Hearst continued to build his newspaper empire, buying two newspapers in Chicago in 1902, and a Boston paper and a Los Angeles paper in 1904. But his fervor for journalism at this juncture may have been more of a prop for a new passion for politics. The same year found him running for president and losing the Democratic nomination to Alton Parker, who would lose to Teddy Roosevelt.

B y today's standards, the crimes of the yellow journals were minor. Things that seemed outrageous at the time—large headlines, vivid illustrations, newspapers running holiday charity drives and sponsoring contests—are now commonplace. And what is wrong with a paper solving a murder or putting together a committee to investigate a bad law? These are things we now value, though they go under different names—activist journalism, solutions journalism, immersion journalism. But the notion that yellow journalism was uniquely terrible and worthy of censure lingers like ancient varnish.

Condemnations of "yellow journalism" included the work of the female undercover reporters, neatly folding their writing into a genre that some were eager to toss into the trash. After the war, the history of these bold journalistic experiments began to be erased. The task was made easier by the fact that, in the case of quite a few reporters, no one knew their real identities. While the anonymity of pseudonyms offered a refuge for stunt reporters, giving them privacy initially, it contributed to the ultimate disintegration and critical dismissal of the genre.

Sometimes the stunt reporters themselves were eager to assist in the erasure. In August 1898, Elizabeth Banks published a piece on "American 'Yellow Journalism'" in *Nineteenth Century* magazine, condemning undercover work and women's role in it. In particular, she blamed editors who would put a reporter in danger and then claim desire for reform as an excuse. Her essay argued that these stunts represented a man taking advantage of an inexperienced writer rather than, as was her case, a journalist choosing to write for a venue that paid well and hired the best talent. Her words echoed, reprinted in papers across the country: "I have yet to meet the woman engaged in even the mildest sort of sensational journalism who loved, indeed, who did not hate her work."

But even she would be dismayed by the eagerness with which her critiques were adopted, the way the journalism establishment was ready to rid itself of its tradition of female-led investigations. A way in to the profession had been sealed off, marked as a scandal or a joke. Several years later, in 1901, when Banks was trying to sell her book *Autobiography of a "Newspaper Girl"* to an American publisher, she sensed that her agent wasn't happy with the manuscript. He wanted her to stress the "seamy side" of the female journalist's life, but she resisted. She'd written the book she wanted and wouldn't make any major changes: "I approve of journalism as a career for women who have talent, strong characters and are obliged to support themselves. I would never dream of 'warning off' aspirants who had what we Americans call 'good stuff' in them."

Sensing the change in the tides, male writers studded their work with negative female journalist characters. A whiff of Hawthorne's fear of the "ink-stained Amazons" lingered. In F. Scott Fitzgerald's *The Great Gatsby*, reporter Ella Kaye used unsavory tricks to get an older rich man to do her bidding. As he confided in a letter to a friend, Fitzgerald based Kaye on Nellie Bly. In his novel *Active Service*, Stephen Crane, who worked at both the *World* and the *Journal*, reporting on the Tenderloin and doing stunts, described the sudden appearance of his hero's romantic interest, the actress "Nora Black," on the field of the Greco-Turkish War. The main character was surprised and embarrassed to see her. "But why are you here?" he asked, to which she coolly responded that she had been hired as a reporter for an opposition paper at a bigger salary than his. As he revised and republished his novel *Portrait of a Lady*, first released in 1881, Henry James made his journalist character Henrietta Stackpole increasingly vulgar, tracking the trashing of female reporters. One character commented, in the 1908 revision, "Henrietta, however, does smell of the Future—it almost knocks you down!"

The yellow did seem like it would stain the entire profession if reporters and editors didn't do something about it. Pelted by disapproval, journalism began to professionalize. Previously, pushback greeted the idea of a reporter getting a journalism degree or even going to college. *New-York Tribune* editor Horace Greeley had said, "Of all horned cattle, deliver me from the college graduate." The pressroom would provide its own education. And in the days of stunt reporting, it did. While many of the men in Pulitzer and Hearst's offices had a college education (at Harvard, more often than not), many of the women, including successes like Bly and Black, had only the most rudimentary high school coursework.

But suddenly, in the wake of the Spanish-American War coverage, formal training seemed like a good idea. Pulitzer, in particular, was passionate about the notion. By the turn of the century, a handful of colleges offered journalism classes, but his vision was larger. He had always spoken eloquently about journalism's potential; launching a school would be a way to promote these ideas and rehabilitate his image. Pulitzer laid out the concept in a 1904 article for the *North American Review*. He didn't want a course of study that provided a mere grounding in business or finance. Journalists are like artists and statesmen, he argued, "whose thoughts reach beyond their own livelihood to some common interest" and warned, "Once let the public come to regard the press as exclusively a commercial business and there is an end of its moral power." Students should learn ethics and study the great newspaper battles of the past to learn the lessons found there, Pulitzer wrote.

In many ways this tightening of standards was a good thing. Unregulated undercover work is open to abuses. Stories in the *World* and the *Journal* and papers they inspired could be highly exaggerated if not outright false. But like the formation of the American Medical Association with its explicit goal of discrediting midwives, and the institutionalization of the natural sciences, which labeled many women "amateur naturalists," while men grabbed government and university jobs as botanists, entomologists, and astronomers, the change erected financial and cultural barriers for all women and racial barriers for those who weren't white.

By 1910, Walter Williams, dean of the newly founded University of Missouri School of Journalism, advised reporters against adopting the role of "private detective" and writing anything they would not like their mother or sister to read, among other sins. Undercover investigations and first-person reporting were frowned upon. Distance and objectivity were prized.

Pulitzer didn't live to see the reality of his educational dream. He died in 1911 at sixty-four on his yacht in Charleston Harbor, after twenty years of trying to outrun his ill health. A year later, funded by $2 million of Pulitzer's fortune, the Columbia Journalism School plotted its September opening. But while the board hashed out details of curriculum, one pressing question remained: Would Columbia allow women? Were they part of this grand vision for the journalistic future? Things didn't look good: the newly appointed director had at one point given a speech against women's suffrage. Trustees were rumored to fear that coeducation would infect other parts of the university. The current building didn't have accommodations for women and the new one wouldn't be completed for several years. And planners seemed to be avoiding the issue.

"Was any decision reached on the question of admitting women to the school?" a reporter pressed the assistant director after an early board meeting. The assistant director brushed him off.

But, finally, Barnard stepped in. The women's college would provide female students with their first two years of courses, at which point they could join the men at Columbia. Pulitzer's journalism school opened in the fall with seventy-nine students, including twelve women.

After the era of stunts ended, exposés continued, though with a different focus, a different framing, and almost exclusively male authorship. Publications like *McClure's* and *Everybody's Magazine* ran lengthy articles by writers like Lincoln Steffens on government corruption, tainted food, and factory accidents. The constant questioning of institutions prompted President Roosevelt to make a 1906 speech condemning this branch of reporting. He lambasted "the man with the muck rake," a figure from *Pilgrim's Progress* who looked only "downward with the muck-rake in his hand." The man with the muck rake was so focused on the filth and grime, Roosevelt said, he couldn't look up to see the possibility of anything better. This attitude discouraged people from public life, promoted cynicism, and stunted the ability to recognize "worthy endeavor." Roosevelt meant it as a criticism, but the term "muckraker" had a long life, and soon became a badge of honor while its progenitor, "stunt reporter" became a badge of shame.

After stunt reporters faded, a new female-branded journalism genre appeared in its place: the "sympathy squad," the "pity platoon," the "gush girls," the "sob sisters." Rooted in Jordan's perception at the Lizzie Borden trial that women, banned from juries, might offer a different perspective on criminal proceedings, and in her experiments at the *World*, empaneling a "jury" of women to weigh in on newsworthy cases, "sob sisters" were female reporters who covered trials. They offered their thoughts and—as implied dismissively in the name— feelings. Winifred Black Bonfils* was one of the most famous, with her coverage of the 1907 trial of Henry Thaw for the murder of his wife's former lover (perhaps abuser) Stanford White.

It was another pejorative label, associating first-person point of view with an unseemly display of emotion, another thing women writers had to scramble to distance themselves from if they wanted to be taken seriously.

---

* She remarried in 1901.

Winifred Black Bonfils

The collapse of the stunt reporter genre might well have been a relief for some female journalists who came after. The door to the newsroom had been pried open by Bly, Nelson, Black, Swan, and others, and women who remained had access to more respected forms. Ida Tarbell, working as one of the few female "muckrakers" for *McClure's*, pored over hundreds of documents for her series about the unethical tactics of the Standard Oil Company. Her reporting resulted in the dissolution of its monopoly. Women continued to report, free to write about business or politics or organized crime with professional detachment, but were open to criticism if they adopted a unique voice or dipped into subjects more closely tied to their sex.

This catch-22 can be seen in the life of Willa Cather, who spent years as a journalist before writing groundbreaking novels about life on the plains—*O Pioneers!* and *My Antonia*, among others. After spending much of her childhood in Nebraska, she worked as a columnist for the *Nebraska State Journal*, then moved to Pittsburgh to edit the magazine *Home Monthly* in 1896, at the height of the stunt reporter craze. She couldn't help but be aware of these writers and the mocking of them. She then became managing editor of *McClure's*, the magazine famous for muckraking, which published some of her first fiction. After leaving journalism, Cather would go on to win the 1922 Pulitzer Prize, not for her inventive work about women but for *One of Ours*, a book with a patriotic male soldier as its hero. She was careful to keep her private world walled off from her writing. As Francesca Sawaya wrote of Cather's attempt to destroy her letters and other evidence of her personal life: "On the one hand, that action conforms to her notion that her work was professional and should be evaluated impersonally; on the other hand, it reveals her sense that her work would not be read impersonally unless she erased all signs of the personal."

IN THE WAKE

In the face of continual and massive discouragement, women need models not only to see in what ways the literary imagination has . . . been at work on the fact of being female, but also as assurances that they can produce art without inevitably being second-rate or running mad or doing without love.

—Joanna Russ, *How to Suppress Women's Writing*, 1983

On steamships from the South, after a disorienting boat ride of often more than twenty-four hours, young women, noise of clucking chickens still in their ears, arrived in this vast city. On the pier at the end of Beach Street, they blinked against the fish smell, the seagulls crying overhead, the sun sparkling off the water, a sea of unfamiliar faces. Stony roads led into Manhattan, lined with high buildings casting long shadows, the winds whipping between them.

Often, during the final years of the nineteenth century, Victoria Earle Matthews would be waiting, hoping to reach these young Black women before the others, also biding their time, who would pounce at the sign of insecurity flickering across a face or a repeated scanning of the crowd for someone who hadn't shown up. These included hansom-cab drivers ready to charge huge fees for a ride around the block, or to load up a person's luggage and run away with it; pickpockets running fingers over a jacket in search of a purse; pimps; agents of the employment service who would whisk them off to an apartment where they would sleep on the floor accruing debt for every night they didn't pay rent.

Matthews and the others she recruited to wait in her place on the docks often felt as if they were doing battle for these rural young women, unguarded against New York scams. The second half of the century had been characterized by women stepping off ships, trains, carriages into the big city and hoping to make their fortune. Matthews wanted to be sure vulnerable Black women from the South were met by a friendly face. The rescue missions were harrowing, she declared, "so brazen and defiant were the agents and ignorant and timid the majority of women who came up, that a woman had little power against the insolent white agents (men)."

If the woman getting off the ship, sometimes holding a toddler or two, insisted her sister would be coming to meet her, Matthews and her coworkers would wait with her until darkness made it hard to see, and the dockworkers shooed the women away. If the new arrival was trying to find her husband, only knowing he was somewhere in Brooklyn, they helped her search for the scrap of paper with the address tucked somewhere at the bottom of a piece of luggage. And if

Victoria Earle Matthews

no one ever showed up? Or the scrap had been torn away by a gust of wind? They would find the newcomers someplace to stay.

For Matthews, articles about home decor had turned to lectures on human trafficking.

Her 1898 speech at the Hampton Negro Conference—"Some of the Dangers Confronting Southern Girls in the North"—warned against the duplicitous employment agencies: "Let women and girls become enlightened, let them begin to think and stop placing themselves voluntarily in the power of strangers." The talk concluded with the suggestion that southern women might be better off staying in the South. But she argued against this position as well, writing a letter to the *Sun*: "The city does not need to throw back from her borders the flocking ignorant, but rather to bring to a sense of duty those whom her bounty, her patience, her indulgence has redeemed from the humdrum of rural common place." Her mother had once been one of these women running to the North after all.

To remedy problems she'd uncovered on her 1895 trip south, she had launched the White Rose Mission, a settlement house promising lodging and food, a chance to socialize, and a better start than the employment agencies offered. The mission provided a kindergarten and classes for adults, including a "race history" course taught by Matthews, featuring a bookcase for the use of her students. It contained a 1773 edition of Phillis Wheatley's poems, a magazine featuring the Harper's Ferry uprising, and an 1836 edition of *Appeal in Favor of That Class of Americans Called Africans* by Lydia Maria Child. As she told the *Evening Telegram*: "The White Rose Mission was organized for the single purpose of breaking up this traffic in Southern colored girls."

It wasn't smooth sailing. Money was a constant concern. Demand stretched the resources of the small building and volunteer staff. She would later use her ability to pass as white to rent a better facility. But at the docks, these concerns fell away as Matthews scanned the disembarking passengers for a woman wearing hope too nakedly on her face, eager to offer her a steady hand.

Matthews had long given up traditional journalism for activism, but as stunt reporting waned, other female journalists cast about for what to do, what role to play, in the new journalism landscape. The decline of the form that launched them, though few commented on it directly, presented a challenge. If they wanted to keep writing, they would have to find something that paid as well as the "sensational" articles previously in such high demand. With yellow journalism now out of fashion, could they turn their skills to new endeavors? For some, this involved parlaying their contacts into different jobs. For others, it meant personal reinvention.

In 1899, Elizabeth Banks did one last stunt. And it didn't involve lying to anyone's face or getting elbow-deep in a stranger's laundry. It was a campaign waged by mail. Two years before, a rumor had begun to swirl about a Vassar student. Right before graduation, Anita Hemmings confided to a faculty member that the speculation was true—she was mixed race. Her roommate had discovered her secret and demanded a new room. After a flurry of meetings, administrators let Hemmings graduate but not without a lot of hand-wringing and newspaper headlines. Banks had noticed that while northern whites congratulated themselves on open-mindedness and condemned atrocities in the South, they often avoided associating with Black men and women themselves. She explored these disparities in a piece for *Nineteenth Century*: "Says the Northerner, 'We have no place for the negro. We don't like him. Take him away!'"

Then she wrote, "Oh no! I forgot! The Northerner does not say this! He *thinks* it and *feels* it." So she put these liberal sentiments to the test. She wrote letters to several dozen colleges in the United States and England, presenting herself as a nineteen-year-old woman with light skin and blue eyes but with a Black ancestor. "Everybody took me for a white girl," she insisted to the schools. Would they admit her?

Results were conclusive. Western colleges suggested she might be more comfortable in the East. Eastern colleges suggested she might fit in better in the West. Oberlin College, one of the first to admit Black students, proud of its abolitionist credentials, admitted her, then recommended a boardinghouse in town run by a mulatto woman. Couldn't she stay in campus housing with the other students, Banks asked? She didn't get a reply. Meanwhile, colleges in England welcomed Banks's imagined student with the lack of prejudice Banks had noted when living there. In *Autobiography of a "Newspaper Girl,"* she drew her Black maid, Dinah, in the broadest strokes as a stereotyped caricature who spoke in dialect. At the same time, when Dinah wanted to return to the States, Banks advised her against it. In London, she said, Black and white servants went shopping together, attended each other's parties, shared sleeping quarters, something not possible in Alabama: "America is not a land of equality for the negroes, Dinah. You and I know that."

The college letter was a perfect Banks stunt, designed to uncover hypocrisy. But the conclusion she drew from her experiment was grim. After revealing the hollowness of the northern attitudes and acknowledging the violence of the southern ones—the deeply imbedded notions of racial inequality, efforts at voter suppression, and lynchings (though she claimed Ida B. Wells-Barnett exaggerated)—her takeaway was that Black people would never be accepted in America and should move. In her mix of patriotism and critique of her home country, she recognized that many white people in the United States were prejudiced, and then admitted she shared those prejudices. The finished piece was called "The American Negro and His Place."

At the same time as Banks was sending out her applications in fall 1898, Ida B. Wells-Barnett reentered the fray, though only months before, the birth of her second son prompted her to publicly declare she was staying home to commit herself to motherhood. Thomas Fortune, editor of the *New York Age*, who had offered her a job after she determined she couldn't return to Memphis, called a meeting to give new energy to the Afro-American League. He wanted Wells-Barnett to attend, and she did, leaving the baby with a grandmother while Wells-Barnett stayed with Susan B. Anthony in her redbrick house in Rochester, New York. The two maintained a relationship, though Anthony's organization, the National American Woman Suffrage Association, was increasingly adopting racist rhetoric in an effort to woo southerners to the cause.

Wells-Barnett noticed an odd tone in Anthony's voice as she pronounced "Wells-Barnett," one she interpreted as distaste.

"Miss Anthony, don't you believe in women getting married?"

"Oh, yes," Anthony said, "but not women like you who had a special call for special work. . . . I know no one better fitted to do the work you had in hand than yourself." The suffragist added that Wells-Barnett's activism and writing had fallen off since she'd married and, rightly so, as her thoughts were probably with her children. It was, Anthony said, necessarily a "divided duty."

Ida B. Wells-Barnett with her son in 1896

What Wells-Barnett felt she couldn't say in response was that organizations hadn't been able to fund her activism as Anthony had been funded. On her trip to Washington to advocate for the family of the postmaster who had been lynched, she'd run out of money, and she and her husband covered the expenses themselves. She needed more support, so an organization like the Afro-American League seemed like a good idea. At the meeting she was elected secretary, and commented, sounding both resigned and energized, "despite my best intentions, when I got back home to my family I was once again launched in public movements."

First, the tool to measure wind speed blew away. Then the rain gauge went. Then everything on the roof. The Local Forecast official watched in increasing anxiety as his instruments vanished, one by one. Sunshine recorders, thermographs, clocks—all gone. At John Sealy Hospital, patients grabbed their bedding to keep it from floating away. Winds stripped the roof off the Tremont Hotel and tossed bricks and stones "like they were little feathers," according to one guest.

In the first few hours after the hurricane tore through Texas's barrier islands in September 1900, killing six thousand people, it was "as easy to get into Galveston . . . as to Mars," according to Winifred Black, who had rushed to the scene to report for Hearst. Journalists were banned. But she tucked her hair under a boy's cap, stepped into boy's shoes, heaved a pick on her shoulder, said she was a construction worker, and climbed into a small boat headed from the mainland across the bay.

On the deck, they moved over the water, now calm and eerily quiet with stars overhead. As the boat approached Galveston, bodies floated by. When it landed, the city was dark, the ground "slimy with the debris of the sea." Picking her way past pools in the middle of streets and the campfires of the newly homeless, holding her breath against the smell, Winifred talked to the survivors. She expected tears, but everyone seemed numb. At a hotel, the clerk mechanically repeated there were no rooms, then someone else said there were plenty of rooms, just no water.

Her dispatches, the first from the wrecked city, showed the country the flooded homes, the drowned children. She reported on the official response, interviewing a US marshal, who admitted there was nothing they could do with the bodies but stack them in piles and burn them. The city was under martial law, and he had stationed men on street corners to shoot looters. (Disconcertingly, she repeated his assertion that none of the looters were Americans, but rather "negroes" and southern European immigrants.) She interviewed the mayor, who commandeered some able-bodied residents for cleanup and sent others to feed themselves at relief stations. She talked with a general who was dismayed at the appearance of a woman on the scene. He requested she ask her readers to donate money and disinfectants. Most of all, she reported the shock in the wake of a large-scale natural disaster. At the Aziola Club across the street from the hotel, she met a man who had been stuck under a pile of debris for four hours while friends walked past: "He told us what he was thinking about as he lay there with a man pinned across his chest and two dead men under him. He tried to make his story amusing and we all tried to laugh."

After filing her stories in the middle of the night through a telegraph office in Houston, Winifred Black returned to her hotel, where stacks of telegrams awaited her, detailing the supplies that were on their way. Now that she'd dressed as a man and reported on a disaster, Hearst asked her to organize the relief effort. And she did, rallying to his cause as ever, arranging for cots in a high school to house the homeless, buying dishes, meeting doctors from Chicago at the Houston train station. It was a new century, coming at the country like a wall of water set to unmoor the past, requiring roles as yet unimagined, and she was ready to take them on.

VANISHING INK

Our journalism has accomplished more than can now be estimated; in fact not until careful biographers make special studies drawn from the lives of the pioneer journalists, shall we or those contemporary with them ever know the actual meed of good work accomplished by them under almost insurmountable difficulties.

—Victoria Earle Matthews

In 1965, a hundred years after Elizabeth Banks, Elizabeth Jordan, and Kate Swan were born, Truman Capote stunned readers with the story of two men who killed an entire family in Kansas for a profit of only a few dollars. The series started with the Clutters going about an ordinary day—baking a cherry pie, feeding a horse an apple core—on a collision course with two disgruntled men who'd heard jailhouse rumors of a rich farmer and his full safe. Magazines throughout the 1950s and '60s, flush with cash in the way New York newspapers had been in the 1890s, paid reporters to do in-depth, risky, expensive stories, and Capote launched the years-long project with *New Yorker* money. He called the book that resulted, *In Cold Blood*, a "nonfiction novel," a genre that applied journalism to "a serious new art form." He interviewed the convicts extensively in prison and watched their execution, taking many of the techniques of sensational nineteenth-century journalism and rebranding them as art.

In Cold Blood begat a New Journalism, tinged with amnesia, and not just in the reuse of an old journalistic term. It relied on many innovations of the late nineteenth-century reporters without acknowledging they'd even existed. In a 1972 article for *Esquire* ("The Magazine for Men"), reporter Tom Wolfe expressed his frustration with an establishment journalism promoted by journalism schools with their focus on distanced objectivity. He found it staid and boring. The writers he liked, by contrast, were taking on what literary novelists of his day avoided: the social life of the great cities. They seized the mantle of realist authors like Dickens to capture the popular imagination: "By trial and error, by 'instinct' rather than theory, journalists began to discover the devices that gave the realistic novel its unique power, variously known as its 'immediacy,' its 'concrete reality,' its 'emotional involvement,' its 'gripping' or 'absorbing' quality." The writing he most admired could be termed "stunts": John Sack going through army infantry drills, George Plimpton training with the Detroit Lions, Hunter S. Thompson hanging out with the Hells Angels. But Wolfe did what the stunt reporters could never do—called this kind of work literature, called it good. In his nonfiction manifesto the next year—*The New Journalism*—he outlined the attributes he thought of as central to this form—a story told in scenes, a distinct point of view, ample dialogue, and use of status detail (which he defined in the *Esquire* piece as "the everyday gestures, habits, manners, customs, styles of furniture, clothing, decoration" that his subjects used to mark their social rank). It was the kind of writing Bly did so well.

One of the authors he held up as an example was Joan Didion, whose reporting on the Haight in San Francisco during the late 1960s had similarities to that of Nelson and Valesh as they visited tenements in New York and New Bedford. The stunt reporters' language isn't as rich—Didion pens an unmatched sentence—but the approach is similar. In 1895, in one of her first stories for the *New York Journal*, Winifred Black wrote of a five-year-old dying of alcoholism—a ruined liver—in the hospital: "Lucia stood and watched the nurse with lack-lustre eyes. When I rose to go she held out her little hand. It shook like the hand of a man in the palsy." Black then visited the family in their tenement home and summarized the conversation. The parents said, about the children: "Why should they not have a little sup of good wine now and then, eh, to warm the blood? . . . Too much, that is bad, but who would give a baby too much whiskey? A drop now and again to soothe it? Ah, yes, that was without a doubt, the best." In "Slouching Towards Bethlehem," Didion wrote about a California five-year-old: "I see a child on the living-room floor, wearing a reefer coat, reading a comic book. She keeps licking her lips in concentration and the only thing off about her is that she's wearing white lipstick.

'Five years old,' Otto says. 'On acid.'"

The quiet shock and condemnation are the same.

The voice-driven first-person narration that Wolfe championed in the 1970s, though not as new as he claimed, combined with effects of the women's movement and the civil rights movement to form another strand of this narrative-based nonfiction writing. The personal was political and, thus, worthy of notice. People who were not famous began to write about their lives. These works tended to be distinct from traditional "autobiographies" in that they skipped the parade of accomplishments in the lives of great men—college, marriage, career—and focused on telling stories. They were memoirs. Maxine Hong Kingston wrote about the ghosts of the past that haunted her Chinese American childhood. Maya Angelou wrote about navigating racism and being assaulted as an eight-year-old. Annie Dillard described a year spent looking closely, ecstatically, at Tinker Creek in rural Virginia. Many of these memoirists were women, and so memoir became another "not quite" literary form. It was too popular, too feminine. In Francine Prose's *New York Times* review of *The Glass Castle* by Jeannette Walls, she described the "sensibility, the tonal range, the lyrical intensity and imaginative vision—that distinguish the artist from the memoirist," and concluded, "*The Glass Castle* falls short of being art, but it's a very good memoir."

In the 1990s, building on New Journalism and increasing interest in memoir and personal essay, MFA programs began offering, in addition to degrees in fiction and poetry, degrees in "creative nonfiction." In his scathing article about the upstart genre, James Wolcott in *Vanity Fair* complained of the "slow drip of petty disclosure" and the "big, earnest blob of me-first sensibility." He dubbed Lee Gutkind "the Godfather behind Creative Nonfiction" after Gutkind started an MFA track in creative nonfiction at the University of Pittsburgh, one of the first in the country. Once again, those credited with launching the genre were male, though many of the most successful practitioners were female. Meanwhile, muckraking had turned into investigative journalism, the most hard-hitting, respected form, generally coded as man's work. Textbooks cited novelist Upton Sinclair and other male writers as its progenitors.

For example, in his book of interviews (and declaration of a new genre), *The New New Journalism*, Robert S. Boynton critiqued Wolfe for ignoring the debt of New Journalism to the reporting of the late 1890s. The introduction of *The New New Journalism* gave an overview of journalism history, praising nineteenth-century writers' "artfully told narrative stories about subjects of concern to the masses," ability to draw an "accurate, sympathetic portrait of the 'vicissitudes' of city life," experiments with dialogue and perspective, and "muckraking exposés." Who gets credit for all this? Jacob Riis, Stephen Crane, and Lincoln Steffens.

Despite this genesis narrative for artistic nonfiction, some did acknowledge the contributions of yellow journalism in general and stunt reporters specifically, though only in the most oblique and slighting ways. To reviewer Sol Yurick, Capote's interviews with convicts sounded familiar. Yurick wrote that *In Cold Blood*, rather than representing a new field, was "in the best tradition of newspaper sob sisterism wedding to Southern Gothic prose." Even the title, he said, is nothing more than "sensational headline imagery." Both descriptions are meant as insults.

While "objective journalism" had been promoted by journalism programs as the answer to the intimate, subjective accounts of the stunt reporters, this, too, was being questioned by the New Journalists. Hunter S. Thompson, who roared onto the literary stage in drug-fueled, formally explosive reporting on being beaten up by motorcycle gangs and infiltrating an antidrug conference in Las Vegas while on LSD, was lauded as inventor of "gonzo journalism"—another new style. He protested vehemently against the idea of objectivity, writing in *Fear and Loathing on the Campaign Trail '72*, "Don't bother to look for it here—not under any byline of mine; or anyone else I can think of. With the possible exception of things like box scores, race results, and stock market tabulations, there is no such thing as Objective Journalism. The phrase itself is a pompous contradiction in terms." Thompson also commented on New Journalism, the form Wolfe claimed to have pioneered, "The only reason Wolfe seems 'new' is because William Randolph Hearst bent the spine of American journalism very badly when it was just getting started."

The traditional account of the genesis of investigative journalism and creative nonfiction obscures not only contributions of 1890s reporters but also innovative works like Zora Neale Hurston's 1935 *Mules and Men*. Hurston, who trained as an anthropologist at Barnard, learned the tools of objectivity. Then she turned what she termed the "spy-glass" of her discipline on her own community, the predominantly Black town of Eatonville, Florida, where she had grown up. In the introduction she wrote, "I hurried back to Eatonville because I knew that the town was full of material and that I could get it without hurt, harm or danger." Stressing that her subjects would tell her truths they would never reveal to an outsider, she studied her hometown, starting by drinking a concoction that made the top of her head fly off and cadging an invitation to a party. The story she told was personal, revealing of town and self. No one else could have gained access or told the tale.

Maybe all claims of minting new literary genres require a certain truncation of the past. But skipping the work of female nineteenth-century reporters is a particularly dramatic oversight. So many of these supposed recent literary breakthroughs can trace their roots all the way back to seeds shoveled into the soil by Bly, Black, Nelson, Swan, Valesh, and Wells. Even at the most ragged edges of the genre, there is no more experimental personal essay than the listing of causes of lynching in Ida B. Wells-Barnett's *A Red Record*: "Hanged for steal-ing hogs," "Lynched because they were saucy," "Lynched for no of-fense." It goes on and on.

Undercover experimentation is ongoing, even as knowledge of the original stunt reporters has faded. For aspiring journalists in the twentieth and even the twenty-first centuries, like those in the nineteenth, it continues to be a way in. And it continues to pose challenges in terms of value and respect.

In 1963, as a freelance writer seeking to gain a foothold in the field, Gloria Steinem responded to an ad seeking "pretty and personable" women between twenty-one and twenty-four. The ad promised glam-our, travel, and $200 to $300 a week for those selected to portray that iconic image of 1960s sex appeal—a Playboy Bunny.

In a shorthand, diary-like narration, she charted the development of Marie Catherine Ochs (a pseudonym taken from a family name) and her experience at the Playboy Club. Using a lighthearted tone, she picked apart the subtle humiliations that made up the Playboy universe. On her way to apply, a building guard clucked at her, "Here bunny, bunny, bunny." At the job interview, when she offered to talk about Ochs's past, so carefully created, the Bunny Mother told her: "We don't like our girls to have any background." A mandatory doctor visit included testing for venereal disease.

As earlier stunt reporters did, Steinem added up the cost to the employees of this allegedly lucrative job: $2.50 per day for costume cleaning, $5 for tights, $8.14 for false eyelashes, three quarters of an inch long. The advertised salary was impossible to reach.

When the piece came out in *Show* magazine, under the title "I Was a Playboy Bunny," Steinem at first regretted it. She was striving to launch a literary career, and the image of her in long ears and a bunny tail overshadowed all her other work, including an article she was particularly proud of about the development of the contraceptive pill. In 1960s culture, like the 1890s, presenting as the wrong kind of woman carried risks. You could be sexy or significant, have a body or a brain. This story and the photos put her on the wrong side of the divide. (A divide that she had internalized. She wrote later: "Though I identified emotionally with other women, including the Bunnies I worked with, I had been educated to believe that my only chance for seriousness lay in proving my difference from them.") Male reporters leered. An assignment to investigate the United States Information Agency was given to someone else. Instead, editors suggested she disguise herself as a call girl and report on prostitution. A Playboy Club fan made repeated, obscene phone calls. The decision seemed like a career-ending mistake.

But, over time, Steinem's opinion changed. "Eventually, dawning feminism made me understand that reporting about the phony glamour of exploitative employment practices of the Playboy Club was a useful thing to do. Posing as a call girl (which I didn't do because I found the idea both insulting and frightening) would have been an assignment worthy of Nellie Bly," she wrote in her essay collection *Outrageous Acts and Everyday Rebellions*. And she included "I Was a Playboy Bunny" in the anthology, one of the few pieces that made the cut from her early career.

In the late 1990s, long after Steinem had metamorphosed into a different kind of icon, journalist Barbara Ehrenreich wondered how single mothers pushed into the labor market by welfare reform might get by on minimum wage.

"Someone ought to do the old-fashioned kind of journalism—you know, go out there and try it for themselves," she mused to her editor over lunch. He agreed, and then suggested that the "someone" should be Ehrenreich.

In the resulting book, *Nickel and Dimed, on (Not) Getting By in America*, the reporter spent months serving meat loaf and iced tea at a hotel restaurant, scrubbing floors with a cleaning service, sorting summer dresses at Walmart. Like Nell Nelson, she kept careful accounts, recording apartment rents, uniform costs, and the occasional fast-food lunch. Like Bly, she documented the physical toll, the back strain, the persistent rashes. And like Banks, who attempted to live on a factory-woman's wage of $3 a week, she concluded it couldn't be done: "Something is wrong, very wrong, when a single person in good health, a person who in addition possesses a working car, can barely support herself by the sweat of her brow."

Nellie Bly, in particular, inspired decades of female journalists. In her memoir *In the Darkroom*, Susan Faludi, author of *Backlash: The Undeclared War Against American Women* and *Stiffed: The Betrayal of the American Man*, among other books, wrote that as a child, journalism came to her early. "I perceived it, specifically, as something I did as a *woman*, an assertion of my female independence," she wrote. Courageous reporters from history loomed large in her youthful imagination: "In my schoolgirl fantasies, the incarnation of heroic womanhood was Nellie Bly exposing the horrors of Blackwell Island's asylum for women."

And, if not Bly specifically, the can-do "girl reporter" character Bly created lingers in the mind of almost every female reporter I know. She lives on in comic-book heroines, like Lois Lane, who disguised herself as a rich widow to report on the Playboy Poisoner, and Brenda Starr, who went undercover to sneak into a party and interview a mysterious baron. Their long legs and flying skirts were prefigured by the illustrations of Kate Swan and Helen Dare leaping across the pages of the Sunday papers. In fact, the role of "girl reporter" became almost a superhero, smoothing out the ambiguities of the real women who did the job. It was a loss of complexity, but superheroes have their purpose.

The idea of going undercover, adopting another identity, hearing what you are not supposed to hear, retains a sinuous power. It particularly appeals to the hypocrisy-exposing instincts of the young. One friend of mine, Mara Hvistendahl, now a Pulitzer-nominated foreign policy reporter, went undercover the year after graduating from Columbia Journalism School. Nannying and waitressing to pay the bills, she also held down an unpaid magazine internship and hoped to end up as a successful freelancer. It was hard to break into the glossy magazines with only clips from a second-tier newspaper, though.

But when she heard that strip clubs were hiring in anticipation of the 2004 Republican National Convention at Madison Square Garden, this seemed like her chance. Inspired by the work of Ehrenreich in *Nickel and Dimed* and Ted Conover in *Rolling Nowhere: Riding the Rails with America's Hoboes*, she asked herself: Why not apply as a strip club server and see what the Republicans—selling themselves as the party of family values—were up to after hours?

For the week of the convention, aided by No Doze, she interned at the magazine during the day and took shifts at the strip club each night. Serving drinks and taking notes, she sidestepped energy company lobbyists looking for a twosome and tallied lap dances requested by those decked in flag-patterned ties. Then she rushed home at four a.m. to Google the house committees of her customers, type up her observations, and send them off to the *Village Voice*'s blog, only to get up a few hours later and do it all over again.

It was a cold (thermostats were set for men in suits), exhausting week, complete with a bout of food poisoning. And yet.

"As I look back on it, it was a good piece. It was a good way to try out my writing," she told me. Her posts were picked up by high-traffic sites. Her parents proudly shared them with their friends. The pieces led to editors getting in touch and additional assignments for bigger outlets.

While she rarely goes undercover now, the skills are the same ones used elsewhere in her reporting life. "I do enjoy going deep into those other worlds," she told me. "You slip into these roles and people forget that you're there."

But a century after the stunt reporters, women's undercover work is often still not taken seriously, even if the disguise is much more fraught than a bunny costume. In 2011, journalist Suki Kim went undercover in North Korea, hiring on as an unpaid teacher at the Pyongyang University of Science and Technology, a school run by American evangelicals with permission of the North Korean government. She had been covering the country for ten years by that point, and had come to the conclusion that disguise was the only way to get at the truth of what she described as "a world of deception." For six months, she taught the sons of the North Korean elite and hid her notes in her lesson plan, typed then erased her reporting on her laptop, after saving it on a USB drive that she carried with her all the time. The book that resulted, *Without You There Is No Us*, documented the stunted lives of her students as they navigated outdated technology and propaganda and detailed the regime change as leader Kim Jong-il died and his son Kim Jong-un took over.

But when she returned, thankful to have survived, her project met a wave of criticism. Instead of "undercover reporting," it was called "lying." One *New York Times* headline infantilized her project as "Tales Told Out of School." Reviewers scrambled to term it anything but investigative journalism: a North Korean defector's tale (Kim wasn't North Korean or a defector; she was born in South Korea and educated in the United States); the journey of a woman finding herself; and, in the phrasing of one foreign policy expert, a "kiss-and-tell" memoir. Over her objections, and with the goal of goosing sales, the publisher had categorized the book as a memoir, a label associated with high readership and little respect. As a memoirist, Kim was ineligible for journalism prizes and fellowships and wasn't considered to be a North Korea expert. She had done something no one else had, infiltrated this incredibly secretive country after a decade of planning, reported from inside for six months, and no one wanted to talk about the subject matter, just critique her methods. The attacks mystified her. It took another female writer, Adrian Nicole LeBlanc, to point out to her that the book's reception might have to do with its placement in the female-inflected genre of memoir. (As well as the fact that, as Kim would come to realize, she was an Asian writer in a field dominated by white experts whose skin color was read as "objective.")

The frustrations came to a head at the 2017 Investigative Reporters & Editors Conference in Phoenix. Kim sat on an undercover reporting panel with Shane Bauer, who had disguised himself as a guard

at a private prison in Louisiana for an article in *Mother Jones*, and Ted
Conover, whose undercover experiments included *Newjack: Guarding
Sing Sing*. Both men had won multiple journalism awards; Conover
had been nominated for the Pulitzer. Throughout the session, the
moderator, an investigative reporter for the *Toronto Star*, ignored Kim
and aimed his questions at Bauer and Conover. When she mentioned
that at a previous journalism conference, she had been dismissed as
"that girl," he followed up by saying, "Great insights from 'that girl.'"
Finally, when the moderator, lauding Bauer and Conover for risking
their lives in the pursuit of the truth, asked the two men what would
have happened if they had been caught, Kim grabbed the microphone
and mentioned that, in her case, if she wasn't executed, she would have
been imprisoned for life.

"You're a little crazy. Tell the truth. That's crazy," the moderator
said.

"I have been described as a crazy girl," Kim answered, composed,
though she was seething, and added that if she were a man, she would
be called "brave." The applause and cheers were gratifying, as were
conversations with women who came up afterward to thank her for
speaking out.

But the sense of betrayal by her profession still haunts her. "I was a
published author and, to be immersed, I courted that organization for
three years before I jumped into North Korea," she said of the school
where she taught. "It's not like I was some naive girl who stumbled
there to teach English then came home to write about it, which is how
it was viewed. No one gave credit that I actually planned it, that it was
a professional pursuit."

ANONYMOUS SOURCES

I started forth to test experimentally what treatment a girl whose chastity had been blighted but who was not yet publicly disgraced would receive from physicians in this city.

—Girl Reporter, *Chicago Times*, 1888

When I first read about the Girl Reporter and her *Chicago Times* abortion series, I had just quit my job as a journalist. When I was racing around, chasing down leads, friends had called me "Girl Reporter," a motivational tool, a rallying cry, designed to propel me out the door to battle the interminable city council meetings waiting for me in the Seattle suburbs. It was the mid-1990s, and I had never heard of Nellie Bly, but I knew what "Girl Reporter" implied. Everyone did. She was a character plucked from movies and comic books, and implied fearlessness, a glamorous exterior with a do-gooder heart, all that I wanted to be. But it was a hard image to live up to in an industry that often didn't have space, or even a framework, to tell the stories I found most important. Among the cute Mother's Day features, was there room for a reckoning with substandard day care? In the "personal essay" column on the op-ed page, could a colleague write about abortion? The answer at the time seemed to be no.

The Girl Reporter of the 1888 *Chicago Times* exposé, though, offered a different picture, more complex, no less compelling. Here was someone writing about the reality of women's lives on the front page. When I encountered excerpts of her articles in Leslie Reagan's

When Abortion Was a Crime, I found, rather than a roughly drawn cartoon, a flesh-and-blood young woman, trying to puzzle out sex and writing and her place in the world. One wasn't supposed to discuss abortion (and the Comstock Act banned it), and if one did, it should be a tragic tale of regret, not reports of well-off women mapping out their lives. Yet somehow, the Girl Reporter managed to tell this radical tale.

Like the readers of the *World*, the *Examiner*, or the *Tribune*, who raced out to pick up the next issue featuring stunt reporters' escapades, after reading the Girl Reporter's investigations and growing to admire her wit and nerve, I wanted to find out what happened next. But I couldn't, because after writing the *Times* piece, the Girl Reporter vanished. No one ever took the credit. But her identity seemed key to the nature of her story. Was it a cautionary tale about a country girl who came to the metropolis and was taken advantage of by a money-hungry editor? Or a rags-to-riches fable about a reporter "trying to make a reputation," as one of the doctors accused her of doing, on the path to a blazing career? A call to action about the birth of an activist? Or a romance where the heroine finds the right man and disappears into domesticity? The Girl Reporter posed some questions, about writing, about myself, I needed to answer.

The Girl Reporter's frank wrestling with the desire to tackle issues particular to women and her concern about condemnation stayed with me. So much so that, years later, with a few hours to kill in downtown Chicago, I found myself drawn to a cavernous room in the Harold Washington Memorial Library, dominated by banks of microfilm machines, half of them broken. The reels for the *Chicago Times*, a dreadful paper no one cared about, nestled in a cardboard box. "If I read the whole series, from promotional banner to the final outraged letter to the editor," I told myself, threading the film through with methodical optimism, "I bet I can find her."

The deeper I read, the more I became drawn into the buried tale of the Girl Reporter. Her voice was so vivid. Her series so shattering. She couldn't just be lost. Then as I moved on from articles to letters, pamphlets, and court cases, the documents pulled me into the whole busy, dirty, electric turn-of-the-century world of the stunt reporters, who, through grit and charm, redefined what it meant to be a woman with something to say.

I still wanted to know who she was, and the *Chicago Times* only offered so much. How to piece together a picture? The Chicago Medical Society seethed about the exposé at several meetings but never described the Girl Reporter in any depth. The *Times*'s teasing illustration with the caption "Guess which one of the above is the 'girl reporter,'" showed five young white women who looked remarkably alike, though they glanced inquisitively in different directions. Scattered hints hid in the text of the articles themselves. Back at my hotel, I made a list:

What I Know About the Girl Reporter

She was the right age to be pregnant.

The *Times* described her as "a woman of intelligence, nerve, and newspaper training," though she said the exposé was her first assignment.

She liked puns, particularly those involving doctor's names. "Oh Hale fellow," she addressed Dr. Hale in an imaginary confrontation.

She loved alliteration. One doctor's "shrewd Scotch sense scented danger."

She repeated herself with dashes: "a sin—a sin, alas."

She attended family worship with her grandfather.

Her parents were "respectable" and "well-to-do," not wealthy, not poor.

She described herself as well educated with moral training.

She told one of the doctors she was twenty-three.

She studied French.

She referred to "my prairie home."

She was a huge fan of Amelie Rives's novel *The Quick or the Dead?*

She larded her prose with references to poetry, the Bible, detective
tales, the *Aeneid*, and Shakespeare plays.

L ist in hand, I ran her pet phrases and misquotations through online newspaper search engines: "dollars to dirt," "shots and slings
of invidious fortune," "smell a mouse," but came up with nothing useful. As I read contemporary newspapers, searching for mentions of
the Girl Reporter, it became clear that the high profile of the series
attracted lawsuits. One Dr. Reynolds had sued the *Times* for libel and
$25,000 because his name could be confused with another Dr. Reyn-
olds listed under "Physicians Who Recommend Others Who Would
Commit Abortion." Days later, Dr. Walter Knoll sued for $25,000. In
January, Dr. Silva sued the *Times* for $50,000 and the *Chicago Mail*,
also owned by West, for another $50,000.

Surveying the litigation landscape, the *Rochelle Herald* commented,
"That lady reporter of theirs will have a mighty heap of trouble on her
hands if she has to attend to all their cases in court as a witness."

A witness with a name, I realized, one who might have been called
to testify.

I n the Circuit Court of Cook County Building in Chicago, citizens
wandered through with kids in tow, looking confused, asking for
traffic control or divorce court. But the archive was quiet. An older
man searched for records of a relative's name change. The archivist
wasn't encouraging, saying people often just adopted a new name and
didn't bother with the paperwork. "You're applying today's standards
to yesterday's life," he suggested, and sent him to another building to
look for miscellaneous deeds.

It was my second visit. I'd first come to request court files of the libel lawsuits. Old as they were, the papers were kept off-site—it would take several weeks to recall them. While waiting for documents to arrive, I'd searched through online databases of the *Chicago Times*'s rivals, newspapers that might have been eager to out the Girl Reporter. The *Daily Inter Ocean* mentioned that Silva didn't sue just the paper and its publisher; he sued two men and a woman: "Florence Noble, alias Margaret Noble." Another paper also wrote up the lawsuit, and after the woman's name added, in brackets, "the girl reporter."

Then the archive called. The papers were in, the man on the line told me, though the files were thin and the handwritten documents hard to decipher.

Does anyone mention a "Florence Noble?" I asked.

"No, nothing like that," he'd said.

Then, as I was saying thank you and asking if he would Xerox the files and mail them to me, he added: "But there is a Margaret Noble." A pause, and then: "The Florence is under an ink blot."

Now the files for Silva's lawsuits against the *Times* and *Mail* sat on the table in front of me, frail pieces of dingy cardboard, folded into thirds, holding court documents. The Girl Reporter might be right there, details of her testimony revealing clues to her life after the exposé.

But the archivist had been right, the files were thin. Cases would usually have a narrative, where the plaintiff presented the complaint. A handwritten note on the front of the *Mail* narrative said the enclosed was a copy of the original, which was lost. The narrative for the *Times* lawsuit was missing entirely. And there wasn't much else. Before the end of 1889, West had been sentenced to prison for overissuing stock certificates of the Times Company. Five years after that, the *Chicago Times* was defunct. The rest of the legal file was lawyer after lawyer excusing himself from the case.

Tucked inside one file, though, was a summons for "The Chicago Times Company, James J. West, Joseph R. Dunlop, Florence Noble alias Margaret Noble and———Bowen." On the back, the deputy sheriff scrawled that he had served the summons to the paper, West, and Dunlop, but made no mention of Noble or Bowen. It meant, most likely, they couldn't be found in the county. A few weeks later, one newspaper claimed to have spotted her four hundred miles away in Ashland, a Wisconsin town on Lake Superior, declaring: "The Girl Reporter of the Chicago Times Is Here." But the identification seemed based on a stray comment from a railroad man and the fact that a small, attractive, brown-haired woman showed up asking pointed questions about local dives, lying about her lodgings and her name. Then, nothing. Once again, the Girl Reporter, possibly known as Florence Noble, had slipped away.

No online searchable newspapers or magazines from the 1880s or 1890s have a reporter named Florence Noble. The archives of the Illinois Woman's Press Association didn't list any member with that name. No Florence Noble appeared in the Chicago directory for those years. A Margaret Noble did write a piece on presidential hopeful Benjamin Harrison's Indiana home during the summer of 1888, but wrote nothing else that I could find.

Of course, Florence Noble could also be an alias. Certainly, "Florence" calls to mind Florence Nightingale, a medical heroine. And "Noble" would be an obvious choice. One of the *Times*'s editorials was headlined, winkingly, "A Noble Work."

Or the series might have been too scandalous to launch a career. Maybe she had abandoned journalism. Stunt reporting in general had a dubious reputation, operating at the margins of decency; pretending to be pregnant out of wedlock and seeking an abortion may have been over the line of what a reporter might do and emerge unscathed. Was she the actress Florence Noble who read the balcony scene from *Romeo and Juliet* in New York during a week of Italian opera? Or the Florence Noble who sailed on the *Olympic*, the twin ship of the *Titanic*? Or the Florence Noble who had been a Chicago schoolteacher for thirty-two years before, according to the *Tribune* in 1924, being "committed to the Joliet asylum" because she "suffered from delusions." I hoped not.

Anonymity seems unfortunate in hindsight, but maybe it was

essential. Or so I thought, until I read Elizabeth Banks's critique of yellow journalism in the *Nineteenth Century*.

In her indignation at the treatment of women reporters, Banks referenced the abortion series and declared: "That the young woman filled the assignment, wrote her exposé, was the means of having sent to prison several of Chicago's leading physicians, and had her salary doubled the following week is now a matter of journalistic history." So, according to Banks, the Girl Reporter did have a career, or at least she stuck around long enough to get a salary bump. Another writer confirmed this. In her 1897 piece "Women in Gutter Journalism," essayist and suffragist Haryot Holt Cahoon blasted editors who assigned female reporters undercover work under the pretense they were doing "legitimate journalism."* Her prime example was the Girl Reporter, though she seemed to misidentify her city: "Years ago, a degenerate public was nourished by the newspaper story of a young woman who called upon the various prominent physicians of New York, representing to them that she wished to lend herself to a criminal operation at their hands. As the tangible fruits of her canvass, she gathered an interesting collection of prescriptions. Then she published, together with the prices she paid for each prescription, the name of each physician and the interview." This same reporter went on to other stunts, according to Cahoon, including showing up at the door of Reverend Parkhurst, after the 1893 Tenderloin raids that threw prostitutes out in the snow, claiming to his wife to be "a homeless fallen woman" needing shelter. So even a decade after her abortion series, her fellow journalists knew the identity of the Girl Reporter.

I thought of all the writers who had passed through Chicago in 1888. Nelson, hired by the *World* after her *Times* reports, had just left town. She might have lingered to do one last Chicago piece. Nora

---

* Cahoon may have known this firsthand. An article in the *Arena*'s "Some Newspaper Women" column suggests that she and Eliza Putnam Heaton were both "Kate Kensington" of the *Recorder*.

Marks, who had worked with Ada Sweet to report on prison conditions and the need for an ambulance service, had the perfect training as the *Tribune*'s stunt reporter. Elizabeth Jordan hadn't yet left Milwaukee for New York and the *World*, and in the meantime, she wrote for Chicago outlets. Eva McDonald and Elizabeth Banks worked for papers in Minneapolis and St. Paul, not a far trip on the train. Winifred Sweet was still an actress, but her sister had *Tribune* connections and would soon be pushing her to publish. Could one of them have done the stunt, then gone on to flourish under another name?

None, that I could find, went to Reverend Parkhurst's house in disguise in late 1893, in the aftermath of the brothel closings. The *Recorder*, the newspaper that ran Kate Swan's interview with Lizzie Borden and hired Cahoon at one point, did send "Kathryn Krew" to the Florence Crittenden Mission, the Home for Fallen and Friendless Girls, and other places overrun with homeless women and frustrated with Reverend Parkhurst. Krew wasn't in disguise, though, just accompanying two women looking for a place to stay. All the shelters were full.

In recent years, computer-based stylometry (authorship analysis) has been used to show, for example, whether William Shakespeare wrote sections of the play *Arden of Faversham* and which Supreme Court opinions were penned by clerks. I reached out to digital media experts at the University of Minnesota, Benjamin Wiggins and Cody Hennesy, to see if this type of analysis would yield any clues to the Girl Reporter's identity. We took articles from eight female stunt reporters published in the late 1880s and early 1890s: Bly, Valesh, Jordan, Stackhouse (Nora Marks), Cusack (Nell Nelson), Banks, Black, and Elia Peattie (a writer for the *Chicago Tribune* whose husband, in a tantalizing detail, edited the *Chicago Times*; the couple moved to Omaha in late 1888). We also added in one male reporter—Allen Kelly, the *San Francisco Examiner*'s grizzly bear hunter—as a control. He did stunts, but couldn't have been the young woman the doctors reported pleading in their offices.

The Burrows Delta method of stylometry takes the most frequently used words by one author and compares them to the most frequently used words by another author. (For example, for Author A, 5 percent of their text might use the word "horror";* for Author B, the number might be only 2 percent.) Then it compares those percentages with the average use of "horror" in the pool of words contributed by all the authors. Another method, called the "imposter's tool," allows the results of this analysis to be mapped on a scale from 0 to 1, where 1 is a strong match. A comparison of known writing by J. K. Rowling to *The Cuckoo's Nest* by "Robert Galbraith" (her pseudonym) earned a 1.

A analysis of text by our eight known authors versus the Girl Reporter's articles using the Burrows Delta method with three variations indicated Nora Marks and Elizabeth Banks were the most likely Girl Reporter candidates. One variation gave Stackhouse a score of .94; another gave Banks a score of .63. Allen Kelly earned a score of 0, indicating that the methods could ferret out a clear pretender.

On the one hand, these results make sense. Marks was from out of state (Indiana), as the Girl Reporter claimed to be, and began her stunt reporting at the very moment the Girl Reporter came on the scene. She first appeared in the *Chicago Tribune* at the end of August, feigning to look for a job with an employment agency. She would have had to walk only a few blocks to end up at the *Times* office. Her tone, swinging between casual and formal, sometimes sounded like the Girl Reporter, with a fondness for throwing in a snatch of poetry or a religious phrase. She liked alliteration—one room was "dark, dingy, and dirty"—and addressing the subjects of her investigation directly—"O, Mrs. Carpenter and Mrs. Colby and diverse other keepers of intelligencers." At one point, she speculated, as the Girl Reporter did, that she found herself slipping so deep into her role that she almost forgot her true identity. But the Girl Reporter specified that she wasn't a working girl or a servant: "I would feel myself lost among them. I wouldn't know what to say to interest them," and Marks cheerfully stepped into a servant's shoes, then later chatted with the jail urchins.

---

* I use "horror" as an example here because it fits with the stunt reporter aesthetic. A more realistic example might be use of the word "the."

Also, she had an in at the *Tribune*. Why would she jeopardize it by freelancing for a competitor?

Banks was also from a nearby state—Wisconsin—and in late 1888, like Marks, like the Girl Reporter, she was at the start of her career, penning society stories for the *St. Paul Globe*. Easy enough to take the train to Chicago for a few weeks. It might explain her disgust at the Girl Reporter's abortion work years later as she reflected back on her younger self. Maybe she felt she'd been taken advantage of. She also loved literature, as the Girl Reporter did. At the same time, though, the Girl Reporter had a confidence, sometimes arrogance, that Banks lacked, even at her most famous; and the Girl Reporter loved to moralize, while Banks railed against do-gooders.

Ultimately, though, the stylometry results weren't conclusive enough to say positively that any of these writers visited doctors on behalf of the *Chicago Times*.

So Florence Noble? Without her identity, her series is less like a novel and more like one of Jacob Riis's photographs from *How the Other Half Lives*. For his flash photography, he would barge into a dark tenement room, wake the residents, sprinkle magnesium powder on a frying pan. The circumstances had to be just right: maybe a cub reporter foolishly brave; a newspaper with nothing to lose; an industry reinventing itself; a community of doctors and midwives willing to buck a recent law. Then open the shutter, touch flame to powder, and get a burst of illumination.

I returned to Chicago frequently as I was working on this project, searching along State Street in the rain for the location of the doctor's offices the Girl Reporter visited, standing outside the rough-hewn stones of the hotel where Nellie Bly dined with her husband-to-be, looking up at the new sign declaring "Ida B. Wells Drive." The archivist had told me my quest was a search for a "needle in a haystack." What I found, though, was more like a gleaming pile of needles. The real discovery of my search for the Girl Reporter was how many courageous journalists there were in the decade after Nellie Bly's first stunt. The eight we compared with her writing were not, by far, the only candidates. Every time I unscrolled the microfilm of a new publication, there was another. The handful I ended up writing about here was only the smallest beginning. They had all left traces, sometimes in bound volumes, sometimes in the mere suggestion of life's rich possibility.

A COLLECTION OF ENDINGS

Nothing is so humiliating as to be forgotten, and when I think that if I had wavered in my purpose, a twentieth century office boy in turning over the dusty files might have exclaimed as he woke the night editor from his peaceful slumber, "And who was Caroline Lockhart?" Yes, to be gone and forever forgotten is indeed a terrible thing.

—Caroline Lockhart, *Boston Post*, 1895

VICTORIA EARLE MATTHEWS

In September 1899, a *Sun* reporter toured the White Rose Mission, the brainchild of Victoria Earle Matthews. It had only grown in the years since she first concocted the idea after her trip south. The reporter followed as Matthews led the twenty squirmy four- and five-year-old girls in song, visiting sewing and cooking classes. Matthews described the trips to the docks, the confused passengers she met there, her work to get police detectives to cut off employment agency representatives before they could take the girls away. The mission teachers do what they can, she said, but are hoping to expand. "Think of what a greater amount of good we could do if we were properly equipped for the work, as we will be when our building gets up," she told the reporter.

By 1907, the White Rose Mission had housed 304 young women, found jobs for 204, met 250 at the docks, distributing carfare and escorting them to meet their friends and relatives. The organization stayed in operation for almost ninety years, closing in 1984.

KATE SWAN MCGUIRK

In 1901, in a Brooklyn basement, an expert on the use of the gas cooking stove gave a demonstration of the appliance's abilities, preparing Indian egg short cake, broiled fish, and huckleberry ginger cake at eleven, and roast beef, potato rose balls, and peach short cake at three thirty. The lecturer was listed as "Mrs. Katherine Swan."

After the Spanish-American War and the backlash against Pulitzer and Hearst's papers, Kate Swan McGuirk dropped suddenly from view.* Her name and image were so publicly identified with the *World*'s stunt reporting, it would have been hard to forge a new identity. At first, the name "Katherine Swan" seemed a break from her earlier personas, a fresh start. She'd divorced her husband not long after returning from New Bedford in 1898 and had gone back to school to get a bachelor of science degree. Paid by gas companies, she traveled the East, exhibiting the new stove technology, burying her past fame. But a decade later, her earlier reporting became—if not a matter of pride—a matter of interest. The New York Summer School of Cookery in 1908 mentioned that one of their speakers played a key role in the epic battle between Pulitzer and Hearst, and said the lectures would be of particular interest to those who remembered "the famous 'Kate Swan'" of the *New York Sunday World*.

WINIFRED (SWEET) BLACK BONFILS, "ANNIE LAURIE" AND "COLUMBINE"

In April 1906, Winifred Black Bonfils read the morning paper in Denver in shock. A massive earthquake had torn through San Francisco. She barely had time to absorb the news before a telegram arrived from

---

* One report has her leaving the *World* for the *Journal* along with Brisbane. But while Brisbane left in the fall of 1897, Swan was still reporting on the New Bedford strike for the *World* in early 1898.

Hearst, saying, "Go." In Oakland, as she disembarked the train, an *Examiner* boat waited to escort her across the Bay. She stepped into San Francisco as she had almost twenty years earlier, though this time she had to pick her way through smoldering hunks of wood. A few years after the Galveston hurricane, she stood in the ruins of her own beloved city. Smoke hung in the air. Those left homeless, still in burned clothes, flooded down Broadway to the ferry depot, dragging their trunks. A mist crept in, chilling the thousands who slept in Golden Gate Park. The Examiner building, site of so much journalistic exhilaration, was damaged by fire and would have to be dynamited. Wandering past wrecked husks of mansions, she looked for signs of spirit, the impulse to rebuild, material she could use to write San Francisco back into existence. Her observations appeared in the Sunday paper: "Annie Laurie Tells of the Spectral City."

Her personal life heaved and crashed, stormy waves. After divorcing Orlow Black, she married Charles Bonfils, brother of the publisher of the *Denver Post*. She had two children with Bonfils, Winifred and Eugene. Eugene, never healthy, died at age nine. Jeffrey, the son from her first marriage, drowned off the California coast at thirty-two. But writing was a constant. She never apologized for her stunts (though she hated the term "sob sister"), just used them to launch herself into a sparkling journalistic career, something she and her sister could be proud of. She was unabashed about her mutually beneficial professional relationship with Hearst. She declared her debt to him until the end; he chose her to write a biography of his mother. Over her many decades as a reporter, she did everything—covered trials, edited the children's page, reported on World War I. Her highly syndicated advice columns, sometimes by "Annie Laurie," sometimes by Winifred Black, offered pointed advice to young women trying to navigate the world. She warned one not to be taken in by the romance of a man with a hidden past, and another to avoid sympathetic lunches with the boss who claimed to be misunderstood at home. To three young women desperate to marry and asking for tips on winning a man, she replied: "Get the idea out of your heads that marriage is the aim and end in life. Unless a woman is happily married she is far more likely to be happy when busily earning her own way."

ELIZABETH JORDAN

In 1907, Elizabeth Jordan, editor of *Harper's Bazaar*, found herself deluged with scathing letters. She had ventured into an experimental literary form: the composite novel. Each chapter of *The Whole Family*, written by a different author, would offer a single family member's point of view. Jordan launched the project full of hope, with a blizzard of requests to authors she respected, planning to write the young girl's chapter herself. But problems arose immediately. Samuel Clemens, the writer she'd counted on to pen a young boy's chapter, said no. Some authors said yes, only to quit. And then the woman tapped to write the old-maid aunt presented her character (only thirty-four) as lusty rather than doddering, scandalizing some of her collaborators. Jordan made the mistake of sending each new chapter to all the other contributors, who offered generous edits and criticism. So each mail delivery brought a heap of biting commentary and bruised feelings to Jordan's desk. It took all her tact to keep the manuscript moving forward. Fortunately, she had plenty. Henry James, who wrote through the eyes of the married son, offered barbed critiques, but acknowledged the whole fraught disaster was Jordan's to direct: "You will smile it out, I am sure, all successfully."

The final product was a mess, Jordan freely admitted, but it was one of her own making and it was just the kind of chaos, held in check by tendrils of charm and good organization, that she relished. In fact, she dove right into another composite novel, *The Sturdy Oak*, a 1917 book about women's suffrage, with contributions from her friend from the *World*, Anne O'Hagan, and the western novelist Mary Austin. During her editorship of *Harper's Bazaar* from 1900 to 1913, a position she felt was finally a perfect fit, though the pace seemed painfully slow after late nights in the Pulitzer Building, she spent her days soliciting stories from Stephen Crane and opinions on fairy tales from Jane Addams. When Hearst bought the magazine, she moved over to Harper's Book Publishers, where she edited Sinclair Lewis's first novel. Her own literary production never slowed. She was a prolific novelist and short-story writer, work that included *Tales of Destiny*, *Tales of the Cloister*, *Young Mr. X*. Several of her books were turned into movies: *Make Way for a Lady* and *The Girl in Number 29*.

CAROLINE LOCKHART, "THE POST WOMAN"

After writing for the *Boston Post*, and then the *Philadelphia Bulletin*, Caroline Lockhart ran off with her editor and lover, A. C. McKenzie, to Cody, Wyoming. There, she palled around with Wild Bill Hickok, had a parade of boyfriends, bought and ran a newspaper, and wrote seven popular Westerns, including, *The Man from the Bitter Roots*, *The Fighting Shepherdess*, and *The Lady Doc*, which featured both lesbian characters and abortion. *The Lady Doc* met with a generally glowing reception, though one tremulous reviewer commented, "The story itself is almost too strong for the average reader; it will haunt a man, and what it will do for a nervous woman is not nice to think about."

EVA (MCDONALD) VALESH, "EVA GAY"

After the *New York Journal* fired Valesh, she moved to Washington DC to write for a syndicate, churning out lengthy pieces analyzing policy details—postal thefts, tariffs, an increasing push toward imperialism that she felt was misguided. "It was the happiest work I ever did in my life," she said later. She moved on to the American Federation of Labor's magazine, but when Samuel Gompers refused to credit her, she went to the magazine *American Club Woman*. In 1907, her divorce from Frank Valesh was finalized. She remarried, and when her fun-loving, debt-ridden second husband died in 1923, Valesh renewed her Typographical Union membership, then spent long years as a proofreader for the *New York Times*.

A 1950s photograph of her with her adult son shows them sinking into a comfortable couch, in front of a window full of tree branches and light, his arm slung around her. It's much more relaxed than the stiff 1890s portraits, high collars and tight fabric, photos taken while she struggled to balance her health, her child, and her ambition. In the later picture, her hair is still cropped short, and she wears a boldly patterned shirt. She's leaning back and laughing.

ELEANOR (STACKHOUSE) ATKINSON, "NORA MARKS"

In 1909, Eleanor Stackhouse, now Eleanor Atkinson after her marriage, wrote a letter explaining the story behind a famous portrait of Abraham Lincoln. Even all these years later, after she'd penned a slew of history books, including *The Boyhood of Lincoln*, *The Story of Chicago*, and *Johnny Appleseed*, her undercover exploits loomed large in her mind. Signing the letter, underneath her real name, she still scribbled, "Nora Marks." The two years in journalism, faux fainting in the street and investigating prison conditions, were a vital part of her life story. When one of her daughters published a novel with a plucky, mystery-solving heroine who worked as a reporter in Chicago, the daughter told an interviewer that writing ran in the family: "During the 90's mother . . . was a sob sister on the *Chicago Trib*."

HELEN (CUSACK) CARVALHO, "NELL NELSON"

On a warm June afternoon in 1915, New Jersey women gathered at the lovely Plainfield house of Mrs. S. S. Carvalho. An art gallery filled with old masters opened out into a garden where summer dresses swished across the grass. A thirteen-year-old girl played rousing music on the piano. A local suffragist leader gave a speech, warning the women to prepare for the fight ahead, and expressing gentle scorn for those who declared themselves neutral. "You know what the Lord said about them?" She asked the audience, nodding in their chairs. "It wasn't pretty talk."

Helen Cusack, unless she hid herself under an as-yet-undiscovered pseudonym, wrote little after her marriage in 1895. If she'd ever imagined herself in the tenement houses she visited, worried that one economic downturn or lost job could put her there, those concerns were long past. She raised her two daughters, Sarah and Helen, both teenagers at the time of the suffrage tea, and drove her husband to the station, where he continued to manage the business affairs of Hearst's papers; the couple attended Hearst's wedding in 1903. Her home became a site for fundraisers for the soldiers fighting in Europe during World War I and lectures on topics like "What the Women Are Doing in the War."

ELIZABETH BANKS, "POLLY POLLOCK"

During World War I, while sales of her book *Dik: A Dog of Belgium*, featuring a Red Cross dog, funded wounded soldiers, Elizabeth Banks traveled back to Wisconsin, site of her lonely childhood. After writing her condemnation of stunt reporting, Banks had a long literary career. Despite her early reservations about do-gooders, she became overtly political, campaigning for woman's suffrage and other causes. Tromping through meadows, she peered at the experimental farm where her uncle tried to pay the mortgage by tinkering with the latest scientific theories of making molasses. Old habits die hard and even here, for no real reason, she disguised herself, telling a man leaning against a fence drinking water from a dipper that she was unfamiliar with the place: "As a stranger, I could better get the information I wanted." Cars chugged down the road and telephones interrupted conversations, but the creek was the same, the oak trees, the yellow brick church that awed her as a child. Wandering in, she listened as the preacher described how the world was created in six days and disparaged anyone who thought differently as in league with Satan. What would have become of her if she'd stayed? she wondered. Then she went out to the car, where the hearty college student who was her driver paged through Ernest Haeckel's lecture on the views of Darwin. After spending a lifetime searching for the definition of "American" and where she might fit within it, the contrast between church and parking lot answered some fundamental question about her country. "Where else in the world could such an incident as this have taken place?" she wrote.

Private to the end, though the author of three memoirs—*Campaigns of Curiosity, Autobiography of a "Newspaper Girl,"* and *The Remaking of an American*—Banks demanded in her will that her papers and photos be destroyed, her body burned, and the inscriptions rubbed off her jewelry. She kept her secrets.

IDA B. WELLS-BARNETT, "IOLA"

In 1920, Ida B. Wells-Barnett returned to the South for the first time since her friend was killed and her printing press smashed so viciously twenty-eight years before. She took a train from Chicago to Little Rock, Arkansas, where she met up with the wives and mothers of men who had been jailed during a "race riot" in Elaine. Several of the men had been sentenced to death. She joined the women as they prepared to visit the prison. And though it wasn't her usual method, she donned a disguise, obscuring her own outsize reputation.

"Boys come and shake hands with my cousin who has come from St. Louis to see me," one of the women said. The guards didn't look twice as the famous reporter stepped up to the bars and began conducting interviews. In response to her questions, the jailed men told her their version of events. She pieced together a far different story than the one the papers told, laying bare the cold calculations undergirding the heated violence. It was a good cotton year, and the Black men's arrest had been an excuse to strip them of pigs, chicken, wagons, furniture, hundreds of thousands of dollars' worth of cotton, they told her. Of their accusers, Wells-Barnett wrote: "They are now enjoying the result of these Negroes' labor, while the Negroes are condemned to die or stay in prison twenty-one years." While she was at the jail, the men sang songs, some of which they had written, but she told them the lyrics focused too much on death and forgiveness.

"Pray to live and believe you are going to get out," she advised. And five years later, in part as a result of her efforts, they did.

Throughout her life, along with raising four children, Wells-Barnett continued to fight against lynching, for opportunities for African Americans, and for women's suffrage, founding the Alpha Suffrage Club in 1913. Sometimes her campaigns collided. At the March 1913 parade in Washington DC, when the National American Suffrage Association instructed Black women to march separately from white so as not to upset some delegations from the South, Wells-Barnett ignored the command and marched with the Illinois group, refusing the place they'd deemed fit for her. The parade marked a shift in the suffrage movement, a turn toward radical actions—White House picketing, arrests, and hunger strikes—a tide of anger that would finally sweep the Nineteenth Amendment to ratification in 1920. Wells-Barnett's commitment to her vision of the way things should be never wavered, a fact she detailed in her autobiography, aptly titled *Crusade for Justice*.[*]

ELIZABETH (COCHRANE) SEAMAN, "NELLIE BLY"

The fall of 1914 found Nellie Bly on a hospital train filled with wounded soldiers, traveling from Przemysl to Budapest. At each station, she watched eager young men headed to the front and saw those

---

[*] The autobiography, edited by her daughter, Alfreda Duster, wasn't published until 1970, almost forty years after her death. It was re-released in 2020 with an afterword by her great-granddaughter, Michelle Duster.

returning with hacking coughs, cholera, mangled limbs. Men on the train died in anguish every night. Planes buzzed overhead. Her fifty-year-old feet hurt. At one stop, soldiers ordered a ragged woman to get them some chickens. When she brought four and told them the price, they killed the birds, underpaid her, and mocked her distress. It was just the kind of thing Nellie Bly would notice.

Bly was well out of reporting at the time of the Spanish-American War and the backlash against yellow journalism, but tumultuous life circumstances dragged her back into the profession. For a while, everything seemed to be going her way. After she and Seaman reconciled, he put the Manhattan mansion in her name, made her president of the Iron Clad Manufacturing Company, and willed her all his assets, so that when he died in 1904, her money problems finally seemed to be over.

She attempted to parlay her energy and newspaper experience into running Iron Clad and a second business she launched, the American Steel Barrel Company, modernizing and innovating, adding electricity, acquiring patents, building modern offices. In factories, whose conditions she knew intimately from her journalism, Bly paid a salary rather than by the piece, installed showers with free towels, added a library and bowling alley. But the company was soon mired in financial scandal. The manager, chief cashier, and their allies had forged checks for up to $1.6 million dollars, draining Iron Clad to pay for gambling debts, saloon bills, a yacht. Creditors demanded repayment. During four long years of protracted legal battles, Bly fought for the company, an experience that turned her definitively into a suffragist, as she saw the only help men might offer women in business was the kind predators might offer prey. Iron Clad declared bankruptcy.

At this low point, Arthur Brisbane, a friend from when they were both Pulitzer's protégées at the *World*, and now Hearst's star editor, stepped up. He had hired her back after her marriage seemed about to crumble in 1896. Even when she left the profession, they had remained on good terms. In one letter he recalled a harrowing car trip and signed off with appreciation for her "kind, courteous, and persistent effort to kill me last Saturday." In the middle of the lawsuit, Bly turned to him for advice on lawyers and support from Hearst's editorial pages, but when she lost the company anyway, he offered a different kind of opinion. With her talent, she could be "doing much more useful work than making tin cans," he suggested. So Bly, as she seemed destined to do, returned to reporting, covering political conventions and suffrage marches for Brisbane. When World War I broke out, she went to Europe and took readers into military encampments. She often shared the editorial page of Hearst papers with Winifred Black. In illustrations, she hadn't aged at all.

When Bly died of pneumonia in 1922, Brisbane wrote her obituary. He had always admired her round-the-world trip, her Pullman strike coverage, her compassion and audacity. With his affection for all caps and for the intrepid girl reporter, he concluded, "Nellie Bly was THE BEST REPORTER IN AMERICA."

ACKNOWLEDGMENTS

A book is a monument to an obsession and a tribute to those who helped in the building. Thanks to Hedgebrook for the time to write, the radical hospitality, and the blackberries; and to the Talle Faculty Research Award and the Hawkins Professorship at the University of Minnesota for generous funding in support of this work.

A book is also a conversation, and this, more than my others, was the result of a wide-ranging discussion about writing, about the female body, about efforts to combine the two. For reading drafts and scraps of drafts, and the willingness to point out sentences of particular awfulness, much appreciation to Erica Olsen, Shala Erlich, Jason Albert, Frank Bures, V. V. Ganeshananthan, Emily Sohn, Tanya Barfield, Susan Thurston-Hamerski, and William Souder. In particular, thanks to Mara Hvistendahl and Jessica Nordell, for not just the critiques but the vital digressions. And to Karen Hartman for housing me on research trips and for launching a particularly informative Facebook thread about female comics, what they have to do to succeed, and the backlash that often greets them once they break through. And for the hikes (with Shala, too). Here's to several decades of talking things through on the trail.

For research assistance, I owe a debt to Kristin Collier and Eleanor Garran for combing through the vast troves of articles by stunt reporters and likely wondering, "Must they be so prolific?" And also to Tamsen Glaser for tracking down court records in Chicago. And to

Benjamin Wiggins and Cody Hennesy for their attempts to identify the Girl Reporter using stylometrics, and their research assistants, Janelle Ruth, Kamilla Ruppman, Ella Haugesag, Benjamin Schroeder, Chae Hong, Alyssa Miller, and Molly Bostrom. And to archivists at Minnesota History Center, the Widener Library at Harvard, the YMCA collection at the University of Minnesota, the Bancroft Library at UC Berkeley, the New York Public Library, the University of Tulsa, Syracuse University, Columbia University, the Library of Congress, the Clerk of the Circuit Court of Cook County, San Francisco Public Library, and University of Chicago.

This kind of work stands on what has come before. I am grateful to writers whose books and articles I found particularly influential, some of whom let me interview them about their projects: Brooke Kroeger, Jean Marie Lutes, Leslie Reagan, Paula Giddings, Suki Kim, Rachel Boyle, and Steve Kramer.

Thanks to Alice Whitwham at Elyse Cheney Literary; Sofia Groopman, and Sarah Haugen at HarperCollins for seeing the possibilities in this project; and to Thomas Frail at *Smithsonian* magazine for excellent editing on the article that was the seed of this book. I also have much appreciation for my former students in the creative writing program at Penn State Behrend. Bly's story is inextricable to me from the isolating western Pennsylvania winters that formed her, the same dense snows that heaped outside our classrooms. Your astute responses to the stunt reporters' exploits helped me articulate the contradictions of these writers and the roles they played.

And many thanks to my family: Pete and Gail Todd for careful reading, Ben and Peregrine for their curiosity and optimism, and Jay for his boundless support.

And, finally, my appreciation for everyone who discovers a hidden door of opportunity, slips through, then props it open behind her.

Prologue: The Case of the Girl Reporter (1888)

1   "You must not be scared about it": Girl Reporter, *Chicago Times*, December 15, 1888, 1.

2   "Remember how to take it tonight": Girl Reporter, *Chicago Times*, December 17, 1888, 1.

2   "Inflammation might set in": Girl Reporter, *Chicago Times*, December 16, 1888, 9.

2   "There are enough ways": Ibid.

2   "It will not do for you to feel": Girl Reporter, *Chicago Times*, December 15, 1888, 1.

2   "If I were a girl": Ibid.

3   "Don't prate of virtue": Girl Reporter, *Chicago Times*, December 18, 1888, 1.

4   "Today I have been wondering": Girl Reporter, *Chicago Times*, December 22, 1888, pp. 1, 5.

5   "prostitution of the brains": the *Journalist*, January 26, 1889, 13.

5   by 1900, papers were publishing: Lutes, *Front-Page*, 4.

6   "The natural and proper timidity": Renfroe, "Editor's Introduction," x.

6   "the ink-stained Amazons": Hawthorne, "Mrs. Hutchinson," 18–19.

8   "A careful examination of": Brann, "Women in Journalism," 383.

8   "semipornographic titillation": Lang, *Women Who*, 1999, 37.

8   "cast a spell of infamy": Ibid., 36.

8   "she had thought of something": Woolf, "Professions," 152.

8   "telling the truth": Ibid., 153.

9   they found a 25/75 split: "The 2010 VIDA Count," VIDA Women in
        Literary Arts, May 16, 2011, https://www.vidaweb.org/vida-count
        /the-count-2010/.

Chapter 1: Trials of a Working Girl (1885–1887)

13   "City of Smoke": Muller, "Pittsburgh," 49.

14   "If women would just let up on this sphere business": Wilson, *Quiet
        Observations*, 140.

14   "her home a little paradise": Ibid.

14   "Now what am I to do": *Pittsburg Dispatch*, January 17, 1885, 4.

15   "abnormal" and "a monstrosity": Wilson, *Quiet Observations*, 167.

15   "Your 'Quiet Observer' is a fool": Ibid., 173.

15   "We don't wish to wear": Ibid., 171.

15   "whore" and "bitch" and other details of the stepfather's behavior:
        divorce testimony in *M. J. Ford vs. J. J. Ford*, 1879, Armstrong County
        Courthouse.

16   "Wanted—manager for art publications" and other notices: *Pittsburg
        Dispatch* Want Ads, January 11–17, 1885.

17   "If the writer of the communication": *Pittsburg Dispatch*, January 17,
        1888, 4.

17   "a strain of sound": *San Francisco Examiner*, January 22, 1890, 1.

17   "Girls are just as smart": *Pittsburg Dispatch*, January 25, 1885, 1.

19   "attracted considerable attention here": *Pittsburg Dispatch*, March 1,
        1885, 10.

21   "sparkling, breezy, good-natured tone": *St. Louis Post-Dispatch*,
        April 25, 1883, 8.

21   "chambermaid's delight": James Palmer, "Albert Pulitzer: Notes on the
        Lesser-Known Pulitzer Brother," The Pulitzer Prizes, https://www
        .pulitzer.org/page/albert-pulitzer-notes-lesser-known-pulitzer-brother.

21   "not only large but truly democratic": *World*, May 11, 1883, 4.

21   between 1870 and 1900, 12 million immigrants: Arnesen, *Encyclopedia*, 523.

22   jumping from thirty thousand in 1883: *Journalist*, September 10, 1887, 10.

23   "which appeals to the people": Quoted in Procter, *Hearst*, 41.

23   "Look out for me": Quoted in Kroeger, *Nellie Bly*, 75.

23   "Editor and popular author wants": *Journalist*, September 17, 1887, 8.

24   "I think if they have the ability" and the rest of this conversation: *Pittsburg Dispatch*, August 21, 1887, 9.

25   "get a bachelor and form a syndicate" and the rest of this conversation: Ibid.

25   "I cannot write the utter rubbish": Jane Cunningham Croly "Jennie June" to Pulitzer, January 7, 1884, Box 1, CUWP.

25   "Their dress, constitution and habits" and the rest of this conversation: *Pittsburg Dispatch*, August 21, 1887, 9.

25   "the public demands a different kind": Ibid.

26   "Dr. Hepworth, I want a position" and the rest of this conversation: Ibid.

26   "the empty glory and poor pay": Ibid.

26   "Woman understands women": Ibid.

26   "No editor would like": Ibid.

27   "I don't know what I can do until I try": Bly, "Among the Mad," 20.

Chapter 2: Opportunity in Disguise (1887)

28   "naked ugliness and horror": Dickens, *American Notes*, 37.

28   "assumed the look": *World*, October 9, 1887, 25.

29   "I can see it in your face" and the rest of this conversation: Ibid.

30   "Who Is This Insane Girl?": *Sun*, September 25, 1887, 1.

31   "Poor child" and the rest of this scene: *World*, October 9, 1887, 26.

31   "A good woman can do without blemish": *San Francisco Examiner*, December 18, 1892, 13.

32 "hysterical mania": *Sun*, September 25, 1887, 1.

32 "the sight of licentious paintings" and following list of descriptions: Hayes, *Physiology*, 252–65.

32 "As a general rule, all women are hysterical": Quoted in Grossman, *Spectacle*, 92.

33 "dissolve the paroxysm": Hayes, *Physiology*, 256.

33 "nervous debility" and most of the rest of the asylum account: Bly, *Ten Days*, http://digital.library.upenn.edu/women/bly/madhouse /madhouse.html.

33 "I can't see": *World*, October 17, 1887.

36 "Nellie Bly's Experience in the Blackwell's Insane Asylum": *World*, October 16, 1887.

36 "Can Doctors Tell Insanity?": *Sun*, October 14, 1887, 11.

36 "New York wild with excitement": *Salt Lake Herald*, December 9, 1887, 4.

36 "Smarter Than All of Them": *Hazel Green Herald*, December 9, 1887, 5.

36 "Miss Bly has undoubtedly performed": *Ohio Democrat*, December 17, 1887, 4.

37 "made a sensation from Maine to Georgia": *Iola Register*, December 30, 1887, 3.

37 "I answered the summons with pleasure": Bly, *Ten Days*, http://digital .library.upenn.edu/women/bly/madhouse/madhouse.html.

37 "I was astonished to find": *St. Louis Post-Dispatch*, April 6, 1947, 14.

38 "weak mutton broth" and the rest of the workhouse scene: Greenwood, *Night in a Workhouse*, pamphlet, reprinting of original articles.

39 "He Dug Her Grave": *Daily Arkansas Gazette*, October 15, 1887, 1.

39 "Mrs. Robinson's Fatal Leap": *New-York Tribune*, October 10, 1887, 1.

39 "A Bride Choked with Gas": *Evening World*, October 15, 1887, 1.

39 "I began to have a smaller regard": *World*, October 9, 1887, 26.

39 "In ancient times": *Pall Mall Gazette*, July 6, 1885.

39 "Could I pass a week" and the rest of the asylum article quotations in this chapter: *World*, October 9, 1887, 25–26, except where noted.

40   "Some people have since": Bly, *Ten Days*, http://digital.library.upenn
.edu/women/bly/madhouse/madhouse.html.

Chapter 3: Detective for the People (1888)

43   "a terrible tomboy": Reminiscences of Eva MacDonald Valesh: Oral
History, CUL.

43   "go do something else": Ibid.

45   "Don't know. What do you want": *St. Paul Globe*, March 25,
1888, 10.

46   "when she learned some of the qualifications": *St. Paul Globe*, May 13,
1888, 13.

46   "If your foreman insults you": *St. Paul Globe*, March 25, 1888, 10.

46   Knights of Labor's membership increasing from 104,000: Galenson,
United Brotherhood, 43.

48   "petticoat detective" and "Statesmen Shaking at the Knees": *Buffalo
News*, April 3, 1888, 1.

48   "the spectacle of a brilliant young woman": *Times-Picayune*, March 25,
1888, 10.

49   "If we do go back": *St. Paul Globe*, April 19, 1888, 3.

50   "SHOTWELL, CLERIHEW & LOTHMAN, 6 CENTS" and the rest of this
scene: *St. Paul Globe*, May 11, 1888, 4.

50   "charges of ungentlemanly conduct": *St. Paul Globe*, May 12, 1888, 3.

50   "no character, no principle": *St. Paul Globe*, June 3, 1888, 11.

50   "made by a body of men" and following quotations from the same
article: *Minneapolis Tribune*, May 13, 1888, 4.

51   "What is a boycott?": *St. Paul Globe*, April 29, 1888, 11.

52   "never indulging in laughter" and other quotations from this speech:
Duluth Daily News, June 8, 1888, 4.

52   "The greatest little 'Labor Agitator'": Note in the margins of Eva
McDonald to Sarah Stevens, January 5, 1891, MHSVP.

52   "The Firm of Shotwell, Clerihew & Lothman Embarrassed": *St. Paul
Globe*, June 14, 1888, 3.

52 "one of the most responsible in the city": *Minneapolis Tribune*, May 13, 1888, 4.

53 "large Bankrupt Wholesale Dry Goods": *St. Paul Globe*, October 4, 1888, 2.

53 "a crusade for women": *St. Paul Globe*, April 1, 1888, 9.

53 "Well, we've come to a fine pass": Valesh, Oral History, CUL.

53 "joyfully made my escape": *St. Paul Globe*, May 6, 1888, 9.

Chapter 4: Hunger for Trouble (1888)

54 "silly, flat, and dishwatery utterances": Quoted in Wendt, *Chicago Tribune*, 189.

54 "Scandals in private life": Wilkie, *Reminiscences*, 130–31.

55 "one of the ablest and handsomest journals in the world": *Chicago Times*, April 22, 1888, 4.

56 "a particularly caustic pen": A.S.A., *Indianapolis News*, 1.

57 "pretty blonde secretary" and other quotations from this encounter: *Chicago Times*, July 30, 1888, 1–2.

59 "They stuck in my woolen waist": *Chicago Times*, August 7, 1888, 1.

59 "the sleeve of my 'never-rip' jersey" and other quotations from this encounter: *Chicago Times*, August 2, 1888, 1–2.

59 "miserable bullet-headed sapling": *Chicago Times*, August 1, 1888, 1–2.

60 "I don't think I can tell you": *Chicago Times*, August 2, 1888, 1–2.

60 "But worse than broken shoes": *Chicago Times*, August 1, 1888, 1–2.

60 "Aren't you from the *Times*?" and other quotations from this encounter: *Chicago Times*, August 10, 1888, 1–2.

61 "the true knight errant of today": *Chicago Times*, August 3, 1888.

61 "If they prefer working at starvation": Ibid.

61 "made himself obnoxious to me" and "insolent": *Chicago Times*, August 5, 1888.

61 "an anti-Semitic crusade": Ibid.

61 "The highest compliment paid": *St. Paul Globe*, December 24, 1888, 3.

62   "I think I shall always be": *Times Union*, October 20, 1888.

62   "Occasionally her stories": *Buffalo Sunday Morning News*, October 7, 1888, 5.

62   "she suffered the penalty paid": McDougall, *Life*, 187.

63   "Hangman Joe at Home" and other quotations from this article: *World*, September 30, 1888, 17.

63   "Should women propose?" and other quotations from this series: *World*, November 11, 1888, 12, and *World*, November 18, 1888, 17.

64   "Horrors of a Slop Shop" and other quotations from this article: *World*, September 30, 1888, 18.

65   "They Work in an Inferno" and other quotations from this article: *World*, October 7, 1888, 17.

Chapter 5: Reckoning with the Evil of the Age (1888)

68   "yellowest": Chapin, *Chapin's Story*, 134.

68   "bright man and a woman reporter": Ibid., 135.

68   "Chicago Abortioners": Ibid., 136.

69   "parade her shame" and "a young woman of intelligence": *Chicago Times*, December 15, 1888, 1.

69   "but a step toward divorce": *Chicago Times*, December 6, 1888, 9.

69   "Thousands are doing it": *Chicago Times*, December 15, 1888, 1.

69   "I felt that there was some big": *Chicago Times*, December 19, 1888, 1.

69   "Tonight as I write this": *Chicago Times*, December 17, 1888, 5.

70   "I manage somehow or other": *Chicago Times*, December 22, 1888, 1.

71   one in five pregnancies: Mohr, quoted in Lahey, "Birthing," 486.

72   "They have both been excommunicated": *Buffalo Commercial Advertiser*, November 3, 1837, 2.

72   "the infernal plot": *Buffalo Courier*, May 24, 1843, 3.

72   "Genuine French Female Monthly Pills" and "astonishing success": *New-York Tribune*, September 30, 1841, 4.

72   "Female's Friend" and "relieving and removing": *New-York Tribune*, September 28, 1841, 4.

72   "Dr. Van Hambert's Female Renovating Pills, from Germany" and "They must not be taken": *New York Daily Herald*, October 26, 1837, 4.

73   "the beautiful cigar girl": *Public Ledger*, August 3, 1841, 2.

73   "premature delivery": *New-York Tribune*, November 18, 1842, 2.

74   "obstinate and long-standing cases" and "females in delicate health": *Public Ledger*, February 25, 1841, 4.

74   "Restellism": *Baltimore Sun*, April 3, 1848, 1.

74   "Madame Restell's organ": *Vicksburg Daily Whig*, October 12, 1841, 2.

74   "Restell school": *Public Ledger*, September 1, 1841, 2.

74   "in no case do I engage": *New-York Tribune*, August 24, 1842, 1.

75   "The mails go burdened with the circulars": *New York Times*, August 23, 1871, 6.

75   "articles of indecent and immoral use": Quoted in Werbel, *Lust*, 54–55.

77   "It is a cause for profound thanksgiving": The New York Society for the Suppression of Vice, *Annual Report*, 13. UMLKF.

77   "uterine trouble" and "an internal hemorrhage": *St. Paul Globe*, April 8, 1889, 3.

78   "Wilcox's Compound Tansy Pills" and "afford speedy and certain relief": *Boston Globe*, December 30, 1888, 10.

78   from an average of 7 children per woman: Mohr, *Abortion*, 82.

79   "St. Lawrence to the Golden Gate" and "I don't exaggerate:" *Chicago Times*, January 3, 1889, 5.

79   "lost to shame" and "the method adopted": *Buffalo Times*, December 24, 1888, 2.

79   "Some of the young girls will learn": *Chicago Times*, December 23, 1888, 11.

79   "take the bull by the horns": Ibid., 10.

79   "Bring the Husbands to Book": *Chicago Times*, December 28, 1888, 1.

79   "It is our duty": *Chicago Times*, December 22, 1888, 5.

79   "The social order that permits": *Chicago Times*, December 23, 1888, 11.

80   "A Novel Treatment of Gonorrhea" and quotations for the rest of these meetings: Volume 9, CHMCMS.

80   "many a pearly tear": *Journal of the American Medical Association*, January 12, 1889, 55.

81   "anything happened I could locate it": *Chicago Times*, December 18, 1888, 2.

81   "control of our government": *Chicago Times*, December 16, 1888, 9.

83   "the newspaper reports every day": Stanton and Anthony, *Selected Papers*, 159.

83   "A woman should have the same chances" and "Amen": *Chicago Times*, December 23, 1888, 9.

83   "For the Doctors": *Chicago Times*, December 21, 1888, 4.

84   "small token of esteem": *Chicago Times*, December 22, 1888, 5.

84   "My pilgrimage of disgrace is ended": *Chicago Times*, December 26, 1888, 1.

84   "Many of the brightest women": *Journalist*, January 26, 1889, 12.

85   "A harmless life, she called a virtuous life": Browning, *Aurora Leigh*, 11.

86   "A newspaper girl, a newspaper girl" and "don't think of it": Banks, *Autobiography*, 6.

87   "Please make me a mean": *St. Paul Globe*, November 4, 1888, 19.

87   "are so hideous and disgusting": Banks, "'Yellow Journalism,'" 338.

87   "The exposure made by the *Times*": *St. Paul Globe*, December 20, 1888, 4.

Chapter 6: New Territory (1889–1890)

88   "The whole atmosphere of the place": Bisland, *Flying Trip*, 22.

88   "monthly irregularities": *San Francisco Examiner*, February 18, 1889, 7.

89   "Women who have fallen": *San Francisco Examiner*, August 27, 1889, 7.

89   "Minnie . . . come home; all is forgiven": *San Francisco Chronicle*, June 23, 1889.

90   "Confessions of an Actress" and other quotations from this article: *Chicago Tribune*, December 16, 1888, 26.

90   "I began to think": *Chicago Tribune*, January 13, 1889, 26.

91   "the paper must be built up": William Randolph Hearst to George Hearst, January 4, 1885, BLHP.

91   "The Examiner, with this issue": *San Francisco Examiner*, March 4, 1887, 2.

91   "the fragrance of violets": Bierce, "A Thumb-Nail Sketch," 305.

92   "a very sure instinct about": Finch Kelly, *Flowing Stream*, 240.

92   "the common enemy": *San Francisco Examiner*, January 3, 1889, 4.

93   "The Examiner Does the Work of the Life Saving Service": *San Francisco Examiner*, January 4, 1890, 1.

93   "Monarch of the Dailies": *San Francisco Examiner*, January 7, 1890, 6.

93   "would cover not only myself": Black, "Rambles, Part II," 211.

93   "Don't moralize. Get at your story": *San Francisco Examiner*, July 13, 1890, 13.

93   "Yes, sir," and "walked out into the quiet": Black, "Rambles, Part II," 212.

94   "wholesome and pink": Older, *Hearst*, 99.

94   "wholesome as a May": Winkler, *W. R. Hearst*, 72.

94   "the best boss, the kindest friend": Black, "Rambles, Part II," 213.

95   "If I could do it as quickly as Phileas Fogg did": Bly, *Around the World*, http://digital.library.upenn.edu/women/bly/world/world.html.

97   "distinctive" and "peculiar personality": *San Francisco Examiner*, January 22, 1890, 2.

97   "she is a plain every-day girl, with a wonderful head and warm heart": *San Francisco Examiner*, November 19, 1889, 1.

97   "One was the regular routine": *San Francisco Examiner*, January 22, 1890, 2.

98   "has never done anything" and "Miss Bisland is universally regarded": *San Francisco Examiner*, November 19, 1889, 1.

98   "I didn't realize what a public character": *San Francisco Examiner*, November 20, 1889, 1.

98   "The Star-Eyed Goddess of Reform": Black, "Rambles, Part II," 37.

98 "Influence of the Daily Press": Chicago Women's Club Board Minutes 1876–1891, CHMCWC.

99 "Well, what do you want?" and other quotations from this scene: *Chicago Tribune*, January 13, 1889, 12.

100 "inconvenient individual who keeps abreast": Ibid.

101 "I can't see that there is anything" and other quotations from this scene: *Chicago Tribune*, December 13, 1889, 1.

101 "The city should at once organize": Ibid., 2.

102 "simply sick of hearing these things": *San Francisco Examiner*, January 22, 1890, 1.

102 "queer doings" and "young girls wandered in": Black, "Rambles, Part II," 214.

103 "I kept walking away from it": *San Francisco Examiner*, December 18, 1892, 13.

103 "I am so sick" and other quotations from this scene: *San Francisco Examiner*, January 19, 1890, 11.

104 "She was treated right" and other quotation from this encounter: *San Francisco Examiner*, January 20, 1890, 1–2.

104 "all the numerous complaints" and other quotations from this interview: *Daily Alta California*, January 23, 1890, 4.

105 "The most precious bit of freight" and other quotations from this scene: *San Francisco Examiner*, January 22, 1890, 1–2.

106 "the fact that two young" and other quotations from this page: *San Francisco Examiner*, January 22, 1890, 6.

Chapter 7: Under the Gold Dome (1890–1891)

109 "The American Girl will no longer": *Pittsburg Dispatch*, January 26, 1890, 1.

110 "little newspaper girl": Bly, *Around the World*, http://digital.library.upenn.edu/women/bly/world/world.html.

112 "wonderful things" and "a delicate layer of frost": Jordan, *Cheers*, 23.

113 "A horde of dirty children": Riis, *Other Half*, 29–30.

114   "Miss Virginia Cusack Missing": *Chicago Tribune*, March 18, 1890, 1.

115   "cordial" and "kept very much to herself": Jordan, *Cheers*, 87.

115   "I was out of New York": Ibid., 29.

116   "The first story should deal with": World Sunday Edition Editorial
       Department to Commander Peary, April 26, 1905, NYPLSP.

117   "To me the southern mountain assignment": Jordan, *Cheers*, 41.

117   "In the nineteenth century there are": *World*, November 20, 1890, 2.

118   "the comments not only smirched one": Jordan, *Cheers*, 128.

118   "did sensational stories": Jordan, *Tales*, 223.

119   "nothing but nuisances": Banks, *Autobiography*, 17.

119   "Get in, Miss," and other quotations from this scene: Jordan,
       Cheers, 131.

119   "After all, a woman's place": Jordan, *Tales*, 223.

119   "I beg your pardons" and "drop the damned": Jordan, *Cheers*, 38–39.

120   375 feet tall, 26 stories, and other measurement details: *The World, Its
       History and New Home*, pamphlet.

121   "God grant that this structure": Ibid.

121   "Accuracy! Terseness! Accuracy!": Seitz, *Pulitzer*, 440.

122   "a minister's meeting from ten to twelve": Black, "Rambles, Part II,"
       211.

122   "the 'Nelly Bly' of San Francisco" and other quotations: *San Francisco
       Examiner*, January 5, 1891, 6.

123   "Face Bleach" and other quotations: *San Francisco Examiner*, January
       25, 1891, 14.

124   "pretty and coquettish" and "fool": *San Francisco Examiner*,
       December 18, 1892, 13.

Chapter 8: Exercising Judgment (1892)

125   "families who lived, all of them": Finch Kelly, *Flowing Stream*, 230–31.

126   "It is very hard to have any veneration": *Los Angeles Herald*, August 18,
       1892, 5.

126　"Clever Mrs. McGuirk": *St. Paul Globe*, July 9, 1892, 8.

126　"'Kate,' as her numerous friends call her": *Boston Globe*, July 18, 1892, 8.

126　"How do you get along" and other quotations from the interview: *New York Recorder*, September 19, 1892, 1–2.

127　"masculine looking woman" and "peculiar guttural harshness": Quoted in Kent, *Source Book*, 32.

127　"Her hands and arms": *Boston Post*, August 6, 1892, 2.

127　"a repellent disposition": *Logansport Reporter*, August 6, 1892, 1.

128　"the embodiment of laughter and fun": *Daily Arkansas Gazette*, April 30, 1893, 16.

129　"whose card has taken her": *New York Times*, August 29, 1892, 1.

130　"a magnificent 'fake'": Porter, *Fall River*, 141.

130　"Mrs. McGuirk, that able": *Vancouver Daily World*, November 11, 1892, 7.

130　"an impartial jury of the state": Del Carmen, *Criminal Procedure*, 19.

131　"This danger would be increased immeasurably" and other quotations from this article: Parkman, "Woman Question," 316–17.

131　"indecencies" and "sodomy, incest, rape, seduction": Quoted in Rodriguez, "Clearing," 1833.

131　"Slowly, perhaps, but surely": *Newport Mercury*, July 1, 1893, 3.

Chapter 9: A Place to Speak Freely (1892)

132　lynchers killed 150: Wells-Barnett, *Selected Works*, 29.

133　"Princess of the Press": *Journalist*, January 26, 1889, 4.

134　"I am an anomaly to myself": Wells, *Memphis Diary*, 78.

135　"O my God!" and "It may be unwise": Ibid., 102.

135　"a town which will neither": Wells-Barnett, *Selected Works*, 6.

136　"thread-bare lie" and "a conclusion": Wells-Barnett, *Crusade*, 65–66.

136　"Well, we've been a long time": Ibid., 61.

137　"They could and did fall in love": Ibid., 70.

137   "I felt that I owed it": Ibid., 69.

137   "zealous, watchful spirit": Davis, *Lifting*, 30.

137   "No writer of the race is kept busier": *Journalist*, January 26, 1889, 4.

138   "I do not think our women will object": *Washington Bee*, April 9, 1887, 3.

139   "Peace and security are very good things to have": Matthews, "New York," January 5, 1889, 2.

Chapter 10: Guilt and Innocence (1892–1893)

141   "Public Services Rendered by *The World*" and other quotations: *World*, May 7, 1893.

142   "you have to make up your mind": *World*, June 4, 1893, 13.

142   "Many women—faithful daughters and wives": *World*, June 11, 1893, 20.

142   "Christian attributes" and "Angels, my friends say": Ibid.

143   "a self-constituted jury" and "They sit": *World*, June 18, 1893, 15.

143   "To-day, as yesterday, you squeezed": *World*, June 14, 1893, 8.

143   "plain to the point of homeliness" and other quotations: *World*, June 6, 1893, 8.

145   "I would not be seen doing that, Lizzie" and other quotations from this conversation: *World*, June 15, 1893, 3.

145   "The old man is trying to testify" and other quotations from this scene: Jordan, *Cheers*, 120.

146   "A woman's cunning devised," "It is unjust," and other quotations from this scene: *World*, June 21, 1893, 1, 7.

146   "Miss Borden's vindication was clear": Ibid.

147   "He spent his time devising" and other quotations from this story: Jordan, "Assignment," 365–72.

147   "So, Ruth Herrick, that's the kind": Jordan, *Cheers*, 122.

150   "dream of beauty": Victoria Earle Matthews to Frederick Douglass, August 3, 1894, LCDP.

151   "no news is good news": *Chicago Tribune*, October 27, 1893, 8.

151   "The Usual Result": *Evening World*, December 6, 1893, 1.

152   "lead respectable lives": *Evening World*, December 6, 1893, 1.

152   "merry twinkle" and other quotations from this article: *World*, December 10, 1893, 33.

Chapter 11: Across the Atlantic (1893–1894)

154   "surrounded with dozens of lovers": *St. Paul Globe*, November 25, 1888, 19.

154   "from getting too lonely": Banks, *Autobiography*, 50.

154   "Stitch! stitch! stitch!": Hood, *Works*, 308.

155   "I wear caps and aprons": Banks, *Campaigns*, 3.

155   "in the city whistles are blowing": *Chicago Tribune*, December 17, 1892, 14.

156   "As Housemaid, Parlourmaid, or House-Parlourmaid": Banks, *Campaigns*, 9.

156   "For myself, I knew little or nothing": Ibid., 6.

157   "they have to make quite sure": Bishop and Lowell, *Words*, Letter 218.

157   "there actually breathe a woman": *Pall Mall Gazette*, November 22, 1893, 5.

158   "Now, tell me exactly" and other quotations from this scene: Banks, *Autobiography*.

158   "A Young American Lady": Banks, *Campaigns*, 98.

159   "after all my investigations, my faith": Ibid., 113.

159   "A YOUNG WOMAN wants a situation": Ibid., 159.

159   "I'll help you, Miss Barnes" and other quotations from the laundry scene: Banks, *Campaigns*.

161   "I was beginning to get intensely interested" and other scenes from the laundries in this section: Banks, *Campaigns*.

Chapter 12: Girl No More (1894–1895)

164   "Do you think we're as bad as that?" and other quotations from this scene: *St. Louis Post-Dispatch*, July 13, 1894, 2.

165 "Their only hope is": *St. Louis Post-Dispatch*, July 17, 1894, 2.

165 "While it occupies her": *St. Paul Globe*, September 11, 1894, 5.

166 "Life is growing worse every day": *Evening World*, February 5, 1895, 4.

167 "Why couldn't I write for a newspaper": Quoted in Clayton, *Cowboy Girl*, 33–34.

167 "This Page for the Lords of Creation" and other quotations from this issue: *Boston Post*, February 11, 1894.

169 "Have I not been drinking moxie" and other quotations from this article: *Boston Post*, June 2, 1895, 9, 12.

170 "Is 'Nellie Bly' Married?": *Indianapolis Journal*, April 7, 1895, 2.

170 "The marriage of Nellie Bly": *San Francisco Examiner*, April 15, 1895, 6.

170 "And thus is refuted": *Weekly Pioneer-Times*, April 18, 1895, 4.

170 "He is very old": *Buffalo Morning Express*, April 16, 1895, 4.

171 "everybody knew her but she had very few familiars": McDougall, *Life*, 187.

171 "Nellie was deeply attached": Ibid., 189.

171 "It is a genuine surprise": *Boston Post*, June 21, 1895, 4.

172 "a small man with muscles of iron" and "the most energetic": McDougall, *Life*, 199.

172 "Her reward was great": Jordan, *Cheers*, 87.

172 "You have dealt with": Wells-Barnett, *Selected Works*, 15.

172 "It is like being born": Wells-Barnett, *Crusade*, 135.

173 "attempted robbery" and other quotations from this source: Wells-Barnett, *Selected Works*.

174 "octaroon evangel": *New York Times*, April 29, 1894, 1.

174 "retired to what I thought was the privacy of a home": Ibid., 239.

175 "Next to a great, big bank account": *Boston Post*, February 11, 1894, 19.

176 "In the craft I had chosen": Webb, *Diary*, 252.

176 "She deals only with ballot boxes": *San Francisco Examiner*, May 26, 1895, 13.

177 "There are certain moments in life": Black, "Rambles, Part II," 217.

Chapter 13: Full Speed Ahead (1895–1896)

179   "I had secured very remunerative": Abbot, *Watching*, 137.

179   "It seemed to some of us": Ibid., 147.

180   "Can I help you" and other quotations from this scene: Interview
        with Miss Elizabeth Jordan at her home, April 13, 1938, Brisbane
        2001 Addition, Box 1, Folder "J" Miscellaneous, SULBF.

182   "by turns fire and ice": Jordan, *Cheers*, 136.

182   "I have sometimes wondered": Ibid., 128.

184   "Officer, there is a man in that cab" and "Oh, that is all": *Sun*,
        November 10, 1895, 4.

184   "If I have done anything wrong" and other quotations from this
        scene: *Sun*, November 11, 1895, 3.

184   "Learn to think only": Nellie Bly to Mary Jane Cochrane, October 12,
        1915, Folder Bly, Nellie/Cochrane, Mary Jane, 1914–1915, SULBF.

185   "frightful" and "I really believe women": *World*, January 26, 1896, 4.

185   "I adore the little peculiarities of people": *World*, February 2,
        1896, 10.

185   "Do you pray?" and other quotations from this scene: Ibid.

187   "You know every time" and "Man and woman": *World*, February 16,
        1896, 32.

187   "She fell from the see-saw": *World*, February 23, 1896, 17.

189   "freaks" and "froth" and "your old energy": G.W. Hosmer to Norris,
        May 29, 1896 [with enclosure of Pulitzer to Brisbane], Box 1, Folder
        1896, May–June, LCPP.

189   "Sorry we did not have that": Box 1, Folder 1886–1897, SULBA.

189   "I am not sorry that I endured": *World*, February 16, 1896, 17.

190   "You know perfectly well": Box 1, Folder 1886–1897, SULBA.

190   "an interesting condition" and "disgusting and sickening": Quoted in
        Morris, *Pulitzer*, 380.

192   "The light from Liberty's torch": *World*, April 12, 1896, 29.

192   "Give me two ounces" and the rest of the quotations about the scene:
        World, June 21, 1896, 17.

193   "Byronic fashion" and other quotations from this article: *World*, August 9, 1896, 30.

194   "Semaphore" and other examples of code: Cable Code Book used by H. A. Jenks, New York, ca. 1906, Box 40, CUWP.

194   "I hope you are satisfied": Pulitzer to Norris, June 15, 1896, Box 1, Folder 1896, CUPP.

195   "There was never before anywhere": *Sun*, October 21, 1896, 6.

196   "I used to go to my hotel": Black, "Rambles, Part II," 218.

196   "guttural snarl" and other quotations from this article: *San Francisco Examiner*, June 5, 1892, 13.

197   "fairy bareback rider": *World*, March 8, 1896.

198   "These women are fiercer than the men": *New York Journal*, March 14, 1896, 2.

198   "Shakespearean ballet" and "a chorus of women reporters": *Times*, March 28, 1897, 5.

199   "the furious exploitation of crime" and other quotations from this article: *Chicago Times-Herald*, quoted in *Sun*, March 27, 1896, 6.

200   "If any girl who reads this is ever tempted": Willard, *Occupations*, 290.

200   "intruding their individuality on the public" and other quotations from this article: *Times-Democrat*, April 12, 1896, 22–23.

Chapter 14: A Smear of Yellow (1896–1897)

204   "And behold a Transformation!" Banks, *Autobiography*, 297.

204   "Oh, no; I am not going" and other quotations from this interview: *New York Journal*, October 14, 1896, 12.

205   "financial catastrophe": Banks, *Autobiography*, 195.

205   "sunlight, sparkling on a dome of gold": Ibid., 197.

205   "the most difficult, the most enterprising": Banks, "'Yellow Journalism,'" 340.

205   "Hundreds of them passed": Ross, *Ladies*, 24.

206   "You'll have to write": Finch Kelly, *Flowing Stream*, 138.

206 "clamour of the stunting sisterhood" and "its daring and unsavory exploits": Ibid., 458–59.

206 "My book will not go because": Elizabeth Banks to Wm. Morris Colles, December 11, 1901, UTBP.

207 "But one thing troubles me": Banks, "'Yellow Journalism,'" 335.

207 "Gotham's Great Epidemic" and other quotations from this article: *Indianapolis Journal*, February 4, 1897, 2.

207 "that prurient desire of knowing": "prurient, adj. and n." *OED Online*, Oxford University Press, March 31, 2020. Web.

207 "The smartest ancient rhetorical theorists": Beard, *Women*, 41.

208 "In many institutions where the *World* and *Journal*" and "pernicious and unclean newspapers": *Sun*, March 10, 1897, 1.

208 "the respect and confidence of the public" and "the notion that we are": Pulitzer to Norris, August 21, 1897, Box 1, Folder 1897 July, LCPP.

209 "the wilds of Virginia" and "'Men! . . . why, if I sent a man": Banks, "'Yellow Journalism,'" 336.

209 "delicate, feminine appearance" and other quotations from this scene: Banks, *Autobiography*, 209–11.

210 "breaking down under a very great": Quoted in Banks, *Remaking*, xxxiii.

210 "I had forgotten that you were interested" and other quotations from this scene: Banks, *Autobiography*, 225.

212 "When the educated man of special training": *New York Journal*, July 4, 1897, 13.

213 "You, men, take care of the situation": Prados-Torreira, *Mambisas*, 139.

213 "shy, dark-eyed Cuban maiden": *New York Journal*, October 17, 1897, 45.

213 "Mrs. Victoria Earle Matthews who was once a slave" and other quotations from this page: *New York Journal*, August 15, 1897, 12.

214 "none are more popular": Penn, *Afro-American Press*, 375.

214 "America's great epic": Matthews, "Cedar Hill," 2–4.

214   "The Value of Race Literature" and quotations from the speech: Matthews, *Value*.

214   "Yes I had seen The Hon.": Victoria Earle Matthews to Frederick Douglass, August 3, 1894, LCDP.

214   "torn and disordered": Quoted in Washington, *Papers*, 362.

214   "motherhood and womanhood" and "the same standards of morality": "Colored Woman's Congress."

215   "When I speak of the colored people": Matthews, "Redemption," 57.

215   "fearlessly and unobserved" and "her personality and natural": Davis, *Lifting*, 21–22.

217   "If you are going to try to exist": *Evening World*, December 9, 1888, 5.

217   "No working girl can live comfortably": Ibid.

218   "As the days and the weeks went on": Banks, *Autobiography*, 215.

218   "self-assertive and combative disposition": Ibid., 204.

219   "Above the boards and councils": *New York Journal*, December 3, 1897, 6.

219   "timid and dull, as bankrupt": *New York Journal*, December 31, 1897, 8.

220   "Chief much broken": Alfred Butes to John Norris, December 31, 1897, Box 1, Folder 1897 December, LCPP.

Chapter 15: All Together in New Bedford (1898)

221   "came from the Atlantic, Pacific": Melville, *Moby Dick*, 28.

222   "Friend Doll" and other quotations from this letter: Eva McDonald Valesh to Albert Dollenmayer, July 19, 1891, Folder: Letters 1891, MHSDP.

223   "It is a hard struggle" and other quotations from this letter are from Eva McDonald Valesh to Albert Dollenmayer, August 20, 1891, Folder: Letters 1891, MHSDP.

223   "baby being then considerably older": Frank Valesh to Albert Dollenmayer, May 10, 1892, MHSDP.

223   "I don't think I shall ever be content": Eva McDonald Valesh to Albert Dollenmayer, July 19, 1891, Folder: Letters 1891, MHSDP.

223   "She was the most selfish": Reminiscences of Eva MacDonald Valesh: Oral History, 1952. A letter from her sister is included in the copy held at the Minnesota Historical Society.

224   "loss of self respect": *Star Tribune*, November 6, 1898, 27.

224   "an impossible assignment" and other quotations about reporting this suicide story: Valesh, Oral History, CUL.

225   "terror of work, of monotony": *New York Journal*, September 2, 1897, 5.

225   "I want an exclusive story": Valesh, Oral History, CUL.

225   "She has good looks to recommend her": *New York Journal*, September 2, 1897, 5.

225   "suicide editor" and "it was gruesome work": Valesh, Oral History, CUL.

226   "these things must be done artistically": *Star Tribune*, November 6, 1898, 27.

226   "By taking these liberties": Kois, "Facts," https://slate.com /culture/2012/02/the-lifespan-of-a-fact-essayist-john-dagata-defends -his-right-to-fudge-the-truth.html.

226   "a great paper has a duty" and "may wield an enormous": *Star Tribune*, November 6, 1898, 27.

226   "Of course, we are a bit sensational" and other quotations from this scene: Valesh, Oral History, CUL.

227   "A man, you see": WLHBH.

228   "Sit down!" and other quotations from this scene: Ibid.

228   "the Journal's special commissioner to the cotton strike": *New York Journal*, January 19, 1898, 1.

229   "The woes of the 4,000 women": WLHBH.

229   "Grim Silence Everywhere": Ibid.

230   "her ragged gown about her" and "The New England mill operatives": Ibid.

230   "unutterable degradation—the degradation": Ibid.

230   "a howling wind might blow": Ibid.

231   "Yesterday's story was mainly": Ibid.

231   "a few degrees lower, if such a thing": Ibid.

231   "America's a cruel country": Ibid.

232   "Could you suggest any other plan": Ibid.

233   "Her bravery is not": Ibid.

233   "I will not be fined": Ibid.

233   "interesting and unique personality" and "roused all England": Ibid.

233   "who obtained situations in the homes": Ibid.

233   "a friend of the poor workers": Banks, "'Yellow Journalism,'" 337.

234   "such clean houses they keep" and "I never saw": WLHBH.

234   "Write up some of the happy things": Ibid.

234   "one of the happiest and brightest": Ibid.

234   "Little Lord Fauntleroy": Ibid.

234   "Jolly Strikers Who Don't Whine": Ibid.

235   "Weavers on all common looms": Ibid.

235   "The Mill Weaver's Kiss of Death": Ibid.

235   "One newspaper woman couldn't find enough": Ibid.

236   "These good people claim" and "There may be cases": Ibid.

237   "I have called you together" and other quotations from this scene: Ibid.

238   "pitiable object": Ibid.

239   "You are out on strike in New Bedford?" and other quotations from this scene: Ibid.

239   "The two women were evidently": *Boston Globe*, February 9, 1898, 5.

239   "sensational yellow journalism" and other quotations from this scene: *Boston Globe*, February 11, 1898, 6.

239   "Choke her off" and "This woman carries nothing": WLHBH.

Chapter 16: Reversal of Fortune (1898–1912)

241   "Maine Explosion Caused by Bomb or Torpedo?" and circulation figures: *World*, February 17, 1898, 1.

241   "Blanco Reports to Spain That It Was an Accident": Ibid., 2.

241   "Destruction of the War Ship Maine Was the Work of an Enemy":
        New York Journal, February 17, 1898, 1.

241   "War! Sure!": *New York Journal*, February 17, 1898, 1.

242   "Congress Declares War": *New York Journal*, April 25, 1898, 1.

242   "We Pilfer the News": Quoted in Procter, *Hearst*, 124.

243   "possessed in common the traits": Roosevelt, *Rough Riders*, 19.

243   "services to liberty": Quoted in Procter, *Hearst*, 127.

244   "We are indeed accustomed to finding truth": Hawthorne,
        Evangelina, 17.

244   "Does Our Flag Shield Women?": *New York Journal*, February 12,
        1897, 1.

245   "the American government declines": *New York Journal*, February 14,
        1897, 42.

245   "It is true that I was actively engaged in the conspiracy as far as I
        could be": *World*, February 15, 1897, 1.

245   "The fair young female journalist" and "Every beautiful newspaper
        woman": Brisbane, "Great Problems," 545–46.

246   The "New Woman in Journalism": *Hartford Courant*, March 12,
        1898, 8.

246   "I have always advocated that weavers": WLHBH.

247   "God pity those who could not at command": Banks, *Autobiography*,
        237.

248   "I am not here to detail the serious": Quoted in Freeman, *Kit's
        Kingdom*, 109.

248   "in the grand style such": Ibid., 110.

248   "one hundred and thirty-three men": Ibid., 118.

249   "Old Glory over Santiago," "The ceremony of hoisting the Stars and
        Stripes," and circulation figures: *New York Journal*, July 18, 1898, 1.

249   "You provide the pictures": Campbell, *Yellow Journalism*, 85.

249   "The paper is a jest": Irving Bacheller to Don Carlos Seitz, April 12,
        1900, Box 1, CUWP.

249   "We must heed it in every department": Meeting minutes, November
        28, 1898, Box 1, Folder 1898 August–Dec, LCPP.

249   "corrupts, depraves, degrades, or injures": *Buffalo Weekly Express*, October 13, 1898, 4.

251   "The latter simply prefer scandal": Commander, "Significance," 154–55.

251   "The *Journal* has too sincere a sympathy": Thornton, "When a Newspaper," 110.

253   "I have yet to meet the woman": Banks, "'Yellow Journalism,'" 338.

253   "seamy side" and other quotations from this letter: Elizabeth Banks to Wm. Morris Colles, December 10, 1901, UTBP.

253   "But why are you here?": Crane, *Active*, 160.

254   "Henrietta, however, does smell": James, *Portrait*, 131.

254   "Of all horned cattle, deliver me": Quoted in *Philadelphia Inquirer*, April 12, 1891, 4.

254   "whose thoughts reach beyond their own livelihood" and other quotations from this article: Pulitzer, "College," 658.

255   "private detective": *Editor and Publisher*, August 20, 1910, 5.

255   "Was any decision reached": *New-York Tribune*, March 23, 1912, 7.

256   "the man with the muck rake" and other quotations from this speech: *Bismarck Tribune*, April 16, 1906, 1.

258   "On the one hand, that action": Sawaya, *Modern Women*, 81.

Chapter 17: In the Wake (1898–1900)

260   "so brazen and defiant": *New-York Tribune*, March 30, 1905, 5.

261   "Let women and girls become enlightened": Matthews, "Dangers," 62–69.

261   "The city does not need to throw back": *Sun*, September 14, 1897, 6.

261   "The White Rose Mission was organized": *New York Evening Telegram*, September 20, 1897, 1–2.

262   "Says the Northerner" and other quotations from this article: Banks, "Negro," 459–74.

263   "America is not a land of equality": Banks, *Autobiography*, 157.

264   "Wells-Barnett" and other quotations from this scene: Wells-Barnett,
       Crusade, 255.

265   "despite my best": Ibid., 216.

265   "like they were little feathers": Green and Kelly, *Night*, 24.

265   "as easy to get into Galveston": Black, "Rambles, Part V," 36.

265   "slimy with the debris of the sea" and "negroes": Quoted in Green,
       Flood, 88.

266   "He told us what he was thinking": Ibid., 93.

Chapter 18: Vanishing Ink (1900–Present)

267   "nonfiction novel" and "a serious new art form": *New York Times*,
       January 16, 1966, BR2.

268   "By trial and error" and "the everyday gestures": Wolfe, "Great
       American Novel," 158.

268   "Lucia stood and watched": *Jewell County Monitor*, November 27,
       1895, 3.

269   "I see a child": Didion, *Slouching*, 127–28.

269   "sensibility, the tonal range": *New York Times*, March 13, 2005, G1.

270   "slow drip of petty disclosure," "big, earnest blob," and "the
       Godfather behind": Wolcott, "Me, Myself," 216, 214.

270   "artfully told narrative": Boynton, *New New Journalism*, xi–xxxii.

270   "in the best tradition of newspaper sob sisterism": Yurick, "Sob-
       Sister," 158.

271   "Don't bother to look for it here": Thompson, *Fear*, 33.

271   "The only reason Wolfe seems 'new'": Thompson, "Jacket Copy,"
       108.

271   "spy-glass": Hurston, *Mules*, 1.

271   "I hurried back to Eatonville": Ibid., 2.

272   "Hanged for stealing hogs" and other examples: Wells, *Selected Works*.

272   "pretty and personable" and other quotations from and about this
       article: Steinem, *Outrageous*, 29–69.

273   "Though I identified emotionally": Ibid., 16.

273   "Eventually, dawning feminism": Ibid.

273   "Someone ought to do": Ehrenreich, *Nickel*, 1.

274   "Something is wrong, very wrong": Ibid., 199.

274   "I perceived it, specifically": Faludi, *Darkroom*, 52.

275   "As I look back on it, it was a good piece" and other quotations from this source: Author interview.

276   "a world of deception": Author interview.

276   "Tales Told Out of School": *New York Times*, November 30, 2014, 18.

276   "kiss-and-tell": Haggard, "Suki Kim," https://www.piie.com/blogs /north-korea-witness-transformation/suki-kim-without-you-there -no-us-my-time-sons-north-koreas.

277   "Great insights from 'that girl'" and other quotations from this panel: "From the Inside: A Conversation on Immersion and Undercover Reporting," Investigative Reporters & Editors Conference, 2017.

277   "I courted that organization": Author interview.

Chapter 19: Anonymous Sources (Present)

279   "trying to make a reputation": Volume 9, CHMCMS.

280   "Guess which of the above is the 'girl reporter'": *Chicago Times*, December 21, 1888, 4.

280   What I Know About the Girl Reporter: Details are taken from her *Chicago Times* series in December 1888.

281   "Physicians Who Recommend Others Who Would Commit Abortion": *Chicago Times*, December 27, 1888, 1.

281   "That lady reporter of theirs": *Chicago Times*, January 4, 1889, 4.

282   "Florence Noble, alias Margaret Noble": *Inter Ocean*, January 9, 1889, 9.

282   "the girl reporter": *Sterling Daily Gazette*, January 9, 1889, 2.

282   "The Chicago Times Company, James J. West": Silva vs. *Chicago Times*, January 1889, G-70667, CCCA.

283 "The Girl Reporter of the Chicago Times Is Here": *Ashland Weekly News*, January 23, 1889, 6.

283 "committed to the Joliet asylum" and "suffered from delusions": *Chicago Tribune*, May 8, 1924, 20.

284 "That the young woman filled": Banks, "'Yellow Journalism,'" 338.

284 "Years ago, a degenerate public": Cahoon, "Gutter," 572.

284 "a homeless fallen woman": Ibid., 572–73.

286 "dark, dingy, and dirty": *Chicago Tribune*, September 5, 1888, 5.

286 "O, Mrs. Carpenter": Ibid.

286 "I would feel myself lost among them": *Chicago Times*, December 19, 1888, 1.

Chapter 20: A Collection of Endings (1899–1922)

289 "Think of what a greater": *Sun*, September 24, 1899, 1.

290 "Mrs. Katherine Swan": *Brooklyn Daily Eagle*, June 23, 1901, 2.

290 "the famous 'Kate Swan'": *Star-Gazette*, June 16, 1908, 7.

291 "Go": Black, "Rambles, Part V," 256.

291 "Annie Laurie Tells of the Spectral City": *San Francisco Examiner*, April 22, 1906, 10.

292 "Get the idea out of your heads": *Fort Wayne Journal-Gazette*, July 4, 1919, 12.

292 "You will smile it out": Henry James to Elizabeth Jordan, October 2, 1907, Box 2, Folder 16, NYPLJP.

293 "The story itself is almost": *Tennessean*, October 20, 1912, 43.

293 "It was the happiest work": Valesh, Oral History, CUL.

294 "During the 90's": *Detroit Free Press*, March 22, 1936.

295 "You know what the Lord": *Courier-News*, June 15, 1915, 11.

295 "What the Women Are Doing in the War": *Courier-News*, March 21, 1917, 1.

295 "As a stranger, I could": Banks, *Remaking*, 172.

296   "Where else in the world": Ibid., 182.

296   "Boys come and shake hands": Wells-Barnett, *Crusade*, 401.

297   "They are now enjoying the result": Wells-Barnett, *Arkansas*, 11.

297   "Pray to live": Wells-Barnett, *Crusade*, 403.

299   "kind, courteous, and persistent effort": Arthur Brisbane to Nellie Bly, June 28, 1907, Box 12, Folder Brisbane, Arthur/Bly, Nellie, 1907–1912, SULBF.

299   "doing much more useful work": Arthur Brisbane to Nellie Bly, June 13, 1912, Box 12, Folder, Brisbane, Arthur/Bly, Nellie, 1907–1912, SULBF.

299   "Nellie Bly was THE BEST": Quoted in Kroeger, *Nellie Bly*, 509.

Archives and Special Collections

1898 Textile Strike in New Bedford: scrapbooks of clippings collected by Harry Beetle Hough. Widener Library, Harvard University (WLHBH). (Many of the clippings in these scrapbooks are missing dates and, often, the names of the newspapers where the articles were printed.)

Elizabeth L. Banks Papers. University of Tulsa, Special Collections and University Archives at McFarlin Library (UTBP).

Brisbane Family Papers. Special Collections Research Center, Syracuse University Libraries (SULBF).

Brisbane 2001 Addition. Special Collections Research Center, Syracuse University Libraries (SULBA).

Chicago Medical Society Records, 1852–1912. Chicago History Museum Research Center (CHMCMS).

Chicago Women's Club Records. Chicago History Museum Research Center (CHMCWC).

Circuit Court of Cook County Archives (CCCA).

Albert Dollenmayer and Family Papers. Minnesota Historical Society (MHSDP).

Frederick Douglass Papers. Manuscript Division, Library of Congress (LCDP).

Phoebe Hearst Papers. Bancroft Library, University of California (BLPHP).

William Randolph Hearst Papers. Bancroft Library, University of California (BLWHP).

Elizabeth Garver Jordan Papers. Manuscripts and Archives Division, The New York Public Library. Astor, Lenox, and Tilden Foundations (NYPLJP).

Kautz Family YMCA Archives. University of Minnesota Libraries (UMLKF).

Joseph Pulitzer Papers, Rare Book & Manuscript Library, Columbia University Libraries (CUPP).

The Papers of Joseph Pulitzer, Manuscript Division, Library of Congress (LCPP).

Don Carlos Seitz Papers. Manuscripts and Archives Division, The New York Public Library (NYPLSP).

Eva McDonald Valesh Papers. Minnesota Historical Society (MHSVP).

Reminiscences of Eva MacDonald Valesh: Oral History, 1952. Rare Book and Manuscript Library, Columbia University Libraries (CUL).

Ida B. Wells Papers. Special Collections Research Center, University of Chicago Library (UCIWP).

The World (New York) Records. Rare Book and Manuscript Library, Columbia University Libraries (CUWP).

Works by Elizabeth Banks

Pollock, Polly. "She Aspires to Love." *St. Paul Globe*, September 14, 1888.

——. "Fashions at Home." *St. Paul Globe*, September 23, 1888.

——. "A Womanly Woman." *St. Paul Globe*, November 4, 1888.

——. "Polly's Confession." *St. Paul Globe*, November 25, 1888.

——. "Presents Pinching." *St. Paul Globe*, January 6, 1889.

Banks, Elizabeth. "As Ourselves See Us." *Chicago Tribune*, December 17, 1892.

——. *Campaigns of Curiosity: Journalistic Adventures of an American Girl in London*. Chicago: F. T. Neely, 1894.

——. "First Day on $3 per Week." *Evening World*, December 9, 1897.

——. "What She Eats on $3 per Week." *Evening World*, December 10, 1897.

——. "Hardships of Living on $3 per Week." *Evening World*, December 11, 1897.

——. "Hard Work to Live on $3 per Week." *Evening World*, December 13, 1897.

——. "She Can't Live on $3 per Week." *Evening World*, December 14, 1897.

——. "Can Starve, Not Live, on $3 a Week." *Evening World*, December 15, 1897.

——. "American 'Yellow Journalism.'" *Nineteenth Century* 44 (August 1898).

——. "The American Negro and His Place." *Nineteenth Century* 46 (September 1899).

——. *The Autobiography of a "Newspaper Girl."* London: Methuen & Co., 1902.

——. *The Remaking of an American*. New York: Doubleday, Doran & Company, 1928.

Works by Elizabeth Cochrane

Orphan Girl [Nellie Bly]. "The Girl Puzzle." *Pittsburg Dispatch*, January 25, 1885.

Bly, Nellie. "Mad Marriages." *Pittsburg Dispatch*, February 1, 1885.

——. "Superior Soothing." *Pittsburg Dispatch*, August 7, 1887.

——. "Women Journalists." *Pittsburg Dispatch*, August 21, 1887.

——. "Behind Asylum Bars." *World*, October 9, 1887.

——. "Inside the Madhouse." *World*, October 16, 1887.

——. "Untruths in Every Line." *World*, October 16, 1887.

——. *Ten-Days in a Madhouse*. New York: Ian L. Munroe, [n.d.]. http://digital
.library.upenn.edu/women/bly/madhouse/madhouse.html.

——. "The Girls Who Make Boxes." *World*, November 27, 1887.

——. "King of the Lobby." *World*, April 1, 1888.

——. "Hangman Joe at Home." *World*, September 30, 1888.

——. "Should Women Propose?" *World*, November 11, 1888.

——. "Should Women Propose?" *World*, November 18, 1888.

——. "Among the Mad," *Godey's Lady's Book* 118 (January 1889).

——. *Around the World in Seventy-Two Days*. New York: Pictorial Weeklies Company, 1890, http://digital.library.upenn.edu/women/bly/world/world.html.

——. "Dr. Parkhurst to Nellie Bly." *World*, December 10, 1893.

——. "Rents Did It." *St. Louis Post-Dispatch*, July 13, 1894.

——. "At Pullman." *St. Joseph Daily Herald*, July 13, 1894.

——. "Their Only Hope," *St. Louis Post-Dispatch*, July 17, 1894.

——. "Nellie Bly Says." *Evening World*, February 5, 1895.

——. "Nellie Bly with the Female Suffragists." *World*, January 26, 1896.

——. "Champion of her Sex." *World*, February 2, 1896.

——. "Homeless, Hopeless." *World*, February 9, 1896.

——. "Nellie Bly and Two Woman Contrasts." *World*, February 16, 1896.

——. "Nellie Bly as an Elephant Trainer." *World*, February 23, 1896.

——. "Austrians Joyful as They Go into Battle, Feeling Cause Right." *Buffalo Courier*, January 16, 1915.

Works by Helen Cusack

Nelson, Nell. "City Slave Girls." *Chicago Times*, July 30, 1888.

——. "City Slave Girls." *Chicago Times*, July 31, 1888.

——. "City Slave Girls." *Chicago Times*, August 1, 1888.

——. "City Slave Girls." *Chicago Times*, August 2, 1888.

——. "City Slave Girls." *Chicago Times*, August 3, 1888.

——. "City Slave Girls." *Chicago Times*, August 4, 1888.

——. "City Slave Girls." *Chicago Times*, August 5, 1888.

——. "City Slave Girls." *Chicago Times*, August 7, 1888.

——. "City Slave Girls." *Chicago Times*, August 8, 1888.

——. "City Slave Girls." *Chicago Times*, August 9, 1888.

——. "City Slave Girls." *Chicago Times*, August 12, 1888.

——. "City Slave Girls." *Chicago Times*, August 15, 1888.

——. "City Slave Girls." *Chicago Times*, August 17, 1888.

——. "City Slave Girls." *Chicago Times*, August 18, 1888.

——. "City Slave Girls." *Chicago Times*, August 26, 1888.

——. "City Slave Girls." *Chicago Times*, August 27, 1888.

——. "Horrors of a Slop Shop." *World*, September 30, 1888.

——. "They Work in an Inferno." *World*, October 7, 1888.

——. "Useful Husbands." *Boston Post*, February 11, 1894.

Works by Elizabeth Jordan

Anon. [Elizabeth Jordan]. "In Her New Cottage." *World*, June 28, 1890.

——. "A Mountain Preacher." *World*, November 20, 1890.

——. "Borden Jury Chosen." *World*, June 6, 1893.

——. "Miss Borden Faints." *World*, June 7, 1893.

——. "Lizzie's Dark Day." *World*, June 9, 1893.

——. "Miss Borden's Hope." *World*, June 10, 1893.

——. "Is Lizzie Borden Innocent?" *World*, June 11, 1893.

——. "Murders Re-Enacted." *World*, June 14, 1893.

——. "You Gave Me Away!" *World*, June 15, 1893.

——. "Lizzie Borden Free." *World*, June 21, 1893.

Jordan, Elizabeth G. "This Is the Real Lizzie Borden." *World*, June 18, 1893.

——. "Ruth Herrick's Assignment," *Cosmopolitan* (May–October 1894).

——. *Tales of the City Room.* New York: C. Scribner's Sons, 1898.

——. *Three Rousing Cheers.* New York: D. Appleton Century Co., 1938.

Works by the Girl Reporter

Girl Reporter. "Infanticide." *Chicago Times*, December 15, 1888.

——. "Infanticide." *Chicago Times*, December 16, 1888.

——. "Infanticide." *Chicago Times*, December 17, 1888.

——. "Infanticide." *Chicago Times*, December 18, 1888.

——. "Infanticide." *Chicago Times*, December 19, 1888.

——. "Infanticide." *Chicago Times*, December 20, 1888.

——. "Infanticide." *Chicago Times*, December 21, 1888.

——. "Infanticide." *Chicago Times*, December 22, 1888.

——. "Infanticide." *Chicago Times*, December 23, 1888.

——. "Infanticide." *Chicago Times*, December 24, 1888.

——. "Infanticide." *Chicago Times*, December 25, 1888.

——. "Infanticide." *Chicago Times*, December 26, 1888.

Works by Victoria Earle Matthews

Matthews, Victoria Earle. "Home Circle." *Washington Bee*, April 9, 1887.

——. "Our New York Letter." *National Leader*, January 5, 1889.

——. "Cedar Hill and Its Master." *Woman's Era* 1, no. 8 (November 1894).

——. *The Value of Race Literature: An Address Delivered at the First Congress of Colored Women of the United States, at Boston, Mass., July 30th, 1895.*

——. "The Negroes of New York." *New York Sun*, September 14, 1897.

——. "Some of the Dangers Confronting Southern Girls in the North," Hampton Negro Conference Proceedings, 1898.

——. "The Redemption of Our City—Colored," *Federation* 1, no. 8 (July 1902).

——. "Protecting Colored Girls," *New-York Tribune*, March 30, 1905.

Works by Kate Swan McGuirk

McGuirk, Mrs. "Summer Dress of Congressmen." *Los Angeles Herald*, August 18, 1892.

——. "A Persecuted Woman's Plea." *New York Recorder*, September 19, 1892.

——. "Their Summer Homes." *Salt Lake Herald*, June 25, 1893.

——. "Thrilling Hunt for a Wild Woman." *World*, May 31, 1896.

——. "Mrs. M'Guirk Studies Bryan," *World*, August 9, 1896.

McGuirk, Kate. "The Mill Weaver's Kiss of Death," *World*, January 30, 1898.

Swan, Kate. "Kate Swan in the Death Chair." *World*, February 16, 1896.

——. "Kate Swan's Night on Ellis Island." *World*, April 12, 1896.

——. "Traffic in the Drug That Debases Womanhood." *World*, June 21, 1896.

Works by Eleanor Stackhouse

Marks, Nora. "On the Great West Side." *Chicago Tribune*, September 5, 1888.

——. "Nora Visits the Jail." *Chicago Tribune*, January 13, 1889.

——. "All Jolted Alike." *Chicago Tribune*, December 13, 1889.

Works by Winifred Black

Columbine. "Confessions of an Actress." *Chicago Tribune*, December 16, 1888.

——. "Her Frank Confession." *Chicago Tribune*, January 13, 1889.

Anon. [Winifred Sweet]. "A Peep at Fairyland." *San Francisco Examiner*, April 25, 1889.

——. "Circling the Globe." *San Francisco Examiner*, November 20, 1889.

Laurie, Annie. "A City's Disgrace." *San Francisco Examiner*, January 19, 1890.

——. "Annie Laurie's Experience." *San Francisco Examiner*, July 13, 1890.

——. "San Francisco's Shame." *San Francisco Examiner*, August 17, 1890.

——. "Politics as They Seem." *San Francisco Examiner*, August 24, 1890.

——. "Valueless and Poisonous." *San Francisco Examiner*, January 25, 1891.

——. "As Women Never Know Them." *San Francisco Examiner*, June 5, 1892.

——. "As 'Annie Laurie' Saw It." *San Francisco Examiner*, May 26, 1895.

——. "Annie Laurie Tells of the Spectral City." *San Francisco Examiner*, April 22, 1906.

——. "Advice to Girls." *Fort Wayne Journal-Gazette*, July 4, 1919.

Black, Winifred. "Horror of Horrors." *Jewell County Monitor*, November 27, 1895.

——. "Rambles Through My Memories, Part I." *Good Housekeeping* 102, no. 1 (January 1936).

——. "Rambles Through My Memories, Part II." *Good Housekeeping* 102, no. 2 (February 1936).

——. "Rambles Through My Memories, Part III." *Good Housekeeping* 102, no. 3 (March 1936).

——. "Rambles Through My Memories, Part IV." *Good Housekeeping* 102, no. 4 (April 1936).

——. "Rambles Through My Memories, Part V." *Good Housekeeping* 102, no. 5 (May 1936).

Works by Eva McDonald Valesh

Gay, Eva. "'Mong' Girls Who Toil." *St. Paul Globe*, March 25, 1888.

——. "Song of the Shirt." *St. Paul Globe*, April 8, 1888.

——. "Working in the Wet." *St. Paul Globe*, April 15, 1888.

——. "Eva Gay's Travels." *St. Paul Globe*, April 22, 1888.

——. "Striking Maidens." *St. Paul Globe*, April 29, 1888.

——. "Eva Gay's Travels." *St. Paul Globe*, May 6, 1888.

——. "Girls Make Money." *St. Paul Globe*, May 13, 1888.

——. "Workers in Wool." *St. Paul Globe*, May 20, 1888.

——. "Girls Make Cigars." *St. Paul Globe*, May 27, 1888.

——. "Girls Make Boxes." *St. Paul Globe*, June 3, 1888.

——. "The Sewing Girls." *St. Paul Globe*, June 10, 1888.

——. "How Girls Clerk." *St. Paul Globe*, June 17, 1888.

——. "On the Bright Side." *St. Paul Globe*, June 24, 1888.

——. "The Girls Rejoice." *St. Paul Globe*, July 1, 1888.

——. "The White Cross." *St. Paul Globe*, July 8, 1888.

——. "Behind the Scenes." *St. Paul Globe*, July 22, 1888.

——. "Only One Objection." *St. Paul Globe*, July 29, 1888.

——. "Search for Homes." *St. Paul Globe*, August 5, 1888.

——. "Girls in Politics." *St. Paul Globe*, August 19, 1888.

——. "Looking for a Place." *St. Paul Globe*, September 9, 1888.

——. "Yes, You Know Her." *St. Paul Globe*, November 4, 1888.

——. "Didn't Fit the Bill." *St. Paul Globe*, December 12, 1888.

——. "Makes Girls Blind." *St. Paul Globe*, December 25, 1888.

——. "Life of a Fair One." *St. Paul Globe*, January 13, 1889.

——. "Eva Gay's Inquiries." *St. Paul Globe*, January 20, 1889.

——. "My Lady's Chamber." *St. Paul Globe*, January 27, 1889.

——. "A Chapter on Pugs." *St. Paul Globe*, February 3, 1889.

——. "And So She Flunked." *St. Paul Globe*, February 24, 1889.

Anon. [Valesh, Eva McDonald]. "Girl Victim of Suicide Club." *New York Journal*, September 2, 1897.

Valesh, Eva McDonald. "Journalism in New York." *Star Tribune*, November 6, 1898.

Works by Ida B. Wells-Barnett

Wells, Ida B., and Miriam DeCosta-Willis. *The Memphis Diary of Ida B. Wells*. Boston: Beacon Press, 1995.

Wells-Barnett, Ida B. *Arkansas Race Riot*. Chicago: Ida B. Wells-Barnett, 1920.

Wells-Barnett, Ida B. *Crusade for Justice: The Autobiography of Ida B. Wells*. Negro American Biographies and Autobiographies. Chicago: University of Chicago Press, 1970.

Wells-Barnett, Ida B., and Trudier Harris. *Selected Works of Ida B. Wells-Barnett*. The Schomburg Library of Nineteenth-Century Black Women Writers. New York: Oxford University Press, 1991.

OTHER SOURCES

A.S.A. "A Practical Age." *Indianapolis News*, July 4, 1885.

Anon. "Smarter Than All of Them." *The Hazel Green Herald*, December 9, 1887.

——. "Dr. Van Hambert's Female Renovating Pills." *New York Daily Herald*, October 26, 1837.

——. [No Title.] *Buffalo Commercial Advertiser*, November 3, 1837.

——. "To Females in Delicate Health." *Public Ledger*, February 25, 1841.

——. "Mysterious Murder at Hoboken." *Public Ledger*, August 3, 1841.

——. "Another Arrest in the Miss Rogers Case." *Public Ledger*, September 1, 1841.

——. "Female's Friend." *New-York Tribune*, September 28, 1841.

——. "Genuine French Female Monthly Pills." *New-York Tribune*, September 30, 1841.

——. "John Tyler and the New York Herald." *Vicksburg Daily Whig*, October 12, 1841.

——. "The Case of Madame Restell." *New-York Tribune*, August 24, 1842.

——. "The Mary Rogers Mystery Explained." *New-York Tribune*, November 18, 1842.

——. "Lefever, the Seducer." *Buffalo Courier*, May 24, 1843.

——. "Restellism in Boston." *Baltimore Sun*, April 3, 1848.

——. "News Summary." *Brooklyn Daily Eagle*, March 26, 1872.

——. "News Summary." *Brooklyn Daily Eagle*, October 16, 1872.

——. "Political." *Buffalo Commercial Advertiser*, March 23, 1872.

——. [Morning Journal Ad]. *St. Louis Post-Dispatch*, April 25, 1883.

——. [No Title]. *World*, May 11, 1883.

——. "Want Ads." *Pittsburg Dispatch*, January 11–17, 1885.

——. "Lonely Orphan Girl." *Pittsburg Dispatch*, January 17, 1885.

——. "The City." *Chicago Tribune*, June 25, 1885.

——. "Ownership of the Examiner." *San Francisco Examiner*, March 4, 1887.

——. *Journalist* V, no. 25 (September 10, 1887).

——. *Journalist* V, no. 26 (September 17, 1887).

——. "Who Is This Insane Girl?" *Sun*, September 25, 1887.

——. "In and About Town. A Mysterious Waif. Bellevue Shelters a Girl of Whom Nothing Is Known." *New York Times*, September 26, 1887.

——. "Mrs. Robinson's Fatal Leap. A Louisville Woman's Suicide," *New-York Tribune*, October 10, 1887.

——. "Playing Mad Woman." *Sun*, October 14, 1887.

——. "She Ran Away from Home." *Evening World*, October 14, 1887.

——. "A Bride Choked with Gas." *Evening World*, October 15, 1887.

——. "He Dug Her Grave." *Daily Arkansas Gazette*, October 15, 1887.

——. "Can Doctors Tell Insanity?" *Sun*, October 23, 1887.

——. "Smarter Than All of Them." *Hazel Green Herald*, December 9, 1887.

——. [No title]. *Salt Lake Herald*, December 9, 1887.

——. "An Interesting Book." *Ohio Democrat*, December 17, 1887.

——. "The Times Transferred." *Inter Ocean*, December 25, 1887.

——. "Woman's Department." *Iola Register*, December 30, 1887.

——. "The New Chicago Times." *Marion Star*, January 13, 1888.

——. "Howard's Gossip." *Boston Globe*, January 20, 1888.

——. "Woman's World and Work." *Times-Picayune*, March 25, 1888.

——. "A Crusade for Women." *St. Paul Globe*, April 1, 1888.

——. "Serious Charge." *Buffalo News*, April 3, 1888.

——. "A Case for Eva Gay." *St. Paul Globe*, April 7, 1888.

——. "Our Female Strikers." *St. Paul Globe*, April 19, 1888.

——. [No Title]. *Chicago Times*, April 22, 1888.

——. "Minneapolis News." *St. Paul Globe*, May 11, 1888.

——. "A Committee of Jobbers." *St. Paul Globe*, May 12, 1888.

——. "The Plain Facts." *Minneapolis Tribune*, May 13, 1888.

——. "Our Girls." *St. Paul Globe*, June 3, 1888.

——. "Zenith City Items." *Duluth Daily News*, June 8, 1888.

——. "Very Close to the Wall." *St. Paul Globe*, June 14, 1888.

——. "City Slave Girls." *Chicago Times*, August 6, 1888.

——. "City Slave Girls." *Chicago Times*, August 10, 1888.

——. "City Slave Girls." *Chicago Times*, August 11, 1888.

——. "City Slave Girls." *Chicago Times*, August 13, 1888.

——. "City Slave Girls." *Chicago Times*, August 14, 1888.

——. "City Slave Girls." *Chicago Times*, August 16, 1888.

——. "City Slave Girls." *Chicago Times*, August 19, 1888.

——. "Elopement of a Girl Reporter." *Chicago Tribune*, September 27, 1888.

——. "May Dougherty Didn't Elope." *Watertown News*, October 3, 1888.

——. "Special to the Trade." *St. Paul Globe*, October 4, 1888.

——. "She Journalists." *Buffalo Sunday Morning News*, October 7, 1888.

——. "Kittie Smith's Death." *Inter Ocean*, November 27, 1888.

——. "The Chicago Sensation." *St. Paul Globe*, December 20, 1888.

——. "A Novel Enterprise." *Buffalo Times*, December 24, 1888.

——. "Minneapolis." *St. Paul Globe*, December 24, 1888.

——. "Tansy Pills." *Boston Globe*, December 30, 1888.

——. "Is It a Plot?" *San Francisco Chronicle*, January 3, 1889.

——. "Seeking the Remedy." *Chicago Times*, January 3, 1889.

——. "Mrs. Lowenstein's Story." *Sun*, January 5, 1889.

——. "Circuit." *Inter Ocean*, January 9, 1889.

——. "They're Coming, $250,000 Strong." *Sterling Daily Gazette*, January 9, 1889.

——. "The Infanticide Revelations." *Journal of the American Medical Association* XII, no. 2 (January 12, 1889).

——. "Schaack and Bonfield." *Evening Bulletin*, January 12, 1889.

——. "Taking in the Town." *Ashland Weekly News*, January 23, 1889.

——. "Medical." *San Francisco Examiner*, February 18, 1889.

——. [Entire Issue]. *Journalist*, January 26, 1889.

——. "Found Dead in Bed." *St. Paul Globe*, April 8, 1889.

——. "The 'Journal' on Editor West." *Chicago Tribune*, July 24, 1889.

——. "In Financial Straits." *Sioux City Journal*, July 25, 1889.

——. "Personals." *San Francisco Examiner*, August 27, 1889.

——. "Written in Red." *San Francisco Examiner*, September 8, 1889.

——. "Bly Against Bisland." *San Francisco Examiner*, November 19, 1889.

——. "James J. West." *Sun*, December 24, 1889.

——. *The World, Its History and New Home*. New York: G. W. Turner, [1890].

——. "Saved from Death!" *San Francisco Examiner*, January 4, 1890.

——. "Inefficient Life-Saving Service." *San Francisco Examiner*, January 7, 1890.

——. "He Would Thrash Her!" *San Francisco Examiner*, January 20, 1890.

——. "Dr. Harrison Ousted." *San Francisco Examiner*, January 22, 1890.

——. "Nellie Bly Hastens On." *San Francisco Examiner*, January 22, 1890.

——. "The Receiving Hospital." *Daily Alta California*, January 23, 1890.

——. "Nellie Bly There." *Pittsburg Dispatch*, January 26, 1890.

——. "Miss Virginia Cusack Missing." *Chicago Tribune*, March 18, 1890.

——. "Virginia Cusack Heard From." *Chicago Tribune*, March 19, 1890.

——. "Nellie Bly and Her Book." *Harrisburg Telegraph*, July 24, 1890.

——. "Ethel's Game a Bold One." *Chicago Tribune*, November 16, 1890.

——. "Have You Got the Nerve?" *Sioux City Journal*, December 13, 1890.

——. "Mr. Dana on Self-Education." *Philadelphia Inquirer*, April 12, 1891.

——. "Honeymoons." *St. Paul Globe*, July 9, 1892.

——. "Did She Kill Them?" *Logansport Reporter*, August 6, 1892.

——. "His Daughter." *Boston Post*, August 6, 1892.

——. "Lizzie Borden's Sunday." *New York Times*, August 29, 1892.

——. "Mrs. Leslie." *Standard Union*, November 4, 1892.

——. "Her Many Aliases." *Pittsburgh Press*, November 26, 1892.

——. "The Real Annie Laurie." *San Francisco Examiner*, December 18, 1892.

——. [Entire issue]. *World*, May 7, 1893.

——. "Tompkins May Die." *Chicago Tribune*, October 25, 1893.

——. "His Loved Ones Lost." *Inter Ocean*, October 25, 1893.

——. "Tompkins' Mother Arrives." *Chicago Tribune*, October 27, 1893.

——. "The Wares of Autolycus." *Pall Mall Gazette*, November 22, 1893.

——. "Will Give Them Aid." *Evening World*, December 6, 1893.

——. "The Usual Result." *Evening World*, December 6, 1893.

——. "'Del's'" on His List." *World*, December 7, 1893.

——. [Entire issue]. *Boston Post*, February 11, 1894.

——. "He Saw Nellie Bly." September 11, 1894.

——. "Is 'Nellie Bly' Married?" *Indianapolis Journal*, April 7, 1895.

——. "A Red Hot Debate." *Mansfield News*, April 8, 1895.

——. "She's No Longer a Miss." *San Francisco Call*, April 14, 1895.

——. "A Stroke for Freedom." *San Francisco Examiner*, April 15, 1895.

——. "Oatmeal and Mackerel." *Buffalo Morning Express*, April 16, 1895.

——. "Brighter Outlook." *Weekly Pioneer-Times*, April 18, 1895.

——. "Ida Wells to Wed." *San Francisco Chronicle*, June 13, 1895.

——. "The Observant Citizen." *Boston Post*, June 21, 1895.

——. "A Missing Woman Is Found at Last." *San Francisco Chronicle*, September 25, 1895.

——. "For Dogging 'Nellie Bly.'" *Sun*, November 10, 1895.

——. "Nellie Bly Still at It." *Sun*, November 11, 1895.

——. "Nervy Nellie Bly." *Pittsburgh Post-Gazette*. November 30, 1895.

——. "The National Colored Woman's Congress." *The Woman's Era* II, no. 9 (January 1896).

——. "Daring Deeds by the Sunday World's Intrepid Woman Reporters." *World*, March 8, 1896.

——. "Chroniclings." *Democrat and Chronicle*, March 31, 1896, 6.

——. "Elizabeth Banks Will Write Us Up." *New York Journal*, October 14, 1896.

——. "Notes on the New Journalism." *Sun*, October 21, 1896.

——. "Gotham's Great Epidemic." *Indianapolis Journal*, February 4, 1897.

——. "Tale of a Fair Exile." *World*, February 15, 1897.

——. "Vile Newspapers Put Out." *Sun*, March 10, 1897.

——. "Mask and Wig's New Burlesque." *Times*, March 28, 1897.

——. "How the Great Murder Mystery Was Unraveled." *New York Journal*, July 4, 1897.

——. "Negro Girls Sold into Bondage: Young Women, Decoyed from the South by False Promises of Work, Become Slaves of White and Negro Masters," *New York Evening Telegram*, September 20, 1897.

——. "The People Unite with the Journal to Welcome Miss Cisneros to Freedom." *New York Journal*, October 17, 1897.

——. "Fines Law." *Boston Globe*, February 9, 1898.

——. "Agree or Quit." *Boston Globe*, February 11, 1898.

——. "Destruction of the War Ship Maine was the Work of an Enemy." *New York Journal*, February 17, 1898.

——. "Maine Explosion Caused by Bomb or Torpedo?" *World*, February 17, 1898.

——. "War! Sure!" *New York Journal*, February 17, 1898.

——. [No Title]. *Hartford Courant*, March 12, 1898.

——. "Congress Declares War." *New York Journal*, April 25, 1898.

——. "Ellsworth, His Bill." *Buffalo Weekly Express*, October 13, 1898.

——. "The White Rose Mission." *Sun*, September 24, 1899.

——. "Lectures on Cooking." *Brooklyn Daily Eagle*, June 23, 1901.

——. "'The Muck Rake Brigade'–by Theodore Roosevelt." *Bismarck Tribune*, April 16, 1906.

——. "School of Cookery Will Open Monday." *Star-Gazette*, June 16, 1908.

——. "Equipment." *Editor and Publisher*, August 10, 1910.

——. "Plan Journalistic Course." *New-York Tribune*, March 23, 1912.

——. "The Lady Doc." *Tennessean*, October 20, 1912.

——. "Suffrage Tea on the Lawn." *Courier-News*, June 15, 1915.

——. "What the Women Are Doing in the War." *Courier-News*, March 21, 1917.

——. "Teacher for 32 Years; Sent to Insane Asylum." *Chicago Tribune*, May 8, 1924.

Abbot, Willis, J. *Watching the World Go By*. Boston: Little, Brown, and Company, 1933.

Adams, Katherine H., and Michael L. Keene. *Winifred Black/Annie Laurie and the Making of Modern Nonfiction*. Jefferson, North Carolina: McFarland & Company, 2015.

Arnesen, Eric, ed. *Encyclopedia of U.S. Labor and Working-Class History*. New York: Routledge, 2007.

Bab. "Quill Drivers." *Daily Arkansas Gazette*, April 30, 1893.

Bierce, Ambrose. "A Thumb-Nail Sketch." In *The Collected Works of Ambrose Bierce, Vol. XII*. New York: Neale Publishing Company, 1912.

Bishop, Elizabeth, and Robert Lowell. *Words in Air, The Complete Correspondence of Elizabeth Bishop and Robert Lowell*. New York: Farrar, Straus, and Giroux, 2008.

Bisland, Elizabeth. *A Flying Trip Around the World*. New York: Harper & Brothers, 1891.

Beard, Mary. *Women & Power: A Manifesto*. 1st American ed. New York: Liveright Publishing Corporation, 2017.

Bogart, R. D. "Columbia Politics." *St. Paul Globe*, January 29, 1888.

Boynton, Robert. *The New New Journalism*. New York: Vintage Books, 2005.

Brann, W. C. "Women in Journalism." In *Brann the Iconoclast*. Waco, TX: Herz Brothers, 1898.

Brier, Bud. "Under the Rose." *Boston Globe*, July 18, 1892.

Brisbane, Arthur. "Great Problems in Organization: The Modern Newspaper in War Time." *Cosmopolitan* 25 (September 1898).

Brodie, Janet Farrell. *Contraception and Abortion in Nineteenth-Century America*. Ithaca, NY: Cornell University Press, 1997.

Browder, Clifford. *The Wickedest Woman in New York: Madame Restell, the Abortionist*. Hamden, CT: Archon Books, 1988.

Browning, Elizabeth Barrett. *Aurora Leigh*. London: Chapman and Hall, 1857.

Burrows, J. "'Delta': A Measure of Stylistic Difference and a Guide to Likely Authorship." *Literary and Linguistic Computing* 17, no. 3 (September 1, 2002).

Cahoon, H. H. "Women in Gutter Journalism," *Arena* 17 (December 1896–June 1897).

Campbell, Helen Stuart. *Prisoners of Poverty*. Cambridge, MA: John Wilson and Son, 1887.

Campbell, W. Joseph. *Yellow Journalism: Puncturing the Myths, Defining the Legacies*. Westport, CT: Praeger, 2001.

Chapin, Charles. *Charles Chapin's Story, Written in Sing Sing Prison*. New York: G. P. Putnam's Sons, 1920.

Clayton, John. *The Cowboy Girl: The Life of Caroline Lockhart*. Women in the West. Lincoln: University of Nebraska Press, 2007.

Coey, A. J. "Demands an Investigation." *Inter Ocean*, December 23, 1888.

Commander, Lydia. "The Significance of Yellow Journalism." *Arena* 34 (August 1905).

Conner, Eliza Archard. "A Woman's World in Paragraphs." *Vancouver Daily World*, November 11, 1892.

Crane, Stephen. *Active Service*. New York: International Association of Newspapers and Authors, 1901.

Dare, Helen. "Flying the Flume for Forty Miles." *San Francisco Examiner*, July 26, 1896.

Davidson, James West. *They Say: Ida B. Wells and the Reconstruction of Race*. New Narratives in American History. New York: Oxford University Press, 2007.

Davis, Elizabeth Lindsay. *Lifting as They Climb*. Washington DC: National Association of Colored Women, 1933.

Davis, Richard Harding. "Does Our Flag Shield Women?" *New York Journal*, February 12, 1897.

Del Carmen, Rolando V. *Criminal Procedure: Law and Practice*. 7th ed. Belmont, CA: Thomson/Wadsworth, 2007.

Dickens, Charles. *American Notes for General Circulation*. New York: Harper & Brothers, 1842.

Didion, Joan. *Slouching Towards Bethlehem*. New York: Farrar, Straus and Giroux, 1968.

Dyer, Justin Buckley. *Slavery, Abortion, and the Politics of Constitutional Meaning*. Cambridge, UK: Cambridge University Press, 2013.

Eder, Maciej. "Authorship Verification with the Package 'Stylo.'" Computational Stylistics Group, 2018, https://computationalstylistics .github.io/blog/imposters/.

Ehrenreich, Barbara. *Nickel and Dimed: On (Not) Getting By in America*. New York: Henry Holt and Company, 2001.

Fahs, Alice. *Out on Assignment: Newspaper Women and the Making of Modern Public Space*. Chapel Hill: University of North Carolina Press, 2011.

Faludi, Susan. *In the Darkroom*. 1st ed. New York: Metropolitan Books/ Henry Holt and Company, 2016.

Faue, Elizabeth. *Writing the Wrongs: Eva Valesh and the Rise of Labor Journalism*. Ithaca, NY: Cornell University Press, 2002.

Freeman, Barbara M. *Kit's Kingdom: The Journalism of Kathleen Blake Coleman*. Ottawa: Carlton University Press, 1989.

Galenson, Walter. *The United Brotherhood of Carpenters: The First Hundred Years*. Wertheim Publications in Industrial Relations. Cambridge, MA: Harvard University Press, 1983.

Gardiner, Becky, Mahana Mansfield, et al. "The Dark Side of Guardian Comments." *Guardian*, April 12, 2016, https://www.theguardian.com /technology/2016/apr/12/the-dark-side-of-guardian-comments.

Giddings, Paula. *Ida: A Sword Among Lions: Ida B. Wells and the Campaign Against Lynching*. New York: HarperCollins, 2008.

Gladstone, Rick. "Tales Told Out of School in Pyongyang Cause Stir." *New York Times*, November 30, 2014.

Green, Casey Edward, and Shelly Henley Kelly, eds. *Through a Night of Horrors: Voices from the 1900 Galveston Storm*. College Station: Texas A & M University Press, 2000.

Green, Nathan, ed. *Story of the Galveston Flood*. Baltimore: R. H. Woodward Company, 1900.

Greenwood, James. *A Night in a Workhouse*. London: Office of the Pall Mall Gazette, 1866.

Grossman, Barbara Wallace. *A Spectacle of Suffering: Clara Morris on the American Stage*. Theater in the Americas. Carbondale: Southern Illinois University Press, 2009.

H. F. "Church Scorned by Wales." *New York Times*, April 29, 1894.

Haggard, Stephan. "Suki Kim: 'Without You There is No Us: My Time with the Sons of North Korea's Elite.'" *North Korea: Witness to Transformation* blog, 2015, https://www.piie.com/blogs/north-korea-witness-transformation/suki -kim-without-you-there-no-us-my-time-sons-north-koreas.

Hamlin, Kimberly A. *From Eve to Evolution: Darwin, Science, and Women's Rights in Gilded Age America*. Chicago: University of Chicago Press, 2014.

Hawthorne, Julian. *The Story of Evangelina Cisneros*. New York: Continental Publishing Company, 1897.

Hawthorne, Nathaniel. "Mrs. Hutchinson." *Tales and Sketches*. Library of America, 1982.

Hayes, Albert H. *The Physiology of Woman and her Diseases*. Boston: Peabody Medical Institute, 1869.

Heaton, Eliza Putnam. "The Steerage." *Times Union*, October 20, 1888.

Hood, Thomas. *Works of Thomas Hood*, Vol. XI. London: Edward Moxon & Co., 1862.

Hurston, Zora Neale. *Mules and Men*. New York: Harper Perennial, 2008.

Ireland, Alleyne. "At Home with Family—and Last Voyage of the Liberty." *St. Louis Post-Dispatch*, April 6, 1947.

James, Henry. *Portrait of a Lady, Vol III*. New York: Charles Scribner's Sons, 1908.

Justitia. "Bring the Husbands to Book." *Chicago Times*, December 28, 1888.

Keetley, Charles Robert. *Index of Surgery*. London: Smith, Elder & Co., 1881.

Kelly, Allen. "How He Was Captured." *San Francisco Examiner*, November 3, 1889.

Kelly, Florence Finch. *Flowing Stream: The Story of Fifty-Six Years in American Newspaper Life*. New York: E. P. Dutton & Company, 1939.

Kent, David. *The Lizzie Borden Source Book*. Boston: Branden Publishing Company, 1992.

Kim, Suki. "The Reluctant Memoirist." *The New Republic*, 2016, https://newrepublic.com/article/133893/reluctant-memoirist.

Kois, Dan. "Facts Are Stupid." *Slate*, 2012, https://slate.com/culture/2012/02/the-lifespan-of-a-fact-essayist-john-dagata-defends-his-right-to-fudge-the-truth.html.

Koven, Seth. *Slumming: Sexual and Social Politics in Victorian London*. Princeton, NJ: Princeton University Press, 2006.

Kramer, Steve. "Uplifting Our 'Downtrodden Sisterhood': Victoria Earle Matthews and New York City's White Rose Mission, 1897–1907." *Journal of African American History* 91, no. 3 (Summer 2006).

Kroeger, Brooke. *Nellie Bly: Daredevil, Reporter, Feminist*. New York: Times Books, 1994.

———. *Undercover Reporting: The Truth About Deception*. Evanston, IL: Northwestern University Press, 2012.

Lahey, Joanna N. "Birthing a Nation: The Effect of Fertility Control Access on the Nineteenth-Century Demographic Transition." *Journal of Economic History* 74, no. 2 (June 2014).

Lang, Marjory Louise. *Women Who Made the News: Female Journalists in Canada, 1880–1945*. Montreal: McGill-Queen's University Press, 1999.

Lederer, Francis L., II. "Nora Marks: Investigative Reporter." *Journal of the Illinois State Historical Society* 68, no. 4 (September 1975).

———. "Nora Marks—Reinvestigated." *Journal of the Illinois State Historical Society* 73, no. 1 (Spring 1980).

Eric W. Liguori. "Nell Nelson and the Chicago Times 'City Slave Girls' Series: Beginning a National Crusade for Labor Reform in the Late 1800s." *Journal of Management History* 18, no. 1 (2012).

Lockhart, Caroline. "A Mermaid Bold." *Boston Post*, June 2, 1895.

Logan, Shirley W., ed. *With Pen and Voice: A Critical Anthology of Nineteenth-Century African-American Women*. Carbondale: Southern Illinois University Press, 1995.

Lutes, Jean Marie. *Front-Page Girls: Women Journalists in American Culture and Fiction, 1880–1930*. Ithaca, NY: Cornell University Press, 2007.

Manning, Marie. *Ladies, Now and Then*. New York: E. P. Dutton & Company, 1944.

Masterson, Kate. "Weyler Talks to a Woman." *New York Journal*, March 14, 1896.

Mauriceau, A. M. *The Married Woman's Private Medical Companion*. New York: Joseph Trow, 1849.

McDougall, Walt. *This Is the Life!* New York: Alfred A. Knopf, 1926.

McEwen, Arthur. "About 'Annie Laurie'" *San Francisco Examiner*, January 5, 1891.

Melville, Herman. *Moby Dick*. New York: Charles Scribner's Sons, 1899.

Mohr, James. *Abortion in America*. New York: Oxford University Press, 1978.

Morrill, Claire. "Praised and Berated for Frank Novel, Michigan Author Prepares Another." *Detroit Free Press*, March 22, 1936.

Morris, James McGrath. *Pulitzer: A Life in Politics, Print, and Power*. New York: Harper Perennial, 2011.

——. *The Rose Man of Sing Sing: A True Tale of Life, Murder, and Redemption in the Age of Yellow Journalism*. New York: Fordham University Press, 2003.

Muller, G. F. "The City of Pittsburgh." *Harper's New Monthly Magazine* XVII (December 1880).

The New York Society for the Suppression of Vice. *Fifth Annual Report*. New York, 1879.

Older, Mrs. Fremont. *William Randolph Hearst, American*. New York: D. Appleton-Century Company, 1936.

Parkman, Francis. "The Woman Question." *North American Review* 129, no. 275 (October 1879).

Peattie, Elia Wilkinson, and Susanne George-Bloomfield. *Impertinences: Selected Writings of Elia Peattie, a Journalist in the Gilded Age*. Lincoln: University of Nebraska Press, 2005.

Peko, Samantha, and Michael S. Sweeney. "Nell Nelson's Undercover Reporting." *American Journalism* 34, no. 4 (2017).

Penn, Irvine Garland. *The Afro-American Press and Its Editors.* Springfield, IL: Willey & Company, 1891.

Plimpton, George. "The Story Behind a Nonfiction Novel." *New York Times,* January 16, 1966.

Poe, Edgar Allen. *The Mystery of Marie Roget.* New York: R. F. Fenno & Company, 1899.

Porter, Edwin H. *The Fall River Tragedy: A History of the Borden Murders.* Clark, NJ: Lawbook Exchange, 2006.

Prados-Torreira, Teresa. *Mambisas: Rebel Women in Nineteenth-Century Cuba.* Gainesville: University Press of Florida, 2005.

Procter, Ben. *William Randolph Hearst, the Early Years, 1863–1910.* New York: Oxford University Press, 1998.

Prose, Francine. "Outrageous Misfortune." *New York Times,* March 13, 2005.

Pulitzer, Joseph. "The College of Journalism." *North American Review* 178, no. 570 (May 1904).

Ranger, Hal. *Pittsburg Dispatch,* March 1, 1885.

Renfroe, Alicia. "Editor's Introduction." In Davis, Rebecca Harding. *A Law Unto Herself.* Lincoln: University of Nebraska Press, 2014.

Restell, Madame. "The Case of Madame Restell." *New-York Tribune,* August 24, 1842.

Riis, Jacob A., *How the Other Half Lives.* New York: Charles Scribner's Sons, 1895.

Rodriguez, Cristina M. "Clearing the Smoke-Filled Room: Women Jurors and the Disruption of an Old-Boys' Network in Nineteenth-Century America." *The Yale Law Journal* 108, no. 7 (May 1999).

Roggenkamp, Karen. *Narrating the News: New Journalism and Literary Genre in Late Nineteenth-Century American Newspapers and Fiction.* Kent, OH: Kent State University Press, 2005.

———. *Sympathy, Madness, and Crime: How Four Nineteenth-Century Journalists Made the Newspaper Women's Business.* Kent, OH: Kent State University Press, 2016.

Rooney, Alice. "The Girls Heard From." *St. Paul Globe*, May 13, 1888.

Roosevelt, Theodore. *The Rough Riders*. New York: Charles Scribner's Sons, 1899.

Ross, Ishbel. *Ladies of the Press: The Story of Women in Journalism by an Insider*. New York: Harper & Brothers, 1936.

Russ, Joanna. *How to Suppress Women's Writing*. 1st ed. Austin: University of Texas Press, 1983.

Rutland, Lucile. "Catherine Cole Versus Nellie Bly." *Times-Democrat*, April 12, 1896.

Sachsman, David B., and David W. Bulla, eds. *Sensationalism: Murder, Mayhem, Mudslinging, Scandals, and Disasters in 19th-Century Reporting*. New Brunswick, NJ: Transaction Publishers, 2013.

Sawaya, Francesca. *Modern Women, Modern Work: Domesticity, Professionalism, and American Writing, 1890–1950*. Rethinking the Americas. Philadelphia: University of Pennsylvania Press, 2004.

Seitz, Don. *Joseph Pulitzer: His Life and Letters*. New York: Simon & Schuster, 1924.

Srebnick, Amy Gilman. *The Mysterious Death of Mary Rogers: Sex and Culture in Nineteenth-Century New York*. Studies in the History of Sexuality. New York: Oxford University Press, 1995.

Stallard, J. S. *The Female Casual and Her Lodging*. London: Sanders, Otley, and Company, 1886.

Stanton, Elizabeth Cady, and Susan B. Anthony. *The Selected Papers of Elizabeth Cady Stanton and Susan B. Anthony, Volume III*. New Brunswick, NJ: Rutgers University Press, 1997.

[St. Clair, Augustus.] "The Evil of the Age." *New York Times*, August 23, 1871.

——. "The Evil of the Age." *New York Times*, August 27, 1871.

——. "The Evil of the Age." *New York Times*, August 29, 1871.

——. "The Evil of the Age." *New York Times*, September 1, 1871.

Stead, W. T. "Maiden Tribute of Modern Babylon." *Pall Mall Gazette*, July 6, 1885.

Steinem, Gloria. *Outrageous Acts and Everyday Rebellions*. New York: Holt, Rinehart, and Winston, 1983.

Stone, Lucy. "A Flaw in the Jury System." *Newport Mercury*, July 1, 1893.

Thomas, Evan. *The War Lovers: Roosevelt, Lodge, Hearst, and the Rush to Empire, 1898*. New York: Back Bay Books, 2011.

Thompson, Hunter S. *Fear and Loathing on the Campaign Trail '72*. San Francisco: Straight Arrow Press, 1973.

———. "Jacket Copy for Fear & Loathing in Las Vegas: A Savage Journey to the Heart of the American Dream." In *The Great Shark Hunt: Strange Tales from a Strange Time*. New York: Simon & Schuster, 2003.

Thornton, Brian. "When a Newspaper Was Accused of Killing a President." *Journalism History* 26, no. 3 (Autumn 2000).

Tompkins, Elizabeth A. "Saratoga as It Is." *Inter Ocean*, July 30, 1893.

Washington, Booker T. *Booker T. Washington Papers, 1895–98*. Urbana: University of Illinois Press, 1975.

Webb, Beatrice. *The Diary of Beatrice Webb, Vol. 3*. London: Virago, 1982.

Weir Mitchell, Silas. *Fat and Blood: An Essay on the Treatment of Certain Forms of Neurasthenia and Hysteria*. Philadelphia: J. B. Lippincott, 1883.

Wendt, Lloyd. *Chicago Tribune: The Rise of a Great American Newspaper*. Chicago: Rand McNally, 1979.

Werbel, Amy Beth. *Lust on Trial: Censorship and the Rise of American Obscenity in the Age of Anthony Comstock*. New York: Columbia University Press, 2018.

Wilkie, Franc. *Personal Reminiscences of Thirty-Five Years of Journalism*. Chicago: F. J. Schulte & Company, 1891.

Willard, Frances. *Occupations for Women*. New York: Success Company, 1897.

Wilson, Erasmus. "Quiet Observations." *Pittsburg Dispatch*, January 17, 1885.

———. *Quiet Observations on the Ways of the World*. New York: Cassell and Company, 1886.

Winkler, John K. *W. R. Hearst: An American Phenomenon*. New York: Simon & Schuster, 1928.

Wolcott, James. "Me, Myself, and I." *Vanity Fair* 10, no. 446 (October 1997).

Wolfe, Tom. "Why They Aren't Writing the Great American Novel Anymore." *Esquire* (December 1972).

Woolf, Virginia. "Professions for Women." In *Death of the Moth and Other Essays*. London: Hogarth Press, 1947.

Yurick, Sol. "Sob-Sister Gothic." *The Nation*, February 7, 1966.

Page 84: "Guess the girl reporter." *Chicago Times*, December 21, 1888 (Center for Research Libraries, Chicago)

Page 89: Ada Sweet, portrait, c. 1882. (Chicago History Museum)

Page 94: William Randolph Hearst, c. 1904. (Library of Congress)

Page 96: Nellie Bly, c. 1890. Feb 21. (Library of Congress)

Page 99: "Where has 'Nora Marks' Been?," *Chicago Tribune*, October 12, 1888 (University of Minnesota Libraries)

Page 111: "Round the World with Nellie Bly." *World*, January 26, 1890 (University of Minnesota Libraries)

Page 120: Pulitzer Building, New York City, c. 1909 (Library of Congress)

Page 122: Annie Laurie in a Cannery, *San Francisco Examiner*, August 17, 1890 (Newspapers.com)

Page 133: Ida B. Wells, head-and-shoulders portrait, facing slightly right, 1891. Illus. in: *The Afro-American Press and Its Editors*, by I. Garland Penn., 1891. (Library of Congress)

Page 138: Victoria Earle Matthews portrait, *Journalist*, January 26, 1889 (University of Minnesota Libraries)

Page 144: Elizabeth Jordan, *Tales of the Cloister*, frontispiece, 1901 (University of Minnesota Libraries)

Page 156: Elizabeth Banks, *Campaigns of Curiosity*, frontispiece, 1894 (University of Michigan)

Page 168: Caroline Lockhart, Diving Suit, *Boston Post*, June 2, 1895 (Library of Congress)

Page 181: Arthur Brisbane portrait, Brisbane Family Papers (Special Collections Research Center, Syracuse University Libraries)

Page 183: "To the North Pole by Balloon," *World*, February 16, 1896 (University of Minnesota Libraries)

Page 188: "Nellie Bly as an Elephant Trainer," *World*, February 23, 1896 (University of Minnesota Libraries)

Page 190: "Kate Swan in the Death Chair," *World*, February 16, 1896 (University of Minnesota Libraries)

Page 194: "Kate Swan Drives the Electric Engine," *World*, May 31, 1896 (University of Minnesota Libraries)

Page 197: "Flying the Flume," *San Francisco Examiner*, July 25, 1896 (Newspapers.com)

Page 198: "Dorothy Dare's Wild Ride on the Snow Plough," *World*, March 22, 1896 (University of Minnesota Libraries)

Page 228: Eva McDonald Valesh (listed as 1886, but likely 1890s) (Minnesota History Center)

Page 234: Elizabeth Banks illustration (Harry Beetle Hough Scrapbooks, Widener Library, Harvard University)

Page 256: Frederick Burr Opper, artist. The fin de siècle newspaper proprietor / F. Opper, 1894. N.Y.: Published by Keppler & Schwarzmann, March 7. Illus. from Puck, v. 35, no. 887, (March 7, 1894), centerfold. (Library of Congress)

Page 257: Head and shoulders, facing slightly right. "Annie Laurie." Winifred Black, 1936. , c. 1913. Jan. 18. (Library of Congress)

Page 260: Quarter-length portrait of journalist and social worker Victoria Earle Matthews, 1903. Schomburg Center for Research in Black Culture, The New York Public Library. Used with permission.

Page 264: Ida B. Wells with her first son, 1896 (Special Collections Research Center, University of Chicago Library.) Used with permission.

Page numbers of illustrations appear in italics.

KIM TODD is the award-winning author of several books, including *Chrysalis: Maria Sibylla Merian and the Secrets of Metamorphosis*, and *Tinkering with Eden: A Natural History of Exotic Species in America*, winner of the PEN/Jerard Award and the Sigurd Olson Nature Writing Award. Her essays and articles have appeared *Smithsonian*, *Salon*, *Sierra* magazine, *Orion*, and *Best American Science and Nature Writing* anthologies, among other publications. She is a member of the MFA faculty at the University of Minnesota and lives in Minneapolis with her family.